It's a mad, mad, mad, mad Mac

To
Milton Berle, Jonathan Winters, Buddy Hackett, Sid Caesar,
Phil Silvers, Peter Falk, Ethel Merman, Buster Keaton,
Jimmy Durante, Edie Adams, and Stanley Kramer.

It's a mad, mad, mad, mad Mac

Carla Rose

Windcrest®/ McGraw-Hill

New York   San Francisco   Washington, D.C.   Auckland   Bogotá
Caracas   Lisbon   London   Madrid   Mexico City   Milan
Montreal   New Delhi   San Juan   Singapore
Sydney   Tokyo   Toronto

FIRST EDITION
FIRST PRINTING

©1994 by **Windcrest**, an imprint of McGraw-Hill, Inc.
The name "Windcrest" is a registered trademark of McGraw-Hill, Inc.

Library of Congress Cataloging-in-Publication Data
Rose, Carla.
    It's a mad, mad, mad, mad Mac / by Carla Rose.
        p.   cm.
    Includes index.
    ISBN 0-8306-4535-7
        1. Macintosh (Computer)   2. Computer games.   I. Title.
    QA76.8.M3R654   1993
    794. 8'15365—dc20   93-33691
                                                                   CIP

Acquisitions editor: Brad J. Schepp,
Editorial team: Joanne Slike, Executive Editor
                Barbara Minich, Book Editor
Production team: Katherine G. Brown, Director
                Wanda S. Ditch, Desktop Operator
                Joan Wieland, Proofreading
                Joann Woy, Indexer
Design team: Jaclyn J. Boone, Designer
                Brian Allison, Associate Designer
Cover design: Sandra Blair, Harrisburg, Pa   MAC2
Cover photograph: © Orion Press/Westlight   4482

Acknowledgments

There are dozens, if not hundreds, of people who helped make this book a reality. Thanks (in no partcular order) to: Bob Nordling, National Home and School Mac User Group, Brad Schepp and Jennifer DiGiovanna, and all the Windcrest/McGraw-Hill people for doing such a great job of putting these books together, and especially to the game publishers and shareware authors for giving me something to write about.

Special thanks and love to Jay, Josh, and Dan for playing all these games—even the ones they didn't like—for getting great screen shots and tips, and for keeping the house and family together while I worked. Without them, this would have been ten times as difficult. Thanks to the Village Smokehouse, Bo Shing, and the Village Pizza House, for keeping us well-fed and happy.

About the Author

Carla Rose has been playing games on the Macintosh since 1984. A professional writer for more than 20 years, she is a senior contributing editor of *Portable Computing* magazine, and is the author of *The First Book of PageMaker 4* and *The Essential PageMaker 5*, and coauthor of *The First Book of Mac* and *Everything You Wanted to Know about the Mac*. She is also author of *Mac Online! Making the Connection* and *Turbocharge Your Mac!*, both published by Windcrest/McGraw-Hill. She lives in Brookline, Massachusetts with her husband and coauthor Jay Rose, two teenage sons, and asssorted pets.

Contents

Introduction

The games people play

If you've ever watched a kitten and a ball of yarn, an otter and a strand of kelp, monkeys on the zoo trapeze, or dolphins surfing on a ship's bow wave, you've seen the behavior we humans call "play." Play is instinctive. When the other basic needs are met, and there's no immediate danger to trigger a "fight or flight" response, most animals and humans engage in some form of play. It might be engaging in a "sport" activity like chasing a ball or some other object, mock fighting with another, solving a puzzle, or just daydreaming. Play lets body and mind take a break from the challenges of survival.

Playing is also a way to refine one's survival skills. The ancient Greeks knew it. The Olympic games were about becoming better warriors: running faster, throwing the javelin further, jumping higher. . ... It's likely that prehistoric people also had their games of strength and skill. Who could throw the rock the longest distance? Who could hit the target with the spear? Who could out-wrestle the tribal leader? These games were more than just fun. They honed the skills needed for hunting and self-defense. Unlike a real battle or a real hunt, though, losing wasn't fatal. Of course, winning had its advantages. Winners got what they wanted—the best parts of the slaughtered animal, the seat near the fire, their choice of mate. Losers got the leftovers, and came back to compete again and again, until they won.

Today, the stakes, and the games are different. We live in the age of technology. Computers and other electronic devices supervise much of our lives, from the fetal monitor that determines when it's time for a baby to be born, through the machines that keep track of our academic standing, bank balance, credit history, fingerprints and medical records, on down to the microwave ovens that feed us and the programmable VCRs, cable boxes, and electronic games that entertain us. We're not catching our dinner with a hand-held spear, we're choosing it from the freezer and zapping it until it's warm. The days of defending oneself and one's home with a rock or a javelin are long gone. The tools of work and of defense have changed. So have the tools for play. But we work just as hard, or harder, and play is still important. The difference is that today we play with technology.

Where it started...

If you go back to the early days of computing, computers were entire rooms full of mysterious circuits that required their own air-conditioned, humidity-controlled environments, even floors mounted on springs, in order to do very little more than you can do today with a pocket calculator the size of a credit card. Their cost was measured, not in dollars like the credit-card calculator, or even hundreds of dollars, but in the hundreds of thousands of dollars. And the entire system could be brought to its knees by something as trivial as a spark of static from a nylon sweater, or a beetle snacking on the insulation around its wires. Small wonder that people were nervous about computing. Most people didn't even understand *what* a computer did, much less how or why it did it.

It was easy to develop a full-blown case of computer anxiety if you read the papers or the magazines. Such famous future predictors as Marshall McLuhan and Bucky Fuller told us that what we most feared would come true. . .. Computers would take over. They would be everywhere. Big Brother. 1984. Well, as it turns out, 1984 brought us the Macintosh. But that's jumping ahead. . .

Meanwhile, these strange creatures with names like ENIAC and UNIVAC flourished. ENIAC, which used 18,000 vacuum tubes and required 1,800 square feet of floor space, could multiply two 10-digit numbers 300 times per second, and gave you the totals on a stack of punched cards. That is, if you'd given it properly punched cards with the numbers you wanted multiplied, and provided that you'd strung together the individual components of ENIAC that contained the instructions for the operation in an order that let the numbers go in one end of the chain of operations and come out the other. Sometimes it worked; often, it didn't. So that they could figure out what ENIAC was doing, its designers assigned different beep tones to different functions. The first computer "amusement," though not technically a game, came from the beeps. In 1957, at Bell Labs, a bunch of programmers figured out how to make a computer beep "Daisy, Daisy. . .give me your answer, do. . ." just by carefully plotting which tones came from which operations. (It was no coincidence that HAL, in Stanley Kubrick's *2001: a Space Odyssey*, played the same song.) Their next solo was "Hail to the Chief," just in case the President dropped in.

UNIVAC, introduced to the public a year or so later, was much smaller and very much faster. Using 2,500 small electron tubes, it fit into a case about the size of a grand piano. Much more important, for the future of game playing, UNIVAC could be programmed. You could tell it, in machine language, how to multiply two numbers, and it would remember the instructions and apply them to all the numbers you gave it. You still had to give it numbers by punched card or punched tape, but progress had been made.

Artificial intelligence was the buzzword of the day, and most of us feared that it would replace human intelligence. People wore buttons taken from the legend printed on the punched cards that gave orders to these early digital behemoths. The buttons said, "I am a human being. Do not fold, spindle, or mutilate." Defensive? You bet.

The late '50s and early '60s brought us smaller and more adept computing machines, and much more important for game play, it brought us the cathode ray tube (CRT) display. Now, you could see what was happening in the "brains" of the computer by watching the screen instead of waiting for a punched card. This in turn led to the development of some of the early computer games. Probably not the earliest, though. Rumor has it that technicians working on the ENIAC used to place bets on the outcome of some of the computer's calculations—computer gaming, of a sort.

The computer as a toy

What is there about the computer that makes us want to play with it? It's a very expensive toy. Certainly ENIAC technicians knew the value of even a couple of seconds of number-crunching on their behemoth. And that gives us part of the reason. Computers, as a concept, are so overwhelming, so powerful, that in order to coexist we perhaps need to find ways to trivialize them. We need to be able to move from word processing and number crunching to chasing interplanetary bad guys, solving puzzles, or conquering fictional territories. It helps us feel more in control—of our machines, of our time, and perhaps even of our fate. For many of us, the threat of computers taking over the world is lessened if we beat them at chess, Go, or tic-tac-toe.

Computers usually attract people of above average intelligence and creativity. These are also the people who tend to like their work, even to perceive it as "fun." For these folks, finding ways to play with the work tool (e.g., computer) is as natural as doodling with a pencil. So playing computer games serves a similar function—occupying the fingers while letting the brain slide into "neutral" temporarily, to daydream, solve a problem, or just relax.

Also, just as the ancients used their games of chasing and throwing things to improve their hunting and fighting skills, many of us play computer games to hone our computer skills. Physical therapists often use computer games to teach eye-hand coordination. Teachers use them to increase a child's attention span. Games can teach you to type, to speak a foreign language, to manage a city. . .. Games let you experience piloting a jet fighter or a spaceship, a racing car, submarine, or paper airplane. Games take you back or forward in history. Games let you try your hand at brain surgery, managing a multi-national conglomerate, or dropping blocks into a well. Games let you pit your own intelligence, speed, or skill against that of the computer, and occasionally come out on top. Most of all, they're fun.

About this book

For purposes of convenience, each chapter in this book explains a different type of game. Text-based games are the oldest type, and come first, followed by graphic adventures and so on, up to the latest CD-ROM releases. Throughout the book, icons will help you find the kinds of games you're looking for, and will identify multi-player games, shareware and freeware games, and games that aren't for the sandbox set. The exclamation point icon indicates a hint for a specific game. The full set of icons is shown on page xvi.

About the disk

In choosing games for this disk, I looked for the ones that would run on all Macs, black and white as well as color. You'll find a sampling of different types of games including arcade, adventure, and some classic card and board games for the Mac. They've all been compressed with Compact Pro into self-extracting files. Copy them onto your hard drive, double click to open, and "Let the games begin!"

IT'S A MAD, MAD, MAD, MAD MAC

 Fantasy

 Strategy

 War simulation

 Sport simulation

 Game of chance

 Game of skill

 Puzzle

 Other simulation

 Commercial game

 Shareware

 Freeware

 Historical background

 Hint

PG 13 Not for Kids

 Author's favorite

 Two (or more) player game

1

In the
beginning . . .

An oscilloscope is a device that makes electronic signals visible. Engineers use them to trace signals through circuits. If you wander into any place where work is being done with any kind of electronic circuitry, you'll probably find one. So, it's not surprising that there was one in the computer lab at the Massachusetts Institute of Technology (MIT).

Late one night, in the fall of 1961, a bored graduate student watched the scope flicker as the computer chewed its way through the batch of punched cards it was processing. He noticed that some operations seemed to make it flicker in one direction and others in a different direction. He realized that it would be possible to make the blips on the screen move right or left according to the numbers he asked the machine to crunch. But it needed a better display than the oscilloscope, and a more efficient computer than the hulking IBM 704.

In another part of the building was a brand-new PDP-1, a gift from a new company called Digital Equipment. It had several things that might make the goal easier to reach. Instead of cards, it read punched tape, and it had an actual cathode-ray-tube (CRT) display. He talked his way onto the PDP-1 team.

Many days of programming, and many rolls of punched tape later, Steven Russell had created Spacewar, the first true computer game. By today's standards, it was crude. One spaceship shot a torpedo, represented by a blob of light, at another spaceship. The ships had different shapes, so you could tell them apart. One was shaped like a vacuum tube, the other like a short, fat cigar. Each could maneuver a bit. If you flicked switches on the front panel, you could turn right or left, accelerate, and fire the torpedo.

When you fired at the enemy ship, a subroutine for *collision detection* scanned the area. If the torpedo and the ship occupied the same area, the ship was replaced by a shower of tiny dots signifying an explosion. Figure 1-1 shows a Macintosh version of the Spacewar screen. The ships and scenery went through many changes from version to version.

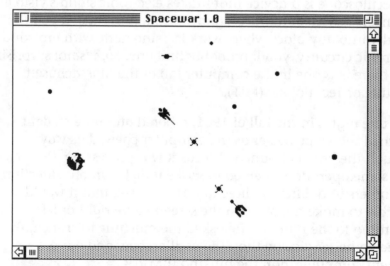

1-1 *Spacewar was usually played with white graphics on a black screen. (This picture has been inverted for printing purposes.)*

Back in those days, there was no such thing as a copyright for computer programs. The ethic, especially at places like MIT, was to share as much as possible and let group efforts create new improvements to the program. Russell knew that other MIT computer users would *hack* Spacewar, and improve on it, but that was the purpose of writing the program. Improvements came quickly. One programmer added an accurate, *scrollable universe* using actual star charts. Another, a fan of science-fiction writer "Doc" Smith, applied Smith's concept of hyperspace and gave the ship the ability to *warp* out of harm's way. Yet another hacked in a central sun, giving the ships gravity to fight against.

Spacewar proved highly addictive. Championships were won and lost late at night, when only MIT's dedicated corps of hackers roamed the halls. The paper tapes holding the game were widely distributed. Digital Equipment got copies and used it to test all the new PDP-1s before they were sent out to customers. The engineers in charge of testing always left the game loaded, so soon every PDP-1 site in the country had it up and running.

California dreamin'

A good many MIT graduates headed west, forming the nucleus of what today we call Silicon Valley. Many went to work on the SAIL program, named for the Stanford Artificial Intelligence Labs, and it wasn't too long before a copy of Spacewar reached California. But it never really caught on.

"The concept of computer games is reasonable," thought the Californians, "but the concept of torpedoes in outer space, well . . . no."

There's a philosophical difference between the East and West coasts that can't be explained by the four time zones that separate them. In Cambridge, the hackers' preferred reading material was hard-core science fiction. In Palo Alto, it was fantasy. The works of Tolkien were quoted, memorized, and even memorialized in the names given to rooms in the new SAIL building. The lab printer was rigged to handle three different Elfish type fonts. It was only natural that when computer gaming finally achieved a toehold in Palo Alto, it would be a different kind of gaming.

Adventure first surfaced at the Xerox Palo Alto Research Center. The basic concept came from programmer Will Crowther, who wrote a simple text-based game about looking for treasure in a cave. A Stanford programmer named Donald Woods took the concept and developed it into a full-scale game called Adventure in Colossal Cave. Instead of flicking switches to torpedo enemy spaceships, you typed simple one- or two-word commands, like Go east or Fight troll. These used a different—less mathematical—kind of programming. Instead of figuring vectors, the computer simply followed a logic script. "If A, then B. If not A, then C," and so on.

Text-based games caught on quickly. They were much easier to write. They appealed to those who liked puzzles, since they were essentially descriptions of complex mazes. You had to work your way through, picking up and using objects you found along the way. You earned points by collecting treasure, battling various creatures, and getting out safely. It helped to make a map as you went along. Players would sit in front of the computer with pads of graph paper, sketching the paths and descriptions as they moved through the cave.

As the games got more sophisticated, *randomness* was introduced. When you fought the monster, a random number generator determined the outcome. Other wrinkles were added as programmers thought them up. Today, Adventure can be found in various formats, including one for the Mac. It's also available as an online game on CompuServe and Delphi. Figure 1-2 shows the opening screen of Delphi's version of Adventure.

Gary Gygax's Dungeons and Dragons (D&D) role-playing game had recently been introduced on college campuses. Although not a computer game, it appealed to the same group of computer-hip people who'd fallen in love with Tolkien's Middle Earth. Role-playing games, or RPGs, seemed to be a natural for computers.

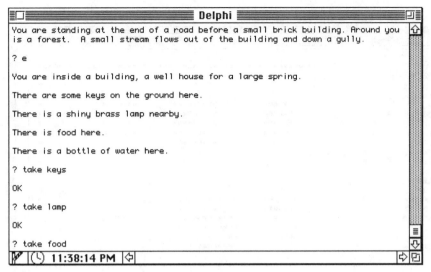

```
≣□□▭▭▭▭▭▭≣ Delphi ≣▭▭▭▭▭▭□□
You are standing at the end of a road before a small brick building. Around you  ⇧
is a forest.  A small stream flows out of the building and down a gully.

? e

You are inside a building, a well house for a large spring.

There are some keys on the ground here.

There is a shiny brass lamp nearby.

There is food here.

There is a bottle of water here.

? take keys

OK

? take lamp

OK                                                                              ≣
? take food                                                                     ⇩
▐ ⟲ 11:38:14 PM ⇦⎸                                                        ⇨▣
```

1-2 *On Delphi, you can also play Adventure in French!*

Along with tightly woven fantasy, there was an element of chance, as in the tossing of dice.

RPGs use a handful of dice, from a pyramid-shaped, 4-sided die to a nearly round, 20-sided die. Throwing dice determine the outcome of battles as well as a character's basic characteristics. Such traits as strength, agility, charisma, and the ability to use magic spells and potions can be built up through combat experience and by finding, stealing, or buying various weapons, armor, and magical items.

The first RPGs on mainframes featured ASCII text-based graphics, mostly maps made out of carefully placed letters of the alphabet and symbols. (ASCII graphics use punctuation marks and symbols such as stars, slashes, and dashes to draw crude pictures on the screen.) As long as your screen width was the same as that of the creator of the game, it was fairly easy to read. Figure 1-3 shows a scene from Moria, one of the better RPGs for the Mac. Although the ASCII graphics aren't remarkable, they are good enough to let you figure out where you are going without graph paper, a definite advantage over text games. The name, by the way comes from Tolkien's *Lord of the Rings*, though the game play is based on D&D.

 File Edit FontSize Moria

```
▤□▤══════════════════ Moria ═══════════════════▤□
                                                          ⇧
        ***********************************************************
Half-Orc *.............................>..............................*
Warrior  *..........................................................*
Rookie   *..........................................................*
         *................*****4.........3********..........*******..*
STR :  18/66 *............******.........*********......6******......*
INT :     5  *............******.........*********........*******.....*
WIS :     9  *............******.........*********........*******.....*
DEX :    16  *............******.........**********.................*
CON :    16  *............******........................*
CHR :     8  *...........................................*
         *.........................@.........................*
LEV :     1  *........................................................*
EXP :     0  *............******2.....................................*
MANA:     0  *............*******....************....*1##..........*
MHP :    19  *............*******....************....####.........*
CHP :     6  *............*******....************....####.........*
         *............*******....5***********.....####.........*
AC  :     1  *............*******....************.....####.........*
GOLD:    60  *............*******....************.................*
         *...........................................*
         ***********************************************************
                                               Town level        ⇩
◁▱                                                          ▷▱
```

1-3 *The @ represents your character. Use the arrow keys to visit the numbered shops in the town square to buy weapons and armor for your quest.*

Zork: The great underground empire

Variations on the theme of Adventure soon came back East and intrigued some of the MIT people who hadn't been overly enthusiastic about Spacewar. Being MIT students, they weren't content to simply play the game. They dissected it and came up with a game of their own. Dave Leibling and Marc Blanc were the co-authors of the original mainframe Zork. Zork, like Adventure, takes place far underground.

The manual states, "You, a dauntless treasure hunter, are venturing into this dangerous land in search of wealth and adventure." You are advised to bring weapons and a light source, and to beware of pickpockets.

Zork was the first game to use an interpretive English parser. It could understand and act upon whole sentences, not just one-or two-word commands. Instead of merely saying Go east, you could tell it Open the panel. Remove the fuse from the socket. Give it to the wizard. **The game was an instant hit.** It was quickly translated to other platforms, and its authors, along with several other MIT programmers, founded a small software company called Infocom.

The parser, now refined and known as Zork Implementation Language or ZIL, let Infocom create a new genre of text games, which became known as *interactive fiction*. Along with Zork, which became the Zork Trilogy, they published a number of games based on science-fiction and fantasy books. Perhaps the best known of these is Douglas Adams' *Hitchhiker's Guide to the Galaxy*. Adams worked with Infocom's Steve Merezetsky on the interactive version of the game, contributing much of the new material. Figure 1-4 shows a scene from the Hitchhiker's Guide.

```
═════════════════════ Hitchhiker's Guide ═════════════════════
Pub                                                Score: 30/29
>listen to music
The song is "Hey Jude" by the Beatles (Footnote 4). It's a particular favourite,
and listening to it calms you down, and cheers you up.

>drink beer
You can hear the muffled noise of your home being demolished, and the taste
of the beer sours in your mouth.

You get drunk and have a terrific time for twelve minutes, are the life and
soul of the Pub, tell some really great stories, make everyone laugh a lot, and
they all clap you on the back and tell you what a great chap you are and then
the Earth gets unexpectedly demolished. You wake up with a hangover which
lasts for all eternity.

We are about to give you your score. Put on your peril-sensitive sunglasses
now. (Hit RETURN or ENTER when ready.) >|
```

1-4 *Never have more than three beers at the pub!*

Atari enters the arcade

During the '60s and '70s, computers had been getting smaller and more sophisticated. What took a roomful of vacuum tubes in the '50s could be managed by a fistful of transistors in the '60s, and by a couple of thumb-sized integrated circuits in the mid-'70s. A company called Atari brought something new to the market, a game that you played with your television set, a black box, and controllers that it called paddles. The game was Pong, and it was an instant success.

Pong had both two-player and single-player versions. As you turned the knob on your paddle, a line representing a Ping-Pong paddle moved back and forth on the screen. If you could manage to bounce back the blip of light and your opponent couldn't, you scored a point. If you missed, the other side got the point.

The actual programming was a lot like Spacewar. It used the same kind of collision detection routine that determined whether the enemy ship exploded, the difference being that here, two things occupying the same space was good news. It meant you'd returned the serve. Figure 1-5 shows an artist's approximation of a Pong game.

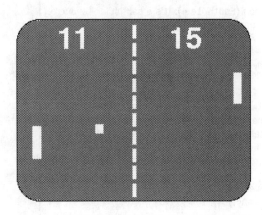

1-5 *Compared to today's games, Pong is unexciting.*

Many of these games are still around in attics and basements. You might find one at a yard sale for a dollar or two. The main circuit is probably still good, although the controllers had a tendency to wear out under the stress of playing.

Pong was intriguing. Before long, entrepreneurs had bought up junked TV sets and combined them with coin boxes and Pong games to make "video games" for bars and penny arcades. Variations on Pong included hockey and basketball games. Atari's original Pong was *hard-wired*. The game box could only play Pong, or possibly Pong, hockey, and basketball, since all were basically the same game.

The next-generation Atari game used plug-in cartridges, containing PROMs (programmable read-only memory). Each cartridge held a different game, and you could switch between them in a matter of seconds. One of the first video-game cartridges to catch on was Space Invaders. It owed a lot to Pong. Your paddle was a missile base that could fire blips of light straight up at descending spaceships. When one landed, the game was over. Figure 1-6 shows a game of Space Invaders, modified for the Mac.

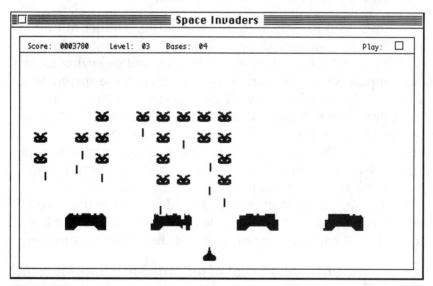

1-6 *In the original Atari version, you got a continuously firing missile launcher by restarting the game with the two-player switch held down.*

About this time, a true version of Spacewar entered the video-game scene. Asteroids had you piloting a spaceship, turning left and right, applying thrust, dodging oncoming asteroids, and firing torpedoes at an enemy spaceship. Unlike Pong clones, Asteroids was played with a joystick that gave multidirectional movement, plus the ability to fire repeatedly by pressing a button. Like Spacewar itself, Asteroids was highly addictive. Players sat for hours, twitching the joystick back and forth, jabbing at the button. The *Journal of the American Medical Association* carried scholarly articles on the treatment of video-game injury.

The next game to make it big on the video scene featured a happy little yellow circle called PacMan, which wandered through a maze, beeping, eating power pellets, and trying to avoid being eaten himself. PacMan entertained those who weren't into shooting things, and became something of a national craze. There were PacMan lunch boxes and T-shirts, PacMan cereal, and even a Saturday-morning PacMan cartoon show.

By this time, both mainframes and the newer, smaller mini-computers were being used for various kinds of games. Many used ASCII graphics and screen displays as well as keyboard or joystick inputs. One intriguing project at MIT in the spring and summer of 1969 used the new PDP-11 to create a chess game called Interactive Kriegspiel (German for war game). This game was developed for the National Aeronautics and Space Administration (NASA), at considerable taxpayer expense, and was intended to entertain the astronauts on long, boring space trips. It played a decent game of chess, although the screen display was simply a list of moves. The idea was the astronaut would be equipped with a magnetic chessboard and could log onto the NASA computer by radio to get the computer's moves.

It was in some ways reminiscent of an early MIT "hack" in which two artificial-intelligence professors were independently told that the IBM 740 had been programmed to play chess. Each was set up in a room with a teletype terminal, supposedly connected to the computer. In reality, the keyboards were connected to each other. One professor entered a move. The other responded. It took a dozen moves before one mistyped and the other caught on to the trick.

Macintosh arrives

Meanwhile, the computer revolution continued. Microchips made it possible to make much smaller, much smarter machines than anyone could have imagined in the '50s. In 1984, the Macintosh was released to the public. Its graphic interface, so very different from the PCs and Apple IIs that preceded it, made it a natural for game programs as well as for word-processing and graphics programs, for which it was (theoretically) purchased.

Every Mac owner had at least two games onboard immediately, the Puzzle desk accessory, and a maze program called Amazing, which was part of the Mac's Guided Tour. Since the Mac was first marketed as a business tool, the avowed purpose of the maze was to teach users how to work the mouse. But it didn't take three levels of complexity or dozens of different mazes like the one shown in Fig. 1-7 to teach mouse manipulation. Even though they might not have admitted it at the time, Apple wanted people to play with their Macs, not just use them.

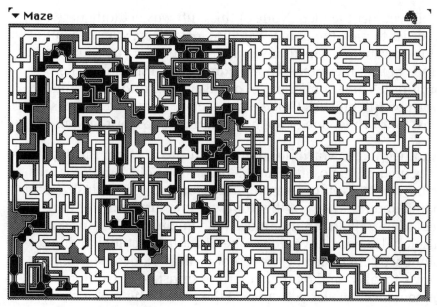

1-7 *There's more to this than just mousing around.*

IT'S A MAD, MAD, MAD, MAD MAC

Some of the first Mac games came from Infocom and from a California software company called Silicon Beach. Infocom's games were text adventures. Zork became a trilogy. Planetfall and Stationfall were interactive science-fiction works by Steve Merezetsky, which were also released as paperback stories. Part of the charm of Infocom's games was the packaging. Each came with an assortment of maps, booklets, and other goodies that might help you play the game, or at least provide some amusing desktop clutter. Hitchhiker's Guide to the Galaxy is a good example. In the box were the following:

- One 400K disk and a few pages of instructions;
- One brochure about the Guide;
- Destruct orders for your home and planet;
- A wad of fluff;
- Super-Chromatic Peril-Sensitive Sunglasses;
- A cellophane package supposedly containing a microscopic spacefleet;
- A genuine Don't Panic! button;
- No tea. . . .

Well, you get the idea. None of this stuff was actually necessary in order to play the game. The sunglasses were stamped out of black cardboard. The fluff was there to remind you that the four kinds of fluff mentioned in the game were important. The buttons became something of a cult symbol and were proudly worn by Hitchhiker's Guide players of all ages. Hitchhiker's Guide was, for a while, one of the best-selling games for the Mac.

Another game, which has remained a success from the day it first appeared, is Microsoft's Flight Simulator. Flight Simulator puts you in the cockpit of a small plane. You can see the instrument panel and the view out the front window, just as if you were in a real plane. Flight Simulator used the medium—the Mac screen display—to good advantage. The illusion of actually flying a plane was enhanced by the motor sounds that came from the Mac's speaker, and by the pattern of smashed glass that appeared whenever you crashed the plane. The motor changes pitch when you move the throttle, just like a real one, and putters and dies when you run out of gas, crash, or stall out.

Silicon Beach was a small software company in southern California that introduced several Mac games in the early days of Macintosh. They also went on to produce one of the best graphics programs ever, SuperPaint. The Silicon Beach games, particularly Airborne, Dark Castle, and Beyond Dark Castle, featured synthesized classical music and realistic sound effects. Silicon Beach also produced World Builder, a tool kit that let Mac users create their own games.

The World Builder system included a set of paint tools for drawing maps and scenery in the graphics windows, a text editor to help you write the story, and a programming editor to write scripts to link the windows and make the game operate. Once completed and saved, the game could stand on its own. You didn't need World Builder to run it. Figure 1-8 shows a typical World Builder game. In this one, you're a would-be actor, trying to succeed in Hollywood.

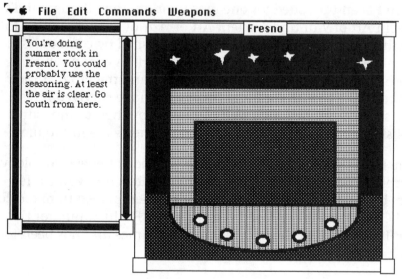

1-8 To go south, type S.

World Builder games were released as shareware or freeware, according to the author's whim. Some were quite intricate and could take hours or days to play out. One popular collection, The MACnificent 7 CD-ROM, contains 71 different World Builder games!

Unfortunately, the success of SuperPaint and Silicon Beach's other graphics programs, notably Digital Darkroom and Personal Press, led Aldus Corporation to buy the company. The Silicon Beach games, which were written in black and white for compact Macs, more or less got lost in the shuffle when Silicon Beach was reorganized as Aldus Consumer Products division. And it appears that Aldus has no plans to continue support for World Builder or Silicon Beach's other games. They haven't been updated for System 7, and probably will not be. However, they will run fairly reliably if you turn off 32-bit addressing on the memory control panel and set the monitor to black and white. World Builder games take a long time to load. Don't assume the game has frozen until you have given it a couple of minutes.

Many games have come and gone since the early days of the Mac. Some aren't compatible with the newer systems, and haven't been upgraded for one reason or another. Brøderbund's Ancient Art of War and Ancient Art of War at Sea regrettably fall into this category. Some games were published by companies that have since gone out of business, like Miles Computing, whose demise left players of Fool's Errand and the Puzzle Gallery with no place to turn for help. Those that have survived have done so because they were well supported by their authors and publishers, but more important, because they were fun to play.

Some have been upgraded to take advantage of new technology. Interplay's Battle Chess, a great game in black and white a few years back, is now even more awesome when played from a color CD-ROM. Microsoft released version 4.0 of Flight Simulator this year. It's still one of the best-selling Mac games and has been for much of the past nine years.

Shareware games—the good news

Today, there are literally hundreds of commercial games for the Macintosh and thousands of non-commercial *shareware* and *freeware* games. Shareware, if you don't know the term, is any program that its creator is willing to share with others. The concept originated way back in the beginning days of computing, when those who had written programs for a particular system passed them around to others.

Today, shareware comes with a price tag. The price is generally quite low, compared to that of any of the commercial games. Typical shareware game fees are in the $5 to $10 range, so it's not much of a strain on one's budget. Freeware, as its name suggests, is free. It's also sometimes called Happyware—"If you like it, smile"—or PostCardware—"Please send the author a postcard from your home town."

You can find shareware games for downloading on all of the commercial online services. That is, all except Prodigy which, as of this writing, doesn't support any kind of downloads for Macintosh. The best sources are CompuServe and America Online's Mac-game forums. Both of these are extremely active, and new games are added nearly every day. Delphi and GEnie also have a fair selection. User-group bulletin boards are another good place to look for games. These groups are likely to publish disks, or even CD-ROMs, of shareware games and other useful and fun applications.

Unlike commercial games, shareware is meant to be distributed. It's okay to share a shareware disk with your friends, to copy shareware programs from anyplace you find them. It's not okay to buy a commercial game and give copies of it to your friends. In many cases, if you own two computers, for instance a desktop Mac and a PowerBook, it's illegal to copy the same commercial application onto both hard drives. Check the wording on the package or in the manual. Some software publishers expect you to buy a separate copy of their product for each computer you use. Others simply say that you can only run the application on one computer "at a time."

Although it sounds contradictory, there are also commercial shareware publishers that put out catalogs of thousands of disks of games and other goodies. Each disk costs a few dollars and has a half dozen or so different programs on it. The important thing to remember when you buy these disks, or when you pay by the minute to download a game from an online service, is that you must pay the shareware fee if you keep on using the program. In the case of the commercial shareware disks, as well as the bulletin-board systems (BBSs) or online service distribution, the program author gets nothing for the use of his or her material unless you pay the fee.

The advantage to shareware is that you can try out something for next to no cost. If you don't like the game or other application, or if it doesn't run on your system, you haven't lost much. On the other hand, if you do use it, you have a moral obligation to pay for it. Shareware authors deserve payment for their work, and especially for choosing to distribute it to the general public. If we don't support the shareware concept, pretty soon there won't be any more new shareware games to enjoy. Remember—If you play, pay! End of sermon.

And now the bad news . . .

There's one other thing to watch out for when you buy, borrow, or download a shareware or freeware game—viruses! A computer *virus* is a nasty bit of code that can do bad things to your system, like erasing the contents of your hard drive, filling the system folder with its own useless non-information, or otherwise messing things up. Some are written by pranksters, and are intended to be relatively harmless. Others do serious damage. We can only speculate as to why someone with enough knowledge to create a virus wouldn't write a useful program instead. Some of the "harmless" viruses actually do quite a lot of harm because of errors in their programming.

You can protect yourself against known viruses by using a virus detection program like Virex or Virus Detective. You can eradicate any bugs it finds with another application such as Disinfectant, which removes the virus from any files that have been infected. The problem is that these, and other similar programs, can only recognize the viruses they've already been taught about. When a new one comes along, it's possible for it to sneak into a number of computers before it is detected. Chris Johnson's GateKeeper works a bit differently from other anti-virus programs and will warn you about any suspicious activity on your Mac. It often finds new virus strains that the other programs miss.

Even though you might be using anti-virus programs, for your own protection get your shareware and freeware from a reliable source. Commercial disks and commercial online services are generally very reliable, as are well-run user-group bulletin boards. Other boards are less so. Sysops (system operators) on private boards might not scan every program for viruses before they release it, and they might not check to see that it works.

Even if you are downloading from a source you believe to be reliable, it's a good idea to scan all incoming programs for viruses. You never know what might appear. Several years ago, two virus-infected games appeared on the InterNet. The bug was spotted in a matter of days, but meanwhile there had been over 1,000 downloads, worldwide, of the infected programs. Fortunately, Mac viruses are less common than PC viruses, but it never hurts to be careful.

The future of Mac games?

If I could really predict the future of computer gaming in general and Mac gaming in particular, I wouldn't be writing books for a living. I'd be rich from investing in some small company with a couple of computers, and some kind of crazy dream. That's where today's classics like Spaceward Ho!, SimCity, and Tesserae have come from. In fact, that's more or less where the Mac itself came from.

IT'S A MAD, MAD, MAD, MAD MAC

My best guess is that the next new wrinkle in computer gaming will be some form of virtual reality (VR) interface for the home-computer market, perhaps a helmet and glove. We're beginning to see VR in the arcade, and it's big in the news media. VR will literally put you in the middle of the action.

CD-ROM has made "bigger" games, with more elaborate graphics, full-color QuickTime movies, and digitized sound, a possibility. There have been a couple of attempts at a 3D Mac game already, and that seems like another area that's worth exploring. Networked games and modem games are yet another area that's seen tremendous growth in the past two years and will continue to grow.

Beyond VR might be direct connection with your computer. Science-fiction writers William Gibson and George Alec Effinger have postulated that perhaps we'll be able to have microchips directly implanted into our brains at some future point. These could be plugged into a central system letting us voyage interactively in cyberspace, or link nervous systems with other users in a vast neural network. This might seem far-fetched, but consider how far we've come since the days of ENIAC. Whatever the future holds, two things are certain: it will be exciting, and it will be fun.

2

Text adventure games

A text adventure is a game in which there's a plot to be followed. You are the hero, or at least the main character. (Some text adventures feature characters who are decidedly unheroic.) You must work your way through the plot, figure out how to solve the puzzles, fight the monsters or bad guys, find the treasure, and get out of whatever situations you get into. During the early days of the Mac, text adventures were published by the dozens, the most prolific publisher being Infocom. Infocom's games read like a good novel.

In fact, *Hitchhiker's Guide to the Galaxy* was a good novel before it became a game, and Infocom even published Planetfall and Stationfall as novels after the games proved popular. Because Infocom specialized in text games, as players and software got more sophisticated, business dropped off, and the company eventually closed its doors.

Recently, though, there has been a resurgence of interest in text games, caused at least partially by the advent of the Mac PowerBook. Text games are ideal for PowerBook play. You don't need fancy graphics or precision mouse control. All you need is a semi-legible screen and a keyboard. Most of Infocom's adventures have been rereleased by Activision in two sets as The Lost Treasures of Infocom, Vols. I & II.

 Volume I of The Lost Treasures of Infocom includes the Zork Trilogy: Zork I, II, and III, as well as Beyond Zork and Zork Zero, two later additions to the series in which Infocom attempted a limited use of graphics. Zork I developed from its mainframe prototype, the Zork game created at MIT by Dave Leibling and Marc Blank, Infocom's founders.

Playing text adventures requires imagination, perserverance, a notepad and pencil, and graph paper for mapmaking. Text adventures tend to be set in some sort of maze-like environment. Part of the game is negotiating your way through the maze. Some games come with maps, others don't. You can sketch out a rough map on graph paper as you go along, remembering that some doors are one-way, and rooms might not always be rectangular. Taking notes might also prove helpful. Sometimes you'll find magic words written on walls, or you'll need a particular word from a line of Vogon poetry to unlock the case and retrieve the Sub-Atomic Plotter. There's no scroll-back function on these games. If you haven't made notes you might regret it!

It's also a good idea to make frequent saves as you play. If you do, when disaster falls you needn't start from square one again. You can opt to restore a saved position. Always save before you head into a risky situation, before a fight, or before you eat or drink an unknown substance.

There's a Script command on the File menu of most games. Selecting it creates a written transcript of the game. Unfortunately, this only works with ImageWriter printers, which can handle a line at a time. It won't work with a laser printer, or with print spoolers. There's no way to save the transcript as a file, either, probably because when these games were written everything had to be saved onto a 400K floppy, which also had the system and the game on it. These games typically occupy only about 100K of disk space.

Communicating with interactive fiction

Since you play a text adventure through your keyboard, communicating with the game means typing simple commands, whenever you see the >> prompt. Most commands are expressed as imperative sentences. Go east. Open the door. Take the sandwich. Give the pickle to the robot. Always press <Return> after you enter a command. When you're deciding what to type, it helps to think in terms of short words. The parser looks only at the first six letters of a word, so Pickle, pickles, and Picklefork are all assumed to be the same.

Traveling from place to place in an adventure game is simple. Type the direction in which you want to go, and you'll be carried along in that direction until there's some reason to stop. You needn't type the whole word. N for north, E for east, SW for southwest, and so on, will get you there. D for down and U for up are occasionally useful. If you try to walk into a wall or get off the beaten path, you'll generally be told "You can't go that way." Sometimes, you'll be told why you can't. "The door is locked." "There is no path in that direction."

Words such as take, open, read, look, examine, hit, drop, get, give, and close will prove extremely useful. Of course, you also have to specify what it is that you want to take, read, or otherwise do. You needn't be too wordy. Take gold will generally do as well as Take the gold coin. Some games keep score according to the number of turns you take, each typed interaction being a turn. So it's to your advantage to combine two commands when you can. Figure 2-1 shows a screen from Zork I, with the current score in the upper right-hand corner. In 41 turns, we have earned 20

```
≣≣≣≣≣≣≣≣≣≣≣≣≣≣≣≣ Zork I ≣≣≣≣≣≣≣≣≣≣≣≣≣≣≣≣
Living Room                                        Score: 20/41

>put egg in trophy case
Done.

>look
Living Room
You are in the living room. There is a doorway to the east, a wooden door with
strange gothic lettering to the west, which appears to be nailed shut, a
trophy case, and a large oriental rug in the center of the room.
Your collection of treasures consists of:
  A jewel-encrusted egg

>read door
The engravings translate to "This space intentionally left blank."

>
```

2-1 *Placing Zorkian treasures in the trophy case earns extra points and keeps them from being stolen by a grue.*

points by finding a jeweled egg in a bird's nest and putting it into the trophy case.

The parser recognizes multiple objects with certain verbs, if you separate them with the word and or with a comma. It also recognizes multiple commands, if you separate them by then or by a period. Thus, you could save a couple of steps in this scenario:

You are on a platform outside the hatch leading into a spaceshuttle. A phaser gun and a can of cola are on a small stand. The shuttle hatch is open to the south. An elevator is to the north.

>>Take gun and can. Go S.

Gun, taken.

Can, taken.

You are inside a spaceshuttle....

If the parser doesn't recognize one of the words you've entered, it
will follow the commands up to that point and then stop.

>>Take gun. Shoot monster.

You can't see any gun here!

So, in the exchange above, you could safely assume that the
monster has not been dispatched. Since you couldn't "take" the
gun, you obviously couldn't "use" the gun.

The parser also recognizes all and it. When there are a number of
useful objects, rather than typing Take pliers, knife, and rope just
say Take all. It only works if all of the objects are visible. If the
knife was in a drawer, you'd miss it.

You can occasionally get some help during the game by asking a
who, what, or where question. Not always, though—you might
also get a less-than-helpful response. If you encounter intelligent
creatures as you work through the game, you can converse with
them by typing a name, then a comma, and whatever you want
to say. Thus, you might try something like:

>>Wizard, give me the sword.

Stranger, what is a grue?

They might help you, or they might not understand you. Some
characters dislike idle chatter, and will attack or leave the area if
you speak to them.

Taking command

All Infocom games, and other text adventures they inspired, use
a set of basic commands. Several of them deal with the way the
scenario is presented to you. Verbose gives you a full description
of each location and any objects in it, every time you enter it.
Brief describes the spot in full the first time you enter, but
subsequent visits are described only by the name of the location
and a list of the objects in the scene. Superbrief gives you only the

place name, even though you might never have been there before. (You can always type look for a description.) Adventures begin in Brief mode, and can be changed to Verbose or Superbrief by typing the command at any >> prompt.

Look always gives you a full description of your location. Examine tells you about an object. Inventory gives you a list of what you are holding. It also tells you what you're wearing if that's significant. Diagnose reports on your health, and in some games, on your spiritual condition as well. Wait makes time pass in the story. Save takes a "snapshot" of your current position. Restore returns you to the saved position, and Restart obviously lets you start at the beginning again. Quit ends the game. If you want to come back to the point at which you left off at some future date, be sure to save before you quit.

Zonked by Zork

The Zork Trilogy comes with an interesting, and highly irrelevant history of the kings of Quendor, and particularly the Flathead Dynasty. You don't need to know any of it in order to win the game. You do need to know a few things, though.

The most important is that objects placed in the trophy case won't be stolen from you. That's why valuable items like the jeweled egg and the painting should be placed there. You can kill the troll with a sword, but you'll have better luck with the Cyclops if you don't fight him. Try feeding him. If you remember your mythology, you'll know whose name to type to get rid of the Cyclops. You must map the maze in order to get through it, to reach the Cyclops. But that's only a small part of the Great Underground Empire.

Zork II picks up where Zork I left off. You begin by finding a familiar-looking sword and lantern. Ever the intrepid adventurer, you head south down a tunnel, across the usual assortment of footbridges, caverns, and tunnels to the strange world of the

Wizard of Frobozz. Your task here, as in Zork I, is to collect treasure. You also must locate and collect three colored spheres. The blue one is easy. It's in the Dreary Room all the way due north from the Carousel Room. But you'll need to have visited the Gazebo first. The key to the Dreary Room is in the lock, unfortunately on the other side of the door.

To retrieve the blue sphere you'll need a letter opener and a paper placemat. The red one is more difficult. Read the instructions for the robot, and be sure he's in the room when you attempt to take the red sphere. You can tell him to lift the cage. Don't push any buttons yourself! Let the robot do it. The tricky part of getting the white (clear) sphere is finding it. One might even say there's something fishy about it. And neither fish nor sea serpents can live long out of water.

In Zork II, the Demon is there to help you. If you die, he'll bring you back. Summon him by placing a black sphere in a pentagram, in the Wizard's Workroom. But, you know what they say about giving the Devil his due. In this case, you'll need to surrender your treasures, but you'll be able to get a better one. Type Demon, give me the wand.

In Zork III, you awaken from a dream to find yourself at the foot of an endless stairway, with your faithful friend the brass lantern in front of you. The passageways are as damp and medieval as before, but this is a more technological dungeon. You'll encounter strange machines, moving walls and boxes, and a touch-sensitive table as you work your way through this one in your quest to become the Dungeon Master. You'll need to acquire his clothes and tools—the hood and cloak, amulet and ring, the lore book, the key, and the wooden staff. Grue repellant would be helpful, too, but you'll need to find a way back to Zork II to get it. You can do it if you try.

Zork Zero departs from the "text-only" mode of the previous games. It supports color and graphics, both in a very limited form compared to games like King's Quest 6. The text is simply framed by a set of pillars that change color depending on where you are. Figure 2-2 shows you inside the castle. Over them is a

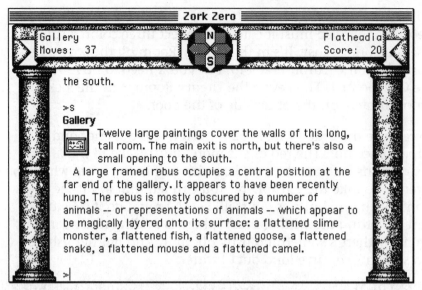

2-2 *Make a note of the location of the rebus. You'll need to come back here many times.*

compass rosette that indicates which directions you can travel in. No maps, no animation, no QuickTime movies . . . nevertheless, it's quite intriguing.

In the first scene, you are a servant at Lord Dimwit Flathead's castle. During the celebration over the completion of Lord Dimwit's statue, the wizard Megaboz casts a Curse that destroys Dimwit, his family, and most of the guests. You avoid the ensuing fireball by diving under a table, but have presence of mind enough to take the scrap of parchment left behind when the Wizard vanishes. Some 90 years later, you awaken to find yourself reborn as a descendent of that servant, and the only person who knows what can and must be done to stop the Curse. Your quest requires finding 24 items and tossing them into a cauldron, and then reciting the magic word from the scroll. It's not trivial. Your travels will take you into the torture chamber, up to the parapet, to the King's Solar, the Baily, and parts of the castle you probably never knew existed. But you won't be alone, at least not all the time. The Jester flits in and out, speaking in rhyme, offering you occasional help in the form of riddles and puzzles to solve, and games to win. You'll even master Double Fanucci and Peggleboz!

The Jester sometimes drops clues for you, too. If scraps of paper are blowing around, be sure to read them carefully. By the way, the word you need is on the scroll that comes with the game. (No, I am *not* going to tell you what the word is. If you bought the games, you have it. If you "borrowed" them, you don't deserve to win.) Hints are built into the game. Type hint when you get stuck, and follow the instructions.

Beyond Zork is the last of the "trilogy plus two." It bridges the gap between text and the later graphic adventures you'll learn about in chapter 3. Beyond Zork features a crude map that expands as you explore the countryside. It also features a Dungeons-and-Dragons-type character generator. You create your own hero by using one of six existing characters, or by letting the game roll the dice and create a new character for you. Your character has the attributes shown in Fig. 2-3. If you create a character from scratch, you can determine his or her attributes, but, as in real life, there's a limit to the character's potential. If he

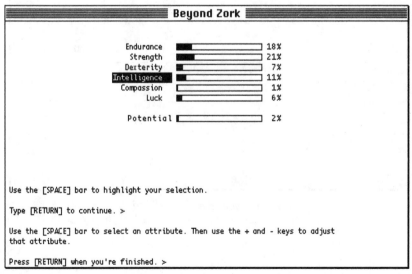

2-3 *There are, alas, limits. You can't make a character super strong and super intelligent. That only happens in real life.*

or she is tremendously strong, you won't be able to apply much intelligence, dexterity, or luck. The most successful game characters are those with a good balance of skills.

 The game preface hints that you must find the fabled Coconut of Quendor, not because you crave a piña colada, but because it contains the accumulated Magick wisdom of dynasties. Since you'll need some equipment for this quest, the game presents you with the opportunity to retrieve a wooden club, a lantern, and a dagger within the first few turns. Use your numeric keypad to move around, or use the mouse to click on a likely spot on the map. The game screen looks different from that of previous Infocom games. The scene is described in the upper box, and your interactions take place in the lower one. The map on the right changes as you move along, though it never gives you any more detail than you see in Fig. 2-4.

```
========================= Beyond Zork =========================
                          Shady Wall

  The air is cool here, beneath the shadow of a towering
  wall of rock.




North Market

>s
South Market

>s
Intersection

>sw
Shady Wall

>
```

2-4 *This looks like a dead end.*

And now for thumb thing completely different . . .

When Douglas Adams first wrote the *Hitchhiker's Guide to the Galaxy*, it was intended to be a radio drama, not a video game. Hitchhiker's Guide was originally broadcast in serial form by the BBC, and is heard occasionally on public radio stations in the United States (Adams' other broadcasting credit was as a writer for the Dr. Who series.) He admits to falling in love ("Well, strong like . . .") with the Zork games, and several of Infocom's other interactive stories, and consented to turn the Hitchhiker's Guide into a game.

As the scene opens, you find yourself in bed and feeling rather awful, in a "morning after" sort of way. You get up, take an aspirin that's in the pocket of your dressing gown, and go outside to see what's making that awful racket. It seems your house is about to be torn down to make way for a highway bypass. You fling yourself down into the mud to stop the bulldozer, and things go from bad to worse. Several turns later, you're in the local pub drinking beer with your friend, Ford Prefect, who has somehow convinced Mr. Prosser of the Village Council to lie down in your place. Prefect tells you that he's actually from another planet, and that earth is about to be bulldozed for an intergalactic bypass. *Déja vu* all over again.

Hearing a crash, you run outside. Your house is in ruins. You toss a cheese sandwhich from the bar to a passing dog, and rush to confront Prosser. The sky grows dark and Ford Prefect drops a small device with buttons. You pick it up and push the green one, as wind swirls around you. You awaken in the dark, onboard a Vogon warship. The device was a Sub-Etha signaling device, better known as a thumb. You've hitched the first of a number of rides. Your task is to collect tools, bits of fluff, and equipment of various kinds, and a cup of Advanced Tea Substitute. Figure 2-5 finds you and Ford in the Vogon ship. Ford has decided to take a nap, while you attempt to get a Babel Fish from the dispenser.

```
═══════════════════════ Hitchhiker's Guide ═══════════════════════
Vogon Hold                                           Score: 45/55
─────────────────────────────────────────────────────────────────
>put mail on satchel
Okay, the loose pile of junk mail is now sitting on the satchel.

>push dispenser button
A single babel fish shoots out of the slot. It sails across the room and hits
the dressing gown. The fish slides down the sleeve of the gown and falls to
the floor, landing on the towel. A split-second later, a tiny cleaning robot
whizzes across the floor, grabs the fish, and continues its breakneck pace
toward a tiny robot panel at the base of the wall. The robot plows into the
satchel, sending the babel fish flying through the air in a graceful arc
surrounded by a cloud of junk mail. Another robot flies in and begins madly
collecting the cluttered plume of mail. The babel fish continues its flight,
landing with a loud "squish" in your ear.


>|
```

2-5 *If the cleaning robots are so efficient, why is the Vogon ship such a mess?*

 That thing your Aunt gave you . . . it's a shopping bag, with magical properties. It stays with you no matter what, and holds an unlimited amount of stuff. Put the things you collect into the thing, and you won't ever be overloaded.

After you deal with the Bugblatter Beast of Traal, you'll be able to get a cup of real tea. Eventually, after an identity crisis or two, you obtain everything you need including a flowerpot. If you eat the fruit from the plant that grows when you plant the fluff, you will fall asleep and dream about one of the tools you've collected on your travels. When you wake up, you'll be able to give Marvin the Paranoid Android the correct tool to fix the hatch on the spaceyacht Heart of Gold. Opening the hatch permits you, Ford, Trillian, and Zaphod Beeblbrox to live happily ever after on the planet Magrathea. Earth? Well, it was only a "minor" planet . . ..

Hitchhiker's Guide has two different kinds of built-in hints. There are footnotes scattered throughout the game that will give you bits of useful information. When you reach one, you'll be told. To read it, simply type footnote. You can also consult the Guide, once

Ford has given it to you onboard the Vogon warship. Type Consult guide about . . .. Try consulting the Guide about fluff, thumb, babel fish, brownian motion, tea, and anything else that occurs to you. And don't take the towel in the very first scene when Ford tries to give it to you. If you do, the game's over.

More lost treasures

There are, in all, 20 different games in Lost Treasures, Volume I, and 11 more in the second volume. In addition to those already described, you'll find the following in Volume I:

Enchanter—A showdown between wizards leaves you, an Apprentice Enchanter, attempting to free the land from the clutches of an evil Warlock. Armed with Magick, you set out to vanquish Krill the Warlock.

Sorcerer—Having defeated Krill and earned a seat in the circle of Enchanters, you continue your studies under Belboz the Necromancer. Alas, Belboz has recently changed. Your concern for your friend and mentor grows. Then, he disappears.

Spellbreaker—Only you can break the mysterious curse . . .. Perhaps the key lies within a cube, but which one?

Suspended—You are the Central Mentality on a semi-automated planet. You are supposed to be in cryogenic suspension, asleep, for the next 500 years. But something has gone wrong . . .. The planet is in chaos. You have six robots with which to save yourself and your world.

Starcross—As a black-hole miner, you search the galaxies in your mining ship Starcross, hoping to harness a black hole that will make you rich. Instead, you meet an alien spaceship . . . .

Planetfall—Stellar Patrol: It's not just a job, it's an adventure? Somehow not the adventure you'd hoped for . . . .

IT'S A MAD, MAD, MAD, MAD MAC

Stationfall—Broom pushing leads to pencil pushing. Your excellent work as an Ensign 7th Class earned you a promotion. Now, you're a Lieutenant First Class, in charge of picking up forms to ask for more forms. Until things get exciting . . ..

The Lurking Horror—Set at GUI Tech (which bears a striking resemblance to MIT), you must find out who . . . or what . . . has made the computer eat your term paper.

Witness—It's 1938. You are a police detective, and you have 12 hours to solve a murder and arrest the killer. Your assistant, Sgt. Duffy, will help you prepare an ironclad case . . . if you can prove the murderer had a motive, the method, and the opportunity to commit the crime.

MoonMist—Something strange is going on at Tresyllian Castle. A ghost, a treasure, and a beautiful woman test your detective skills.

Suspect—There's a Halloween Ball at Ashcroft Farm. You're having a wonderful time, until you're framed for a murder you didn't commit. Can you find out who did, and why? Your time is limited, and the murderer is right behind you!

Ballyhoo—Who knows what evil lurks under the Big Top? Certainly not you—you're just an innocent spectator hanging around after the show. The circus owner's daughter has been kidnapped! Is it an inside job? Perhaps.

Infidel—How can anyone lose anything as big as a pyramid? You'll find out, when you locate the lost pyramid and match wits with the ancient Egyptians to capture a treasure. Or will the sun bake you into a pretzel first?

Volume II brings 10 more works of interactive fiction, adventure, fantasy, and mystery, plus a puzzle collection that almost defies description. Presenting:

A Mind Forever Voyaging—You are PRISM, the world's first sentient machine. Your life until now has been that of a normal child, teenager, young adult. You've developed humor, compassion, and a conscience, as well as formidable knowledge. Now, you must test a future simulation. If it works, it will save the planet. If not . . ..

Cutthroats—As a skilled diver, you will try to salvage a treasure from one of four shipwrecks near your home port of Hardscrabble Island. Some characters in the story can help you. Others will try to stop you.

Wishbringer—As postal clerk in a small village, you deliver a strange envelope to the Magic Shop. Soon you are locked in a battle between the forces of Good and Evil. A magic stone called Wishbringer can help you make the town safe again, but only if you find it and use it correctly.

Seastalker—Save the Aquadome from the attacking sea monster, and from the traitor who sabotages it from within.

Trinity—You are an American tourist, strolling through Kensington Gardens in London, when World War III starts, and ends, with a bang. Perhaps you'll end with it, perhaps you'll enter a different dimension and somehow wind up in the Nevada desert as Operation Trinity, the testing of the first nuclear weapon is about to occur.

Hollywood Hijinx—Your uncle, Buddy Burbank, was a Hollywood movie mogul. His wife Hildy was fabulously wealthy. Their palatial home and fortune will be yours if you can locate the 10 "treasures" from Uncle Buddy's film career. You have only one night to do it . . ..

Sherlock—"Dr. Watson, I presume? Well, perhaps you'll be good enough to give me a hand with the case of the Missing Crown Jewels."

Bureaucracy—Scarier than the Lurking Horror, more fatal than a thermonuclear device . . ... If you don't have a credit card, you're a non-person, and if you don't fill out the forms correctly, you don't have a chance.

Plundered Hearts—As a young English noblewoman in the late 1600s, you have been summoned to the bedside of your ailing father. Alas, dear old Dad is in the West Indies. Your ship is attacked by pirates, and you are carried off by a dashing pirate captain. Danger, excitement, and romance follow, in this computerized bodice-ripper.

Border Zone—East meets West. You'll visit scenic Frobnia, in the Eastern Bloc, and neutral Litzenburg. In each chapter you're a different character—an American businessman, an Eastern spy, a Western spy. This game comes with a Frobnian phrasebook and tourist guide.

Nord and Bert Couldn't Make Head or Tail of It—It's not a story, exactly. It's a collection of the most outrageous puns and puzzles, spoonerisms, cliches, and word plays you'll ever encounter. Part of the game is figuring out how to solve the puzzles. Figure 2-6 gives you a taste of Nord's and Bert's particular brand of humor.

```
═══════════════════════ Nord and Bert ═══════════════════════
Location: Aisle of Manicotti              Bizarre score: 7 out of 22
Other aisles: Desserts, British, Write, Meets, Misc
You toss the mints down the aisle to him. He summarily bites them, then flings
them away over the shelves. There's a noticable improvement in his breath, even
from here.

The pallid gentleman continues his rampage by murdering, in cold red dye #2, a
package of Froot Loops.

>kill vampire with steak
The pun is mightier than the sword.

The pallid gentleman continues his rampage by devilishly ripping into a package
of pasta primavera.

>kill vampire with stake
Under your gaze, the meat starts sizzling and smoking wildly, licking flames
into the air till nothing is left to it but a charred and pointed stick.

With a powerful thrust, you drive the stake deep into the heart of the now
horrified cereal murderer. He collapses to the floor, blood trickling out of the
sides of his mouth. Then he vanishes with a puff of pale blue smoke.

>
```

2-6 This is the oddest grocery store you've ever been in.

Build your own adventure game

Text-based adventure games were popular. The only problem was that once you finally "solved" one, you were through with it. And you wanted another and another . . . they were like salted peanuts. Aside from the expense of buying new games, Infocom wasn't publishing fast enough for truly dedicated players, who kept wanting more. It wasn't long before programmers created systems for writing text adventure games, so ordinary people without programming skills could also write their own adventure games.

The most popular of these game-creation systems are Text Adventure Development System (TADS) and Adventure Game Toolkit (AGT). Both are shareware, and both are still available from the usual shareware sources. TADS includes a game called Ditch Day Drifter, plus the compiler to assemble your own games. Paying your shareware fee gets you a manual that tells you how to use the compiler. While you're waiting to receive it (and frankly, you won't be able to do anything without it), try out Ditch Day Drifter. A scene from the game is shown in Fig. 2-7. It's a

```
  File  Edit  Commands  Travel  Fonts  Sizes
═══════════════════════ TADS ═══════════════════════
Laundry Room                                    10/161
Laundry Room
   You are in the laundry room.  There is a washing machine against one wall.  The
exit is to the south.

>examine washing machine
The washing machine is closed.  There's nothing in the washing machine.

>open washing machine
Opening the washing machine reveals a blue jeans.

>take jeans
Taken.
>take key
*Some* adventure games would try to impose their authors' misguided sense of ethics on you at
this point, telling you that you don't feel like picking up the key, or you don't have time to do
that, or that it's against the rules to even possess a master key, much less steal one from some
other student's pants that you happened to find in a laundry, or even more likely that you are
unable to take the key while wearing that dress.  However, you're the player, and you're in
charge around here, so I'll let you make your own judgments about what's ethical and proper
here...  You've already got your hands full.

>
```

2-7 *One of the nice things about interactive games is putting your personality into them.*

cleverly written game, and somewhat difficult to win. Unnkulian Adventure is another TADS game that's exceptionally well done and can be found in many shareware game collections.

AdventureMaker is a very good shareware text-game creator for the beginner. It has the distinct advantage of coming with the necessary documentation, and in fact is free, as its author says, " . . . for your own pleasure and use. However, if you create an adventure that you are particularly proud of and wish to distribute publically, then you must pay the registration fee for AdventureMaker which is $30."

How the games work . . ..

All text adventure games function in more or less the same way. Games have Rooms, within which are Objects, upon which Actions can be performed. These three parameters—Rooms, Objects, and Actions—determine everything that takes place during the game. Each parameter has its own type of record— RoomRecords, ObjectRecords, and ActionRecords—and all of the records are linked. Rooms call objects, objects call actions, actions call objects, objects call rooms. The hard part in writing an adventure is making sure that you have all the links right.

When you begin a game, you'll see an opening screen and be prompted to ask for instructions. If you type Y, they'll be displayed; if not, you'll be given a description of Room 2 of the game. (Room 1 is your pocket, and contains whatever you're carrying, wearing, or wielding.) The RoomRecord holds the room description, and links to any objects that might be found in the room.

Each time you type in a command and <Return>, the input line goes to the *parse* module. The parser takes the input line and breaks it down to separate words. First, it checks to see if the command is being directed to another character. Then, it looks for a verb, a noun, a preposition, and another noun as the object of the preposition. It does this by eliminating extra words like the and please; and by checking and then eliminating adjectives. For example, suppose you typed Slave, give bottle to me. First, it would verify that slave is a character in the story, and that slave is a listed object in that room. Then it would check the verb, and the first noun. Give...to is a known action, so it would look to see what is given.

The program then calls the execute module, which selects a procedure to call based on the verb (give, take, eat, wield, wear, etc). Then, is bottle on the list of objects that can function with that verb? If it is, what happens to it? Giving it to yourself effectively transfers it from the current room's object list to the Room 1 object list, since you now posess it.

The parser examines up to five words at a time: addressee, verb, noun, preposition, and an object of the preposition. If any of these elements are missing, the *empty string* " " is returned in its place, and you are told "There doesn't seem to be any . . . in that sentence."

Nouns can have attributes of various types. Each noun has a location, of course. It can be wearable, edible, moveable, etc. If a noun lacks the attribute necessary to interact with a particular verb, you'll generate a response like this:

>>Eat castle.

Silly, you can't eat a castle.

Certain verbs invoke "special" responses. Examine brings up a text file description of the noun. Look restates the description of a room. Directions are entered as verbs, with the go command understood. Some "specials" will cause other events to occur. For instance, if you enter Blow up castle, you'll find yourself blown up with it, either ending the game or carrying you many rooms away.

To create a good game, you must design puzzles that can be solved, and tools or treasures that can be obtained by applying skill and luck. Randomness can be effective. If the plot calls for the player to fight a creature, the results of the fight can be random or predetermined. Once you've played a dozen or so text games, you'll be familiar enough with the structure to begin mapping out your own.

Games can be pure fantasy, mystery, science fiction or even instructional, like the infamous Templates of Doom, which introduced new users to the functions of Lotus 1-2-3. If you intend to publish your game, even as freeware, avoid "borrowing" someone else's story for it. The author of your favorite thriller might be flattered to discover you've turned his or her work into a game, but you might also end up in jail for copyright violations. Be original—it's safer and more fun.

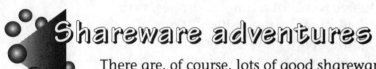

Shareware adventures

There are, of course, lots of good shareware adventure games that other people have written and posted to bulletin boards, or submitted to user groups and other shareware distribution services. Many have been written using one of the game construction sets above. A few seem to be completely original.

One of the more unusual ones I've found is called Murder in the Stacks. It's set in a library, where you have come to do some research. The point of the game, according to its author, is to figure out the point of the game. It's whimsically written and very clever. Figure 2-8 shows a typical interaction. The only drawback is that if you make a mistake, you must start from scratch. There's—deliberately—no way to save, but as the game's creator points out, "You can save yourself by not making dumb moves. This is called Reality Training."

Hypertext games

Hypertext is a remarkable writing tool, and can be used for gaming as well as creating serious interactive fiction. Hypertext works by letting you annotate certain keywords in a page of text, and by creating a complex system of links and branches that

```
▼ ⬤ File  Score  Inventory  Time  Tips  Save  Sponsor          11:10⅞

? up

You are now at the north stairs on the History/Religion Level.  To the west
you see stacks and stacks of history books, to the east is a glassed-in area
entitled 'Special Collections,' and a corridor extends south.
? s

Reference Desk, Level 4.  You converse with the friendly library help,
and learn about the American modes of research.  Suddenly you look at your
 Swiss watch and realize it is 23:10:31 in the real world.  You feel the need
to finish your task, since your glorious folk are depending on you.
A hallway leads east, and the lobby runs north and south.  Actually,
the lobby is standing still.  It's the people that are running north and south.
? s

You approach a study carrel on the 4th floor.  The carrel is unoccupied.
To the west you see Microform Readers, to the east you see stairs,
and the ever-present north and south lobby lies to the north and south.
? s
```

2-8 This game even checks the clock on your Mac, and reminds you of the time occasionally.

might take you from one part of the story unexpectedly to another, or keep bringing you back to the same spot. Hypertext lets you explore a work of fiction much as you explore a cave in Adventure.

The prime example of Hypertext gaming is an interative novel called King of Space, by Sarah Smith, published by Eastgate Systems. King of Space is both an erotic (adult) work of fiction, and a collection of puzzles, made more difficult because there are no directions for solving many of them. It's possible to get through the story, or at least to reach one of the endings of the story without solving most of the puzzles. The nature of Hypertext allows the story to have animated illustrations, puzzles, and even music and sound effects. It's literally interactive fiction. Figure 2-9 shows an example.

PG 13

Eastgate also publishes StorySpace, a Hypertext authoring tool for linking ideas into a coherent form, with notes, pictures, maps, commentary, and other related elements joined in a way that lets

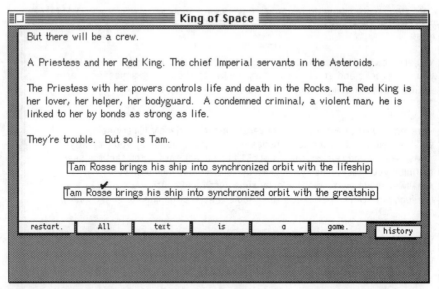

2-9 *These two choices represent a fork in the story path. You must choose one or the other.*

you access them in any order you wish. You could use it to create your own interactive fiction, complete with as many maps, puzzles, and other goodies as you want to put into it. The only thing more fun than putting words on a screen is putting words and pictures together on a screen.

3

Adventure goes graphic

Text games made sense when text was all a computer knew how to put on the screen. But the Mac's graphic environment, along with the proliferation of video games, suggested that maybe games on a computer screen didn't necessarily have to be composed of ASCII characters. Spacewar and games of that type are generally considered to be *arcade* games. Like the games at a carnival or amusement park, the object is to score points by shooting something.

Graphic adventures, although point scores and occasional shooting sprees might be involved, are much more like text adventures. You work your way through various scenes, figuring out what you need to do to get the object, kill the monster, and get out of the cave, dungeon, or whatever you've gotten into. Your character is determined by the game you are playing. You might be a spaceship pilot, an explorer, a detective, or just a lonely guy in search of a date. Most graphic adventures rely quite a bit on text. The graphics illustrate the action, or provide a map to help you find your way around. In current versions of graphic adventures, you can navigate your way through the scenery by clicking rather than typing a direction. Click on an object to use it, or to add it to your inventory.

Sierra On-Line and the quest for fun

Many of the original graphic adventures came from Sierra On-Line. And Sierra On-Line came from a shy Californian housewife named Roberta Williams, her hacker husband Ken, and an Apple II. Ken Williams had worked his way up in the computer world as a self-taught programmer, then as a computer consultant for banks and similar institutions. Most of his work was done on large mainframes, but when his younger brother introduced him to the Apple II, he decided it would be a "fun toy." He brought one home. Roberta, busy with two small children, had little interest in computers, beyond knowing that Ken's work paid the bills. One night Ken called Roberta in to look at the Apple II. She saw on the screen:

> You are standing at the end of a road before a small brick building. Around you is a forest....

It was the original Adventure game, ported from the PDP-1 to the Apple. She was instantly intrigued. Ignoring the kids, the housework, and normal sleeping hours, she played Adventure almost nonstop for days; drawing maps, backtracking, and figuring it out bit by bit. A month later she'd solved it, and went looking for more. There were a few other adventure games at the local computer store. She found them ridiculously easy, and set out to write her own.

The game was called Mystery House, and it required some detective work as well as puzzle solving and treasure finding. The premise was that you were at a house party in an old Victorian mansion. Your fellow party guests were being murdered, one by one, and you had to find the murderer. Ken Williams saw some possibilities in the game, and invested in a new gadget that let you draw crude shapes on a tablet that would then appear on the Apple's screen. Roberta sketched out the rooms of the mansion and stick figures to represent the people in the story. In a month, they had produced the first graphic adventure.

After getting "not good enough" offers from several software companies, Ken and Roberta decided to distribute the game themselves. Meanwhile, Ken had hired several part-time programmers to work on a project involving the translation of FORTRAN to the Apple II. The company he had formed for this project was called On-Line. On-Line's first product was Mystery House, distributed in zip-lock baggies with a disk and a photocopied page of instructions. Roberta managed the duplication, packing, and shipping from her dining room table, and at night worked on a second fantasy adventure game.

Dropping FORTRAN to concentrate on game creation, On-Line soon became a successful company, adding more programmers and game authors, an advertising staff, and lots more games. Video games were becoming popular, and On-line started producing arcade-style computer games that were cloned from popular video-game titles, a practice that almost put them out of business as quickly as they'd gotten into it. Lawsuits followed. Wisely, On-Line switched much of its effort back to Roberta Williams' graphic adventures. King's Quest, Space Quest, Police Quest, and Leisure Suit Larry each spawned numerous sequels. In 1983, the company moved to more spacious quarters and at the same time changed its name to Sierra On-Line and adopted the now-familiar mountain logo.

My kingdom for a quest

King's Quest has been one of the most successful graphic adventures of all time. There are now six games in the series, and more to come. In King's Quest I, you are young Gir Graham, bravest knight in the kingdom of Daventry. The three treasures—

a magic mirror that foretells the future, an enchanted shield that protects the kingdom from invasion, and a never-empty treasure chest—have been stolen from the King. You must recover the treasures and save the crumbling kingdom. Your successful quest leads the King to name you his heir and to grant you the throne of Daventry.

In KQ II, as King Graham, you see Daventry again prosperous, and realize that you must find a suitable Queen and establish your royal line. A look in the magic mirror shows a beautiful young woman named Valanice, held prisoner in a crystal tower. You vow to find her and set her free, and then to make her your queen.

KQ III relates the story of a boy called Gwydion, kidnapped as an infant by the evil wizard Manannan. Mastering the Wizard's spells, Gwydion gains his freedom and eventually reaches Daventry, to discover the land ravaged by a fearsome three-headed dragon. He uses his magic powers to rescue a victim from the dragon's lair, and to slay the dragon. A grateful King Graham rewards him.

As KQ IV begins, King Graham is ill. His court physicians can prescribe only one cure—a fruit from a magical tree in a far away country called Tamir. You, as King Graham's daughter Rosella, must go and find the healing fruit and bring it back in time to cure poor King Graham. Along the way you have adventures of all kinds and perform brave deeds.

The King's return to good health at the opening of KQ V attests to your success. King Graham is, in fact, feeling so good he takes a walk in the woods. A sudden cold wind sends him back to the castle, but the castle has vanished. As King Graham you must find the missing castle and your family. The search takes you on some strange adventures, including a visit to the island of the evil Mordack, whom you must defeat in order to get the castle back.

King's Quest VI takes you on a sea voyage. Your ship runs into trouble, and instead of landing in peaceful and familiar Sirenia, you find yourself shipwrecked in the Land of the Green Isles, where you must rescue a kidnapped princess.

Sierra games, and the King's Quest series in particular, feature beautifully drawn illustrations. Figure 3-1 shows a pair of scenes from KQ V. (They're even better in full color.) Quest games also include sound tracks with music and sound effects. The song *Girl in the Tower*, from KQ II has been released as a ballad, making it the first computer-game theme song to be played on the radio. Critics of the King's Quest games object to the plot's lack of "reality." One player comments about KQ V, "Here's this guy who's just had his house and family vanish in mid-air, and he's wandering around wishing he could buy a pie, and browsing in a toy store—and none of the townspeople recognize him as their king? It doesn't make sense."

3-1 *King's Quest and other Sierra games are notable for their detailed graphics.*

Other quests are just as well illustrated as the King's Quest series. Earlier quests are in black and white and later games in full color. Figure 3-2 shows a scene from Space Quest III, in which you, as spaceship pilot Roger Wilco, have landed onboard a space garbage ship and recycling plant. You must find and install

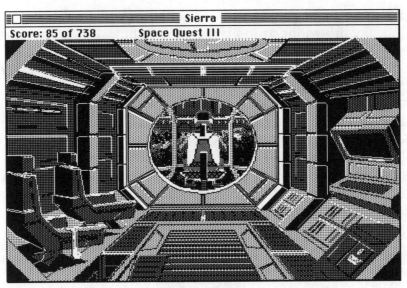

3-2 *The best way out is just to blast through the wall.*

a reactor in the pre-owned spaceship in order to give it enough power to escape from the garbage scow.

The rats have the reactor and you might have to steal it twice.

The newest Sierra Mac game is called Freddy Pharkas, Frontier Pharmacist. The year is 1888, the setting post-goldrush California. Freddy mixes all sorts of elixirs to restore the health of the residents of Coarsegold, (coincidentally the hometown of Sierra On-Line). Freddy's pharmacy is shown in Fig. 3-3. Freddy Pharkas was written by Josh Mandel and Al Lowe, the creator of the Leisure Suit Larry series. Like Larry, Freddy is full of outrageous jokes. It's also picked up on every Western-movie cliché in the books.

The music and sound effects are spectacular, and if you have MIDI or a Roland MT/CM-32 sound module, the game will sound even more awesome. It requires 256 colors, 10M of hard-disk real estate, a SuperDrive to install, and 4M of free RAM, plus System 7 or later to play. It also follows the new trend in Sierra games, in that it comes with very little printed documentation. There's a

3-3 *Freddie's Frontier Pharmacy.*

generic flyer on installation that deals more with DOS than with Macintosh systems. (Among the things it does not tell you, that you need to know, are that you must make sure 32-bit addressing is turned on, and you must set the sound driver to the sound system you are using.) If the sound doesn't run correctly, the game doesn't run at all. There's a Read Me file, which really wasn't much help for troubleshooting, and a Tech Support phone number that operates weekdays only.

Freddie Pharkas comes with a strictly tongue-in-cheek medical guide, which will tell you how to mix up the medicines you must dispense. It also tells you that game hints are available 24-hours a day, at a cost of 75¢ a minute, from a 900 number. It will, of course, take you several minutes and several dollars to work your way through the "If you're calling for hints on . . . push 1 now, for hints on . . . push 2 now," hierarchy to get the hint you need.

One minor difficulty with the newer Quest games is that they require a great deal of memory. The trend for more complex color and sound has brought a generation of what some computer experts disdainfully refer to as *fatware*. King's Quest VI is a case in point. The game comes on nine high-density disks, requires a minimum of 4M of free RAM plus System 7, and you must have 25M available on your hard disk to install it! In contrast, Police Quest I could be run from two 800K floppies, as could the early Space Quest games. The advantage the "larger" games have, of course, is that they can contain more detailed plots as well as 256-color animated scenes, music, and so on. The disadvantage is that unless you have a color Mac and lots of hard-disk space, you can't play. In many cases, you couldn't even load them, since many of the newer games are shipped on 1.4M floppies. A few of the earlier Quest games are still available from Sierra, and will run on older Macs.

! Cutting down on the size of the game files by eliminating sound or color graphics might work in some games, but others will freeze if they don't find the sound resource they're looking for. If disk space is a consideration, look for games that come with a black-and-white version. It will be much smaller.

Risqué business

It seems that every new technology goes through certain stages. One of these is the "sex" stage. Hackers at MIT, Berkeley, and other computing centers, at least those who know that sex exists have created their own programs with a sexual slant. One was a "dirty joke" generator. Another created printouts of naked women using ASCII symbols. Very early in the life of Sierra On-Line, in 1981, a game called SoftPorn appeared on the market. Its programmer had written the game as a way of having some fun while he learned to write in a particular language. Ken Williams bought it and distributed it as an On-Line product. The game required the player to purchase a condom, to have sex with a prostitute, and eventually to find and marry a beautiful blonde whose motto was "No weddie, no beddie." The game was eventually cleaned up from X to PG, and released as Leisure Suit Larry.

There are now five adventures in the Larry collection, with names like Passionate Patti Does Undercover Work. Only two of them have been released for the Mac, though PC users can run the whole set. (I wonder what that says about PC people.) They're only mildly raunchy, by today's standards, but really aren't for kids. Figure 3-4 shows a scene from the original Leisure Suit

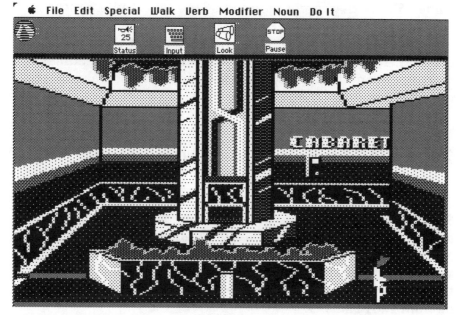

File Edit Special Walk Verb Modifier Noun Do It

Status   Input   Look   Pause

CABARET

3-4 *After winning some money in the casino, Larry heads for the Honeymoon Suite.*

Larry. Now, there's an "enhanced" version with 256 colors and a sound system like the one in Freddy Pharkas. However, like Freddy, it will only run on a Mac II or better.

Virtual Valerie is a "living" doll, but she's not the kind of a girl you'd bring home to Momma. Imagine a Barbie doll on steroids, dressed in black lace lingerie, and you've got a pretty good approximation of Valerie. She first appeared on floppies several years ago, and has been updated to CD-ROM. This, again, is a somewhat raunchy sexual spoof. Valerie's creators call it "cyberotica." Valerie is an example of computerized 3D modelling. She's fully animated, with digitized sound effects and an original musical score.

PG 13

Unfortunately, the trend hasn't stopped at PG. Several software companies have found a market for hardcore porn on CD-ROM, giving us "seedy" CDs. Some incorporate QuickTime movies, most are simply a catalog of the same type of pornographic pictures found in "adult" magazines. A few masquerade as games. Shown at a recent Macworld Expo were The Interactive Adventures of Seymore Butts—bet you can guess what *his* hobby is . . .; Digital Dancing—if you win, the dancer of your choice takes off everything; and Desktop Mistress. If you are a parent, keep an eye on the games your kids bring home. Some games are more "educational" than others.

Native Nick, Willy Beamish, Indy, and more . . .

Sierra is not the only company to produce graphic adventures, although it's easily the most successful. Today's favorites include Mutant Beach, from Inline Design; Dynamix' Adventures of Willy Beamish and Out of This World, from Interplay; as well as the Indiana Jones series, The Secret of Money Island, and Loom— all from LucasFilms Games.

Mutant Beach is sort of a cross between a graphic adventure and an arcade game. As Native Nick, you must find and return the jeweled nose of the great stone idol Mohawk. A greedy tourist took it, and in his wrath, Mohawk has released his control over the 12 idols in Idol City. They have mutated the island's inhabitants into strange creatures. (Nick escaped because he was off on a fishing trip at the time.) You must collect certain items that are hidden on the island, and give them to the idols. If you do so, they will help you find the nose.

Some of the mutants have been turned to stone. Others will try to steal your "stuff" before you can give it to the idols. Figure 3-5 shows Nick in conversation with one of the idols. You can "bonk" mutants to temporarily paralyze them so you can get safely past. Mutants can also bonk you, though, and you might drop your stuff when you get bonked. Oh, yes, and you're also racing against the clock.

If a mutant steals something from you, it will be buried in the same place you found it previously. It might help to keep notes. Mutant Beach requires six disks for a full-color installation, but

3-5 *Nick asks the stone idols for advice.*

the game also runs in black and white, even on color Macs. The black-and-white installation needs only one disk and takes up less than a megabyte of hard-disk space.

Willy Beamish is a typical kid—fond of frogs, Nintari video games, and Slam Dunk cola, but less fond of his sisters, school, and Alicia, the babysitter from Hell. Can Willy save the town of Frumpton from the evil Leona and Louis Humpford? Will Horny the frog win the jumping contest or be disqualified after drug-testing? What do the striking Plumbers have to do with it? And why are we asking all these questions? You'll find out when you play the Adventures of Willy Beamish. Your first challenge will be getting yourself out of detention.

If you wait until the teacher falls asleep, and take the bathroom pass from your desk, it'll be easier. Once you're home, be helpful! Cutting the grass brings you needed money. Pushing Brianna (not too high) in the swing helps keep you out of trouble. If you cut your thumb slicing vegetables, use antiseptic and a bandage. Otherwise you can't win the Nintari championship.

You'll travel around town, hitting some of the high spots including the Pizza store, the T-shirt cart, and the Plumber's Union Hall, just in time for the strike vote. See Fig. 3-6. Eventually, you'll end up in Humpford Mansion, and finally in the Humpford Sludge Works, where your trusty yo-yo will come in very handy. Just don't forget to flush! (Flushing is the only way to save Gordon and rid Frumpton of Leona and Louis.)

3-6 *If the plumbers go on strike, there will be trouble in Frumpton.*

Willy Beamish combines Disney-style (paint on acetate cell) animation with computer animation for unusually accurate motion, and characters with real personality. It's another seven-disk extravaganza though, and won't run in black and white or without a hard drive.

Out of This World also uses elaborate animation including real-time *rotoscoped* art (traced from films of actors going through the same motions), plus the full Hollywood editorial treatment of cinema-style closeups, zooms, and pans. All this is to help convince you that you've been flung into the space-time continuum by a nuclear experiment that went wrong. You must outwit, dodge, or overpower the alien monsters and other obstacles that come along.

Electronic Arts has given us a pair of good space-oriented graphic adventures, Starflight and Starflight II. In Starflight, you must equip a ship, select and train a crew, and then "boldly go where no man has gone before" in search of minerals, artifacts, and information about the origins of your empire. In Starflight II, you follow the intergalactic trade routes to find out why the once meek Spemin have become the most feared race in the galaxy.

A well-trained navigator is your most important crew member. You needn't be familiar with Starflight in order to play its sequel. Each is independent of the other. Both games will play in black and white or color on a Mac Plus or newer computer. Figure 3-7 shows the screen layout in Starflight.

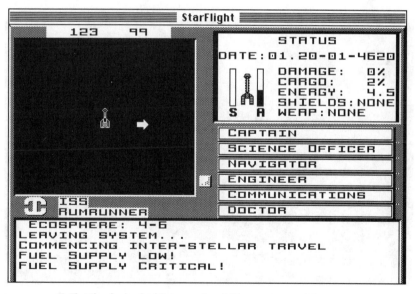

3-7 *Uh oh, looks like you should have stopped for gas.*

Indiana Jones and the Last Crusade was one of George Lucas' biggest hit films, so when LucasFilms opened its LucasArts division and went into the computer-game business, it seemed only natural to adapt the movie to a computer game. As Indy (and occasionally as his father Henry) you must attempt to recover the Holy Grail. Beware of snakes! The latest Indy adventure has our hero, along with the lovely Sophia Hapgood, trying to discover the lost island of Atlantis. Your travels will lead you to Iceland, to the Azores, and to Tikal—and that's just the beginning. In fact, you could say you've hardly gotten your feet wet.

In Fig. 3-8, Indy and Sophia are consulting Dr. Sternhart, caretaker of the ruins at Tikal. You'll be given a choice of several phrases to use each time you speak. Some will get more results than others. At a certain point in the game, you'll be requested to choose one of three paths to follow to reach the solution. Choose the "team" approach to continue working with Sophia, the "wits" path to try to figure it out on your own, or the "fists" path to fight your way to the conclusion.

3-8 Click on the action or the object to use.

 Whichever you choose, save the game before confirming your choice, so you can return and take another path later. Although the paths cross, the outcome is different for each.

In The Secret of Monkey Island, you play the role of Guybrush Threepwood, a somewhat inept pirate, as he goes through one hilarious adventure after another, and finally conquers the evil ghost-pirate LeChuck. Monkey Island II, subtitled LeChuck's Revenge, will also have you in stitches with more high-seas hijinks and gross jokes. This time you must deal with Largo LeGrand, another thoroughly nasty dude. And possibly LeChuck isn't as dead as you thought he was. Meanwhile, you're trying to find the treasure of Big Whoop, which could make you rich beyond belief, but you're not the only one looking for it. Captain Dread might let you charter his boat to help in your search, if Largo lifts the embargo he's placed on Scabb Island.

The Mojo woman will make you a Largo voodoo doll if you gather the right ingredients for her. Visit the swamp to pick up your shopping list, or just collect the items as you go from ship to ship. Use the paper (from the cartographer's shop) to collect a gob of Largo's spit. If you untie the alligator, you can get into Largo's room to steal his toupee and another item. The last one can be found in the graveyard . . . if you dig it, man . . ..

The interface in these games is much like that in the Indiana Jones series. You can talk to other characters, but again, only by choosing from preprogrammed phrases. The graphics are detailed and clever, and you click on actions and objects to use them, as shown in Fig. 3-9. Monkey Island II gives you two modes of play—regular and easy—which, according to the box, is only for "beginners and magazine reviewers." Figure 3-10 shows how to select your play mode.

In LucasArts' Loom, you are a young member of the Guild of Weavers, living on Loom Island. The Elders vanish under mysterious circumstances, and you must learn to weave their magical, musical "drafts" or spells. A draft is four notes long. At first, you can manage only a few notes, but as you gain experience you learn to use more tones and manage more powerful drafts.

3-9 *You've got the voodoo doll . . . Now get close to Largo and put it to work.*

CHECK ONE:

☐ **MONKEY ISLAND 2**
"I WANT IT ALL! ALL THE
PUZZLES! ALL THE WORK!"

☐ **MONKEY 2 LITE**
"I'VE NEVER PLAYED AN
ADVENTURE GAME BEFORE.
I'M SCARED!"

3-10 *The "easy" version lets you finish sooner.*

Write down the drafts in your Book of Patterns as you learn them. (Write in pencil. The drafts will change if you start the game again.) A good ear for music will help you succeed in this game.

Explore the island and click on various parts of the screen to see what's there. Anything that you can use or interact with will have an icon. When you find four owls, you can learn the draft for seeing in the dark, as shown in Fig. 3-11. Drafts are played by clicking the notes on the staff.

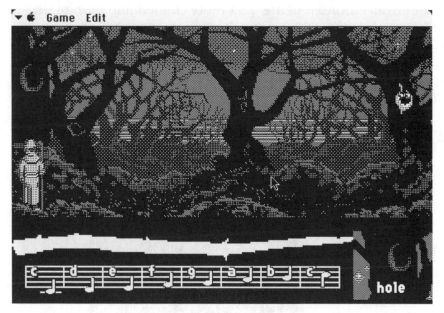

3-11 *Four holes in the trees, four owls, and four notes for your staff . . ..*

Click on the spinning wheel to learn about spinning gold. Click on the waterspout to learn the draft for "winding" and then unwind it.

Unlike most adventures, Loom is nonviolent. You might startle another character, but you won't hurt anyone. The interface is *point-and-click* so there's little or no typing required. If you're new to adventure gaming, Loom would be a good introduction. It was written by Brian Moriarty, author of Infocom's Beyond Zork and

Wishbringer. Loom comes with an audio cassette that gives you a prologue for the game, putting the characters and scene in context. The opposite side contains the original musical score for the game, a nice touch. The plot of Loom seems to indicate that there will be a sequel. Some puzzles are left unsolved, and the ending seems to leave the player hanging in midair. As of this writing, though, no sequel has been announced.

 Shadowgate and Shadowgate II are published by ICOM Simulations. They follow more or less the same format as other graphic adventures, but are a bit more challenging than most. Shadowgate opens with six windows on your screen, as shown in Fig. 3-12. You can drag things into and out of the inventory window when you collect them, or need to use them. The picture shows what you're looking at, and the text window below gives you a description.

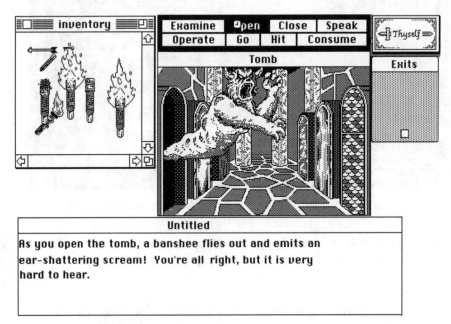

3-12 *Don't ignore warnings that your torch is flickering. If you run out of light, the game is over.*

Clicking on parts of the picture will reveal hidden objects, and will move you into the scene. Click on an object to select it, and

Operate to use it—for instance, click operate with a selected key to open a lock. When you click an object in inventory, the cursor changes to that object. The Exits window keeps a rough map of where you are, and how to get out of there. There might be exits behind you that don't show on the map. ICOM's DejaVu I & II follow the same format, but with a decidedly different plot. Subtitled The Casebooks of Ace Harding, these two adventures pit you against the Mob. You have been framed for murder, and you can't quite defend yourself since you're suffering amnesia— probably related to that lump on the back of your head. Use the commands and objects as in Shadowgate.

"Hit" has two meanings. You can earn a little cash to help you in your investigation by playing Blackjack. To get into the game, place a chip on the table. To get an additional card, use Hit Self.

Dungeons, dragons, myths, and monsters

Many graphic adventures have evolved from Gary Gygax's original Dungeons and Dragons game. D&D became wildly popular on school and college campuses at about the same time computer games started to appear. It's variously called a fantasy game or a role-playing game (RPG). Playing the game requires a handful of dice, a book of tables and character description sheets, and a vivid imagination. The Dungeon Master presents a scenario, which might be based on a science fiction or fantasy story familiar to the players, might be made up "from scratch," or based upon any of the dozens of adventures sold by TSR, the game's publisher.

In D&D and other RPGs, you determine the attributes of your character. There's an element of luck involved, since you begin to create your character by throwing dice. But as you play the game, your character can increase his (or her—RPGs tend to be nonsexist) skill, strength, and other attributes. Conversely, if injured in a fight, the character loses strength though he might gain wisdom.

As you play the game, you act out the role of your character, becoming a lord, an elf-thief, a halfling cleric, a dwarf ranger, or whatever you've chosen. D&D books include descriptions of character "classes," spells, weapons, and other items needed to complete the game, as well as complicated tables that interpret dice throws as hits, misses, ability quotients, and so on.

Because the actual playing of a D&D adventure is dependent on the outcome of dice-throwing and complicated formulas of hit-points and damage, it's an ideal type of game to play on the computer. All of the necessary tables and formulas can be turned easily into algorithms, and the dice can be simulated with a random number generator. So, it's not surprising that there are many computer RPGs available.

The first RPG series available for the Mac was a port from the Apple II, the Wizardry series from Sir-Tech. Only Wizardry I was translated initially into the Mac format, but several years ago Wizardry II was released for the Mac and Wizardry I was given a facelift with enhanced graphics. Sir-Tech also publishes Bane of the Cosmic Forge, another extremely fascinating RPG in the Wizardry series.

Bane of the Cosmic Forge looks interesting, but is difficult to install. My copy of the game came with no installation instructions, and it's definitely nonintuitive. There's an installer, on disk E. (Disks are "numbered" A through F.) But it wouldn't run under System 7.1. It was possible to run the game from disks, although frequent disk swaps were required, and the screen interface was annoyingly PC like: "Insert Disk A into Drive 1." However, the Wizardry I games, Proving Grounds of the Mad Overlord, shown in Fig. 3-13, and Knight of Diamonds, do run quite happily.

The key to success with these games, especially Bane of the Cosmic Forge, is to spend enough time considering the composition of your party and rolling the (computerized) dice to create the perfect characters. You'll want a couple of fighters, a magic user, a thief, and someone who can heal the wounded. Beyond that, the field is wide open. Try for characters who have combinations of skills. For instance, a Ninja is a good fighter who can also use alchemist spells.

3-13 *Monsters are everywhere in the Proving Grounds of the Mad Overlord.*

If you go looking for monsters (to gain experience points before you attempt the next level), they're apt to be scarce. If you want to avoid them, you'll invariably walk in on the Monster Class Reunion. To summon monsters when you can't find them, rest. They'll come find you.

New World Computing's Might & Magic series has also been popular among RPG fans. Might & Magic I and II currently come as a boxed set. M&M I, subtitled The Secret of the Inner Sanctum, and M&M II, Gates to Another World, will run in black and white (M&M II in color, also) and are compatible with System 6.0.5. and higher, as is Might & Magic III (Isles of Terra), which has been released separately. These are well-thought-out adventures with good graphic detail, pregenerated characters for "instant playing," a 3D point of view, and an overhead view window to help you see where you are and where you're going.

The officially sanctioned versions of Advanced Dungeons and Dragons are produced by Strategic Simulations, Inc. Players can

start out with the AD&D Forgotten Realms series: Pool of
Radiance, Curse of the Azure Bonds, Secret of the Silver Blade,
and Pool of Darkness are some of the titles available. SSI's newest
entry into the RPG market is called Unlimited Adventures. It
would be an ideal gift for the Dungeon Master who has
everything. Unlimited Adventures is a Fantasy Construction Kit.
It comes with a full set of instructions for designing your own
D&D adventures on the Mac, as well as a prewritten game (The
Heirs to Skull Crag) to get you started.

Figure 3-14 shows the screen layout from a scene early in the
game. You've gone into the local pub for a drink. The members of
your party are listed in the upper right, along with their hit
points. Navigate by clicking on the direction you'd like to go, or
by using the numerical keypad to designate a direction: 8 is
north, 2 is south, and so on. You can see the attributes of any
member of your party by clicking on the name and selecting
View or typing the letter v. Figure 3-15 shows an example. When
you encounter monsters, as you surely will, your party will have
to fight them. Figure 3-16 shows a scene from a battle.

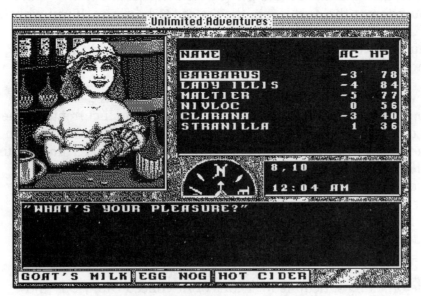

3-14 *Choose your beverage by clicking on it.*

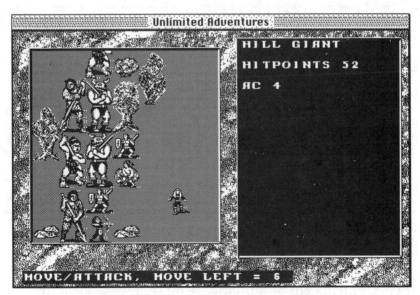

3-15 *To see any character's statistics, select the name and click View or type the letter* V.

3-16 *Battles increase your experience level.*

! Be sure to save the book. Like many games, Unlimited Adventure asks you to locate and enter a particular word from the manual each time you start the application. It's a less annoying form of copyright protection than some, but still a nuisance.

The other "classic" role-playing series, Ultima, has unfortunately not stood the test of time in terms of compatibility. Ultima II and III were the only installments of that series ported to the Mac nearly five years ago. They won't run under System 7 or even 6.0.7. Though Ultima IV through VI have been successful in the IBM and Amiga formats, they were never released for Mac. However, for a feel of what the early Ultimas were like, RPG fans might want to check out the shareware game called Shadow Keep and its sequel, Shadow Spheres (also shareware). A scene from Shadow Keep is shown in Fig. 3-17.

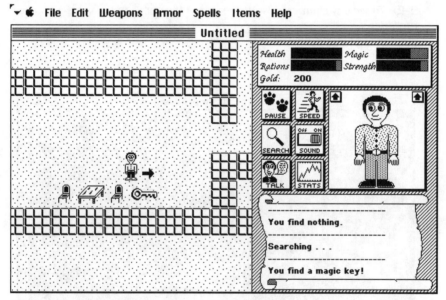

3-17 *The graphics aren't in the same league as a Sierra game, but the plot is nearly as complicated, and the price is a lot lower.*

There's a great deal of similarity to most of these RPGs. In Shadow Keep, as in almost every other fantasy RPG, you must work your way through the maze (castle, dungeon, tunnel, enchanted forest). As you go, you do battle with minor critters, and pick up scrolls, healing potions, anti-spider and scorpion potions, and other useful items including gold, which you can use somewhere else—in this case in the town SW of the castle to purchase such necessities as weapons and armor.

Eventually, in every game of this type, you must be equipped well enough to do battle with the Evil Overlord (witch, monster, prince, etc.) who has taken the Sacred Object (crystal, sword, treasure, etc.), or the Princess or other important person from the good citizens of (insert kingdom here), causing unhappiness, plague, crop failure, banishment to the Vortex of Eternity, etc. If you live through the battle, you will gain the reward, whatever it might be.

Adventure meets arcade

Some adventure games overlap into the arcade category. Although you are still working your way through a maze of some sort, trying to pick up treasure and/or rescue the object or princess, success depends more on combat skills than on luck or having the right spells. Gauntlet first appeared as a video-arcade game, and was quickly adapted to computer play as well as to a Nintendo cartridge for home systems. In Gauntlet, you can choose to be one of four characters. Each has particular strengths and weaknesses. There was a Mac version of Gauntlet released several years ago. Gauntlet was a fairly easy game to copy, and there have been a number of shareware versions released. The most successful of these is Teltnaug. (That's Gauntlet backwards, of course.) Figure 3-18 shows Teltnaug.

A commercial game called Mission Thunderbolt, published by Casady & Greene, is very similar to Gauntlet and Teltnaug. It's shown in Fig. 3-19. The major difference is that instead of looking for treasure and fighting off monsters, you are looking in an underground research lab for an antimatter bomb that you must keep away from the aliens who have taken over earth. You must fight off the mutated animals and alien life forms that lurk at every turn, waiting to take a bite or two out of you.

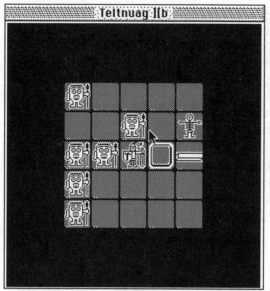

The grunt dies in a fit of agony.

You smeared the grunt to oblivion.

You smeared the grunt to oblivion.

The grunt hits you.

The grunt hits you.

You smeared the grunt to oblivion.

You feel richer.

The grunt dies in a fit of agony.

Ouch...Stop running into walls.

Health: 1363/1500

3-18 *Try not to run into the walls. It costs you health points.*

File Edit Special Commands Help

Character
Captain Hazard

LEV: 3
HP: 29
AC: 0
WC: 3
WT: 66
STR: 10
DEX: 16
SPD: 9
CON: 16
INT: 12
WIS: 15
CHR: 12
EPS: 48

Region: 1

Penalty: 0
Bonus: 0
Score: 48

Mission Thunderbolt™

3-19 *Unexplored territory is dark until you walk on it.*

One of the very earliest of this genre was a little game called
Hunt the Wumpus. It consisted of a labyrinth of rooms. In at
least one room was a critter called the Wumpus. There were also
bats and bottomless pits. The player would be prompted, "I smell
a wumpus," or "I hear a bat." He would then have to guess
which room the Wumpus was in, and shoot an arrow into that
room. If you found and shot the wumpus, you won. If you ran
out of arrows, or fell into a pit, you lost. The superbats could pick
you up and drop you in a different room, causing you to get
disoriented. There's a HyperCard version of Hunt the Wumpus
available from some user groups and shareware collections. It's
shown in Fig. 3-20.

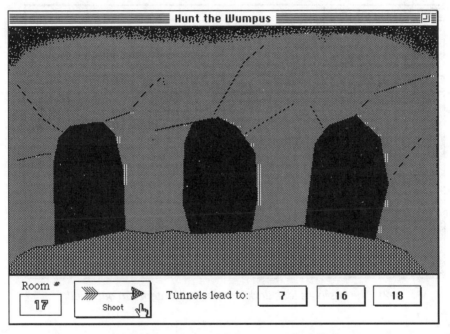

3-20 *If you plan your shot carefully, you might kill the Wumpus.*

Scarab of Ra, which is included on the disk that comes with this
book, puts a slightly different twist on the standard format. These
mazes are inside a pyramid, and instead of the usual pile of
monsters, you must contend with snakes that bite, lionesses that

will maul you, a mummy whose touch is electrifying, and monkeys who are essentially harmless, but will steal whatever you're holding.

The object is to penetrate through as many levels of maze as necessary to locate the three sacred objects: the Crown of Ra, the Staff of Ra, and the Scarab of Ra. Once you've found all three, at the next doorway you'll see a shaft of light, and will be able to exit the pyramid, retaining your treasures and earning a suitable rank in the archaeology department. You can view the maze in perspective, as shown in Fig. 3-21, or as a map.

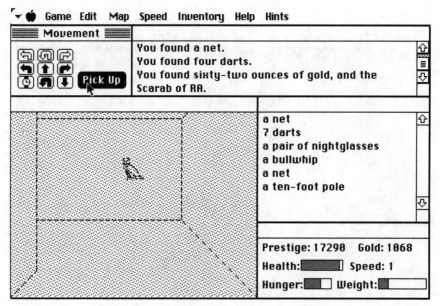

3-21 *The passages look dark because our lantern ran out of oil.*

 The speed at which you travel determines the level of detail on the map. For a more useful map, walk slower.

Along the way you'll be able to pick up many things that will help you. The bullwhip is good for scaring away snakes and lionesses. Gold can be deposited in the Bank of Ra to add to your prestige. (You'll find convenient Bank of Ra depositories throughout the pyramid.) Nets can be thrown over any of the animals to immobilize them. They are most useful when you need to get something important back from a monkey who has stolen it.

If you find a path that heads toward the exit, drop anything you don't need to carry. You can pick it all up on the way out, and you'll be able to explore faster, and not get as tired or hungry, with less of a load.

Orb Mazez is a two-player game. In order to play, tape a piece of cardboard to the Mac screen so players A and B can't see each other's side of the screen. There are two orbs, and a randomly generated maze. You must try to locate the other player while avoiding being found yourself. The color graphics are neat, but the game could use a clearer set of instructions.

Dungeon of Doom is another good shareware adventure. Again, you wander through a multilevel dungeon in search of treasure, try to find the Mystic Orbs, and fight off increasingly nasty enemies as you increase in level and class. When you find the orbs, you are halfway there. Now you must bring them out again, backtracking through all the levels. I don't know anyone who's finished this game, although it's theoretically possible.

Try to save your magic wands and food for later in the game. If you use them up too soon, you might not be able to replace them.

Dark Castle and beyond

Silicon Beach brought out a really clever graphic adventure called Dark Castle back in 1985. The sound and graphics were awesome for the time; although today's CD-ROM games with QuickTime movies kind of leave them in the dust. In order to write the game, the Silicon Beach programmers adapted an application called SuperCard that they'd been working on as competition for Apple's HyperCard. They created a version of SuperCard called World Builder, and made it available inexpensively, to anyone who wanted to design games. It was easy enough to use that ordinary people could write graphic adventures, just as they had used the text-adventure creation system to write their own text games. The games are *stand-alone*; they don't need World Builder to run. There are literally hundreds of World Builder games. Some are terrific. Some are, frankly, lame.

Dark Castle was popular enough to generate a sequel called Beyond Dark Castle. Unfortunately, Silicon Beach's greatest success wasn't in the area of games, but in graphics. They caught the corporate eye of Aldus Corporation, creators of PageMaker, FreeHand, and other graphic programs, and were bought out. SuperCard is still around, and has been given a new lease on life now that Apple has stopped giving away fully featured versions of HyperCard. The Dark Castle games and World Builder haven't been upgraded to be System 7 savvy, and it's doubtful that they ever will be.

State-of-the-art adventuring

Until virtual reality (VR) helmets are available for home use, the closest you can come is a new game from Bungie Software. Pathways into Darkness uses real-time texture mapping to create realistic 3D scenes that seem to bring you right into the middle of the action. You are a member of a secret special forces team, dropped by parachute on the site of a prehistoric asteroid impact. Or was it something even stranger? The President's military briefing has been interrupted by a strange holographic projection. A bizarre creature claiming to be a diplomat from another planet told the assembly that they had eight days left to save the world. The object that had struck the earth so long ago was, he claimed, an immortal creature whose origins predated the Milky Way. Entombed in rock below the earth's surface, the creature was beginning to awaken. The manifestations of its strange dreams were becoming real and had been spotted in the forests of the Yucatan region, along with a pyramid that was neither Aztec nor Mayan.

Your parachute malfunctions. Separated from the rest of your team, you try to locate them. Finally realizing that you're on your own, with earth's survival resting on your shoulders, you go into action. The motion is continuous, as you use the keypad or a joystick to move through the mazes inside an ancient pyramid on the Yucatan Peninsula. There are over 4,000,000 square feet of territory to explore, and many puzzles to solve, monsters to fight, and treasures to pick up. The pyramid is also littered with the corpses of German soldiers . . . and some of the strangest and scariest aliens ever to grace the screen of a Mac. In Fig. 3-22 you're about to be killed by a Headless.

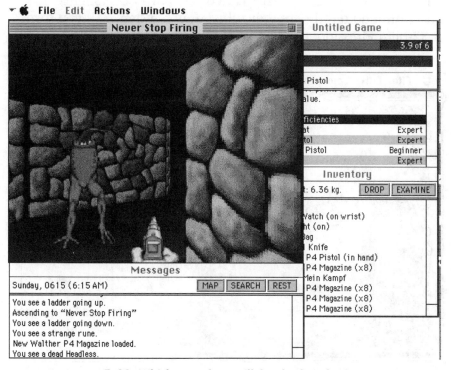

3-22 *Which one of you will fire the first shot?*

Be sure to search any bodies you come across. You might find weapons and other useful objects.

Building worlds

Considering the age of the program, World Builder and its creations are rather amazing. Even though World Builder hasn't been upgraded since 1986, has no color support, and isn't 32-bit clean, it's a remarkably versatile system that allows you to create games with graphics as complex and detailed as you can draw, and plots that are limited only by your own inventiveness.

Figure 3-23 shows a typical World Builder screen. This comes from a cleverly crafted set of puzzles called The Purpose of Silence. It runs, although a little unpredictably, under System 7, if you turn off 32-bit addressing, as do most of the World Builder games.

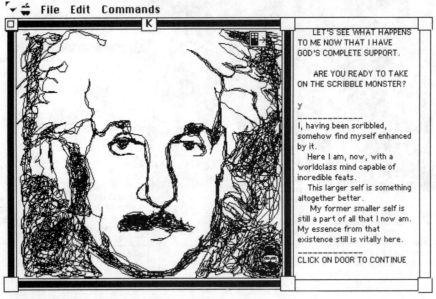

3-23 *This is one of the more existential games . . . . The maze you travel is within the mind of its creator.*

Figure 3-24 shows a different sort of World Builder game, called Mac Spudd! This game is one of the more violent ones, although it also manages to be screamingly funny. The sound effects and music are excellent. Demo versions are available from the usual

3-24 *If you've ever wondered what a jackalope looks like, now you know.*

shareware sources, although you'll have to pay the shareware fee to Mac Spudd's publishers, Smurfs from Hell, to get the fully enabled game.

GrailQuest, from Artworx, is based on the legend of King Arthur and the Quest for the Holy Grail. It follows the Arthurian legends as closely as possible. You play Sir Perceval, one of Arthur's knights. The game itself was assembled for Macintosh using the World Builder system. You'll recognize the format.

You'll need to gather armor and weapons at the castle (along with a few less obvious items like a lump of sugar) to prepare yourself for a long and difficult Quest. The illustrations are very well done, and the game is one of the more challenging ones. Figure 3-25 shows a scene from the game.

Writing your own WB games isn't difficult, as long as you have the World Builder application and manual. Getting these, however, is likely to be a problem. Silicon Beach is now the consumer division of Aldus, and has been out of the game

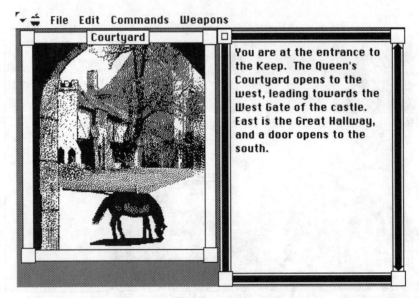

File   Edit   Commands   Weapons

Courtyard

You are at the entrance to the Keep. The Queen's Courtyard opens to the west, leading towards the West Gate of the castle. East is the Great Hallway, and a door opens to the south.

3-25 *If you give the horse a lump of sugar, he'll be your friend.*

business for quite a while. A call to Silicon Beach tech support brought the information that not only do they not publish World Builder any longer, they don't even have a copy of it.

The tech support person suggested that it was "probably available on a lot of bulletin boards," although posting it isn't strictly legal, since it's still under copyright. He also indicated that Silicon Beach wouldn't object too loudly if it were "shared", since they have no plans to update it, and it's been out of print for several years. Of course, tech support people and corporate lawyers might have different points of view about what's fair and what's not. If you "borrow" World Builder, we can't guarantee an Aldus attorney will never come after you,

If you are fortunate enough to have or encounter a copy, it works more or less like the text-adventure games, except that you also have a set of graphics tools to play with. Probably the best way to figure out how it works, if you don't have the manual readily available, is to *reverse engineer* an existing game. First, open World Builder, and then open the game from within WB. If you do so, you'll see the lists of objects, characters, sounds, and rooms that are used. In Fig. 3-26, I'm taking a look "backstage" at the Purpose of Silence. There's a scene map that guides the action, taking the player from one room to another. Objects and sounds are assigned to particular rooms. The player is a character in the game, and will encounter other characters that you create. They might offer puzzles to be solved, give advice, fight, or need to be given something in order to let the player pass by.

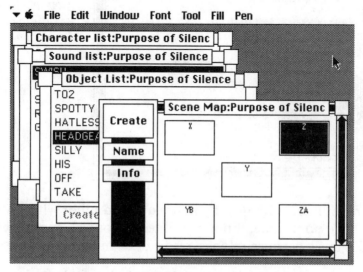

3-26 *The World Builder menus and screens are self-explanatory.*

To create your own WB game, begin by designing the scene map. This will indicate where the game starts and how it moves. Then design the rooms. Import them from your favorite graphics program, or draw them in World Builder. Then create the text that goes with the scene, in the Scene text window. Open Scene data and enter the directions of the exits, and any comments you want to make. For example, if you don't have a door to the east, the game would ordinarily say "You can't go that way" if the player tried to walk east. Instead, you might say "You walk into the wall and break your nose, improving it considerably." You can also indicate in the Scene data window any sounds to be played. Then you use the Scene Code window, shown in Fig. 3-27, to do the actual programming. The programming language used

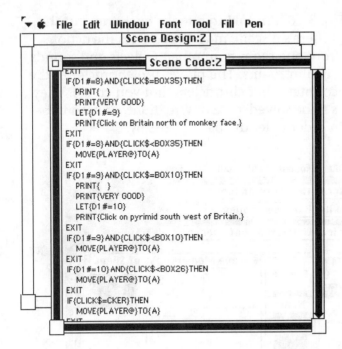

```
     File  Edit  Window  Font  Tool  Fill  Pen
              Scene Design:Z
              Scene Code:Z
 EXIT
 IF{D1#=8}AND{CLICK$=BOX35}THEN
    PRINT{  }
    PRINT{VERY GOOD}
    LET{D1#=9}
    PRINT{Click on Britain north of monkey face.}
 EXIT
 IF{D1#=8}AND{CLICK$<BOX35}THEN
    MOVE{PLAYER@}TO{A}
 EXIT
 IF{D1#=9}AND{CLICK$=BOX10}THEN
    PRINT{  }
    PRINT{VERY GOOD}
    LET{D1#=10}
    PRINT{Click on pyrimid south west of Britain.}
 EXIT
 IF{D1#=9}AND{CLICK$<BOX10}THEN
    MOVE{PLAYER@}TO{A}
 EXIT
 IF{D1#=10}AND{CLICK$<BOX26}THEN
    MOVE{PLAYER@}TO{A}
 EXIT
 IF{CLICK$=CKER}THEN
    MOVE{PLAYER@}TO{A}
 EXIT
```

3-27 *Programming in BASIC is quite simple. The $ symbol means "string."*

in World Builder is BASIC. If you are at all familiar with BASIC, you'll have no trouble. If not, you'll teach yourself very quickly. BASIC is basic because it looks, and works, much like English.

Characters and objects are created in a similar fashion. Characters have physical and spiritual health determined by the combination of speed, strength, armor, and accuracy you give them, and the number of hit points assigned.

Draw objects in the position you want them to appear in the scene, using the drawing tools. If something is supposed to sit on the floor, don't draw it up at the top of the box. Play your game to "de-bug" it. The first few times you'll probably find many things that don't work as you intended, but before long you'll have built a world. It's best to start small, but your world can have as many as 2,500 different scenes, more than 32,000 characters, and as many objects and sounds. If you become as intrigued by World Builder as many people are, send Silicon Beach a note, begging them to reissue it. Perhaps if enough of us do, they'll get the message.

4

Arcade action

While some of us were busy getting to know our home computers, others were hanging out in the video arcade, pumping quarters into video games, pinball machines, and even a sort of overgrown pool table with air vents that let two people compete at "air hockey." Video arcades sprang up like mushrooms in any city that would allow them. Teenagers, business people on lunch breaks, and families all flocked to the arcades to play the newest games.

PacMan was followed by Ms. PacMan and even Baby PacMan. Asteroids generated a whole bunch of similar space-based shoot-em-ups. Centipede led to Millipede, and on and on. Parents who didn't like the idea of letting their kids hang out in what looked like an electric pool hall invested in home video-game equipment. The same games that could be played for a quarter at the arcade could be purchased at the toy store and played as often as one wished, or as often as one's family would allow.

Atari, one of the big names in video games, introduced a line of home computers in the early '80s that could also accept the Atari game cartridges. Commodore brought out its own line of game cartridges for the VIC-20 and the somewhat later Commodore 64.

It wasn't too long before games on floppy disks came along, first for the Commodore, Apple II, and IBM, and soon for the Mac. Many of these were arcade-style games, copied, and in some cases, stolen from their cartridge versions.

It was just such a situation with a PacMan clone that got Sierra On-Line in trouble. Atari owned PacMan, the all-time, best-selling arcade game. One of On-Line's programmers had created an elegant version of PacMan to run on the Atari 800 computer. Sensing a potential fortune in the game, On-Line decided to publish it. Unfortunately, it was *too* elegant, and too close to the original. Atari's lawyers objected. The game went back to the drawing board and the ghosts became "happy faces," chased by a set of clicking false teeth instead of the little yellow guy with the big appetite. The game was retitled Jawbreaker. Atari's lawyers weren't satisfied.

They proposed buying the program code from On-Line, but the game's author objected. Much as he liked writing for the Atari platform, he disliked the company intensely and vowed that no work of his would ever be sold under the Atari logo. Ken Williams, annoyed that Atari's tactics included threats as well as an insultingly low offer for the game, decided to fight back. Eventually the case went to court, where the judge decided that he could tell the difference between PacMan and Jawbreaker, and refused to make On-Line stop selling their game. On-Line had won, but Williams realized that the court's decision also paved the way for other companies to imitate his software, as he privately acknowledged that On-Line had stolen the PacMan concept. The focus of the company shifted back toward the Quests, which were harder to imitate.

Pinball construction set

Before there were video games, the penny arcade featured pinball machines. The earliest pinball games were nonelectric, and fired a ball into a forest of protruding pins with point values marked on them. The player had to add up his score as the ball dropped.

These games, called bagatelles, were first made for children in the early 1900s, and might have originated in Italy. (Bagatelle is an Italian word meaning a toy or amusing trinket.) A coin-operated version was introduced to Chicago bars and speakeasies in the '20s, and proved to be an instant money-maker.

By 1931, there were several companies manufacturing pinball games in the Chicago area. The addition of electrically powered bumpers and kickers enabled score-keeping and made the game more a test of skill than luck. David Gottlieb's BaffleBall sold over 50,000 units at $17.50 each. Today, a working BaffleBall would be worth many thousands of dollars to a collector. Ray Maloney, who started out distributing Gottlieb games, created his own pinball game called Ballyhoo. It was also a success, so much so that Maloney started his own company: Bally Manufacturing.

Early games had no flippers. Once the ball was launched, about all the player could do was to watch it fall, and give a gentle nudge to the box to try and influence its direction. In 1947, a Gottlieb game called Humpty Dumpty introduced the flipper, and pinball became a national craze. By the early '70s though, pinball games were found again mostly in bars, pool rooms, and other semi-seedy places. The only surviving manufacturers of pinball games were Gottlieb and Williams.

But two things happened that reawakened the pinball industry. One was a rock-and-roll song, "Pinball Wizard" from the rock opera *Tommy*, by a group called The Who. The other was, somewhat ironically, the event that just about put it out of business for good—the introduction of the video game. Video arcades opened, but with relatively few video games available, their proprietors also installed pinball games. Electronic sounds and scoring, plus the addition of multiball games, background animation, and other goodies, allowed pinball to compete with video, at least for a while.

A young, self-described hacker named Bill Budge worked out a pinball game for the Apple II called Raster Blaster. It worked by using two keys on the keyboard as flippers, and included realistic sound effects. Hitting particular bumpers and rollovers caused different bells and chirps, as well as scoring points. The game was clever and fun to play, but Budge had an even better idea. He sold what was essentially the system he'd developed to program Raster Blaster to Electronic Arts, who packaged and distributed it as Bill Budge's Pinball Construction Set (PCS). It first came out for the Apple, Atari, and Commodore, and was ported to the Mac platform in 1985 to run on the 128K Mac.

The set featured a tool kit and a collection of parts: flippers, bumpers, rollovers, targets, and pits. You designed your game by dragging the parts onto the play area, which you could paint and add graphic embellishments to, if you chose, by using MacPaint. Then you wired it, added the sounds and decided how much of a score each bumper, or other device was worth. At any time during the course of construction, you could play a single ball to test a feature, or play a full game, if you preferred. Saved games could be played over and over again, swapped with friends, or posted to your favorite bulletin-board systems (BBS) or service.

Figure 4-1 shows a game under construction. All the pieces on the right can be dragged onto the play area, and used as many times as you want. In Fig. 4-2, we've gone from placing pieces to wiring them. Note that the cursor has become a soldering iron. Pieces can add scores individually or in groups, just like the "real" pinball machines. Thus you can wire a target to give 100 points, or 1,000 if all four targets are hit.

Like many early games, PCS wasn't updated for use with more current systems. It will work if you have a Mac SE, or earlier, and use the system and finder that came on the PCS disk, or any system prior to 6.0.x. It's still a lot of fun.

Today's pinball fans must thank a Canadian company, Amtex, for giving us some excellent games, although there's no new construction set coming in the foreseeable future. Amtex has recreated some classic pinball games in the Mac format, including Bally's Eight Ball Deluxe, Gottleib's Royal Flush, and Williams' popular Fun House. Just as in PCS, you use two keyboard keys to flip. You can also use the space bar to nudge the

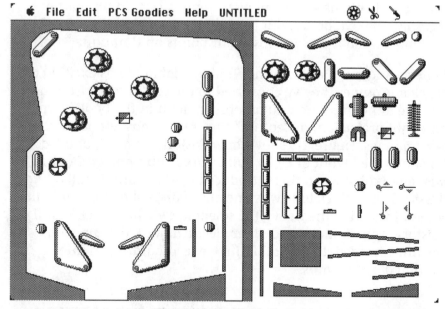

4-1 *Take the "parts" from the right side of the screen and drag them onto the play surface.*

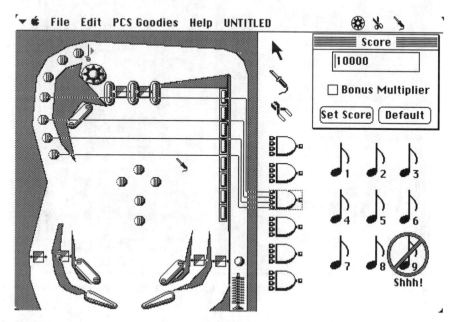

4-2 *If the pieces you've placed will score points, you must wire them into the score counter.*

game a little bit, as serious players apply a certain amount of *english* to the real boxes. But be careful not to hold the space bar too long, or you'll tilt, and lose your points on that ball.

Amtex's original pinball game, Tristan, isn't quite as exciting as the classic games they've converted to the computer. Tristan also uses the annoying "look up an obscure item in the book" form of copyright protection, a "feature" that Amtex has left out of their newer games. Figure 4-3 shows how Tristan is played, and Fig. 4-4 shows the layout of Eight Ball Deluxe, a pinball game that was remarkable when first introduced in 1982, and is still a classic. Eight Ball Deluxe was one of the first solid-state pinball games. Instead of the heavy DC solenoid switches and box full of resistors, transformers, and other electrical junk that previous machines needed, Eight Ball Deluxe was programmed into a handful of microchips.

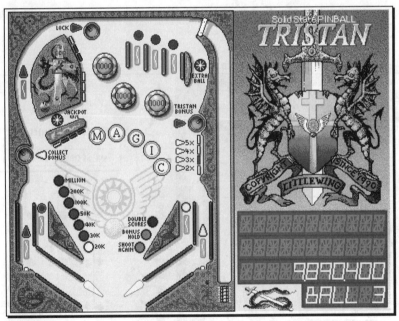

4-3 *Tristan is a typical pinball game, but doesn't duplicate any of the existing ones.*

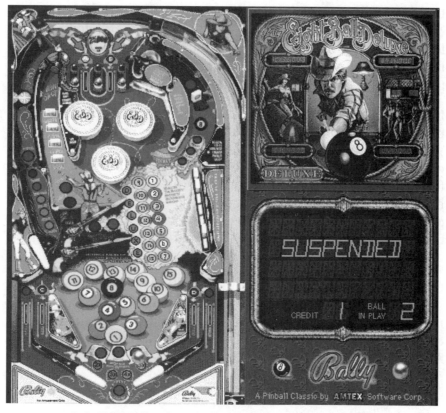

4-4 *Eight Ball Deluxe is an exact copy of the Bally game.*

Remember the Executive Decision Maker that gift shops and novelty shops sold a few years back? Ask a question and click on the 8-ball to the left of the Bally logo.

The best way to master these games, or any other arcade game, is simply to practice them over and over again. Any kid who's worn out a Game Boy will attest to that. There are, of course, tricks to learn. One mistake beginners often make, both in real pinball and in computer pinball, is to push both flipper buttons at once. Always flip alternately to reduce the gap between flippers. If both flippers are "up" at once, you've left a much wider gap for the ball to escape through. Use the flipper to catch the ball as well as to return it. By keeping the flipper button depressed, you "hold" the flipper up, creating a nice, cozy pocket to cradle the ball. Then you can let the flipper go, and the ball will roll down it, letting you to aim it to hit a particular target. You'll quickly learn how far to let it roll before you flip to reach certain areas on the playing field.

If you think of a pinball game as an experiment in applied physics, you'll begin to understand how to make higher scores. You have an inclined playing field, so gravity enters into the equation, too. When you hit the center of the ball with adequate force, it moves in the same direction as the force you apply. If you hit it off center or use less force, it will go off in a vector determined by the combined effects of gravity and off-center thrust. Learning to control the direction and amount of force is the key to becoming a pinball wizard.

One advantage to computer pinball is that you needn't feed rolls of quarters into the disk drive. You can keep on playing until you master the game. And even after you've gotten all of the moves down, it's still a challenge. As 1992 International Flipper Pinball Association (IFPA) Champion Dave Hegge says, "Pinball is 80 percent skill and 20 percent luck."

The early classics

Asteroids, and the "shoot the other rocket ship" games that followed are still around in various forms. Many of them are shareware games, including Megaroids I and II, Staroids, Hemiroids, and Maelstrom. The goal in these games is to blow up the incoming asteroids, satellites, and assorted space junk before it crashes into you. In Staroids, which is typical of the genre, the rocket ship is steered by a combination of keys. One spins it clockwise, the next counter-clockwise. Another key gives it thrust. Various others raise a shield and fire bullets or laser beams. Some games even give you something like a bomb to explode when the situation looks critical.

Andrew Welch's Maelstrom is one of the best of these asteroid games. You pilot a spaceship in the Hormel asteroid belt, somewhere between Alpha Centauri and Beta Carotene. Every time you blow up an asteroid, it turns into smaller fragments, any one of which will explode your ship. You must also contend with steel asteroids, which don't blow apart but can be knocked out of the way if you hit them; and with the alien spacecraft that are shooting back at you. You have a limited amount of power for shields to repel the stuff coming toward you. You can also earn points by rescuing other space pilots in trouble, by shooting down the comets that flash past, and by picking up the supply canisters conveniently sprinkled across the galaxy. Supply canisters might contain extra shield power, rapid fire ammunition, or "luck." The sound effects and artwork also help to make this game spectacular. Unfortunately, it's only for color Macs.

Casady & Greene's new entry into the space shot realm is called Spaceway 2000. The action is just like Maelstrom, and the scenery's pretty much the same. The premise is that your spaceship is trapped on an alien-infested intergalactic highway. You're armed with laser cannons and shields. You can score points by shooting the stuff that's coming at you, and by picking up the crystals, smart bombs, and crates that litter the Spaceway. The graphics are neat, although hard to reproduce in black and white. The sounds are, as the kids say, awesome! There's an original music track, plus realistic noises when you hit an asteroid, alien ship, or get blown apart by a mine. Great fun! And it does play, although slowly, on a Plus or SE, as well as on all of the newer machines. It's equally happy with or without System 7.

OIDS, from FTL/Software Heaven, can also be played on black-and-white, as well as color screens. It's an intriguing game, with many loyal fans. You have to land your rocket ship on a planet and pick up the OIDS, who are little robots about to be recycled into vending machines and household appliances. Most of the fun lies in designing your own planets and swapping games with other OIDS players.

Bulletin-board systems (BBS) and online services always have dozens of OIDS worlds to download.

Space Invaders generated a number of lookalike and/or work-alike games. The closest two are a shareware clone called Space Invaders, an almost exact copy of the original Atari program, and Desk Invaders, a desk-accessory version of Space Invaders, elegantly done in 256 colors for a Mac II. Missile Command was one of the earliest, and even though it was released as a commercial game and is no longer available in that form, the shareware version is still around, and is still a good challenge. It's a good choice for a black and white Mac, too. In Missile Command, your job is to shoot down the incoming missiles before they land on the cities at the bottom of the screen. In early rounds, it's not too difficult. But then whoever's launching these things switches to multiheaded missiles that split off in several directions. They're much harder to shoot down. Eventually all of your cities get nuked and the game ends.

Solarian II is an especially well-designed shareware game, and well worth the money its author, Ben Haller, is asking. Like other "invaders" games, you must shoot at things flying over you. In this game, some look like seagulls, some like Playmate coolers, and some like gift-wrapped packages. Others are more difficult to describe. Many of them give you bonus points if you manage to shoot them in time, and some drop bombs on you. Solarian II is the only game I know of with a user-definable end-game sound. Haller's original game ended with someone (probably himself) saying "damn." Since this brought him complaints from some users, he added other options, including a supposedly Fundamentalist preacher shouting "Praise Jesus," a strange sound to hear coming from a Mac.

Perhaps there's something about the concept of invaders from outer space that brings out the sense of humor in programmers. Although there are quite a few "straight" Space Invader clones, there seem to be even more funny variations. Slime Invaders was written by Swedish programmer Ingemar Ragnemalm. It's shown in Fig. 4-5. You must avoid getting hit by wads of slime as you try

4-5 *Be careful you don't get slimed.*

to shoot down the spooks that are dropping them. Higher levels bring more kinds of spook.

Brick Bats is another funny clone. This time it's a bat flying overhead, dropping bricks. You have a bucket in which to catch the bricks and thus score points. When you miss, play stops and a broom pushed by an invisible hand comes across the screen and sweeps away the brick fragments. MacPork Barrel, shown in Fig. 4-6, has you catching the falling objects, which in this case are Congressional Bills, in your Pork barrel. You try to collect as much money as possible, just like real congresspersons sometimes do. If you miss, it costs you a favor. But you have to be careful. Some of the falling objects are Auditors, and they'll cost you money, as well as a favor. Since you have only three favors to start with, you need to stay on your toes.

Another funny game that probably belongs in this category is Toxic Ravine. Instead of being on the ground shooting up at invaders, you're in a sort of blimp, dropping bombs. Here's the

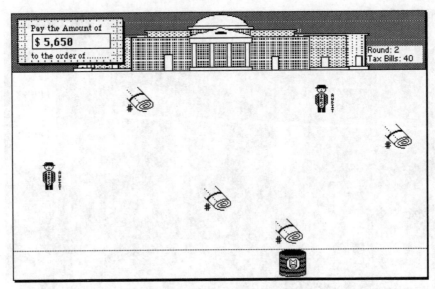

4-6 *Catch the bills in your pork barrel to make money for your district.*

story: the Toxic Ravine has been the dumping ground for all
kinds of genetic experiments and toxic waste. You've been hired
to clean it up, which you do by flying over it and dropping
cleanup bombs. Your blimp can be damaged by toxic vapors that
rise from the muck, so you need to avoid them. You also need to
rescue the good mutant clones that have been trapped in the
muck. They're encased in sort of bubble-shaped things, as shown
in Fig. 4-7. You can release a sort of magnet-like robot to pick
them up, for humanitarian reasons and extra points. (If you
bomb them instead, they flop over and die, holding little daisies.
Cute, but you get no points . . ..) This game is a lot of fun, and
runs on any Mac. It's also environmentally correct.

 Be sure to read all the documentation. (See Fig. 4-8 for a sample.)
It tells the riotous story of Orlando Poon, Jr., who has taken on
the mission of cleaning up the toxic ravine, and hired you to
help. You will also find some good hints on winning Toxic
Ravine.

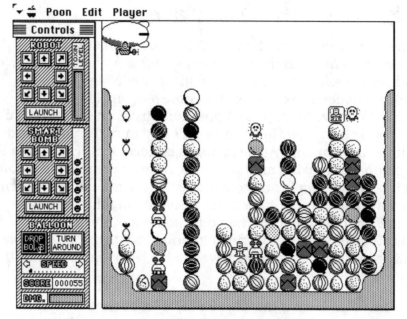

4-7 *Some of the bubbles hold little people who need to be rescued.*

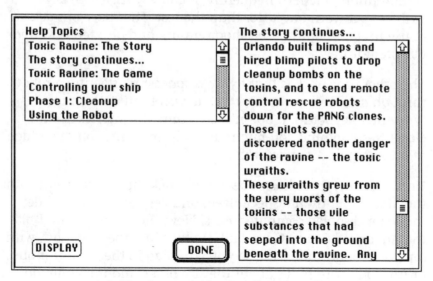

4-8 *The documentation is well worth reading.*

Sticking with the game

One of the things that distinguishes arcade games from action/adventures is the way you give directions to the game. In industrial design terms, it's called the *user interface*. Machines that are designed exclusively for game playing, like the Nintendo, have joysticks and push buttons as an interface. Macs and other computers have keyboards and mice. For some kinds of games, the standard Apple mouse is an ideal tool. The button is right on top, making multiple clicks, as in firing a laser cannon at a bad guy, simple and comfortable. The trackball, which some players prefer, works in a similar fashion. But other kinds of games that require more than directional movement plus one fire button, need a different kind of interface. So, being Mac people rather than Nintendo people, we use the keyboard. This has some drawbacks.

The first drawback is that if you play a lot of games, you are going to wear out your keyboard. Many games use the same combination of letters, frequently JKL or AWSD. These key switches get worn out faster than the rest. The space bar gets a lot of use in a keyboard-based shoot-em-up, and also tends to wear out prematurely.

The other drawback is that flying a spaceship, steering a robot through a maze, or whatever . . . just isn't intuitive on a typewriter keyboard. It doesn't feel right. The joystick is a lot closer to something you might actually encounter on the bridge of an intergalactic spacecraft.

Until recently, there hasn't been a joystick that would work with the Mac, other than a specialized, and very expensive, model made for disabled computer users. Now, there are several. I like the Advanced Gravis GamePad. It plugs into the ADB port, with a pass-through connector, so you can plug in the regular mouse or trackball with it. It's about the size of a standard Nintendo game controller, and has a joystick plus four buttons. It comes with a desk-accessory control panel, and is preconfigured for about two dozen games. You can, of course, add your own setups for your favorite games. It can be used either right or left handed, and it definitely adds to the arcade "feel" of games like Solarian, OIDS, and Tetris.

Diamonds is a Mac's best friend: Variations on Breakout

The original Pong game had two players (or one player and the computer) batting at a square of light with a paddle. Pong got tiresome after a while, and game designers looked for other things that one might do with a paddle. Computer canoeing being impractical, they worked on other paddle games. The best of these was Breakout. The game had the paddle and ball, plus a wall made up of individual bricks. When you bounced the ball into a brick, it vanished, and added to your score. The wall was about six-bricks thick, with higher scoring bricks at the back. If you managed to punch a hole through the wall, and could then put the ball through the hole, it would ricochet off the back wall and knock down lots of bricks.

This game first appeared as an arcade game, like Pong, and was rather quickly rewritten for home-computer and game-machine play. Many shareware clones appeared. One of the best-known is Brickles Plus. It can be configured for anywhere from one to four paddles, and can be played full screen or with a smaller window. A basic game is shown in Fig. 4-9.

UnBreakout reverses the game. There's still a ball and a paddle, but now, instead of hitting the bricks, you're trying to guard them with the paddle. As long as you keep returning the ball, it won't hit the bricks. Fifteen hits and you advance to a higher level. Arkanoid is a similar Breakout-type game, with the added wrinkle that things fall on you while you're trying to smash bricks. Some give you extra points or a larger paddle, others will end your turn.

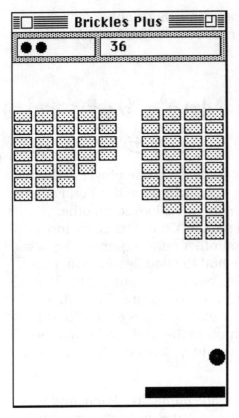

4-9 *Hit the ball into the bricks to get rid of them and score points.*

The ultimate Breakout game, at least so far, comes to us from Switzerland. It's been a real success story for its author, Oliver Dreer, and for Varcon Systems, who picked up the shareware game and packaged it elegantly for commercial distribution. Dreer first released the game as shareware about two years ago. Its colorful screen and rock-and-roll sound track immediately set it apart from the more prosaic games.

The premise is fairly simple. There are bricks in different colors or patterns on a black-and-white screen, as shown in Fig. 4-10. You start with a ball that will only knock out light blue bricks, and you must get rid of all of them before you hit a paintbrush block that will change your ball to a different color. Each color or pattern of brick can only be knocked out when the ball matches

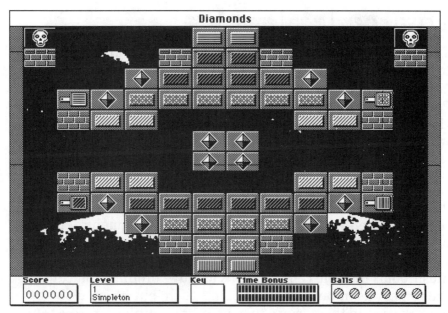

4-10 *Diamonds is beautiful in color, though not too exciting in black and white.*

it. When all of the colored bricks are removed, you can finally knock out the diamond bricks and progress to the next level. There are 30 levels in the game, plus a level editor that lets you invent your own. Higher levels might include obstacles such as locked bricks that can only be unlocked by first hitting the "key" brick, and then the locked brick; and "reverse" bricks that swap the two keys that move the ball left and right, so that the right arrow moves you left, and the left arrow moves you to the right. It's definitely a challenge.

Another great feature of this game, and Varcon's other games, is the recyclable packaging. Since the game publishers (unlike most) apparently realize that you are probably going to stash the master disk in a box with the rest of your masters, they don't give you a large cardboard box to throw away. Instead, the disk comes in a reusable velvet bag, along with a list of 100 possible uses for the bag, ranging from a holder for your sunglasses to a carrier for Bingo chips, gummy bears, or your Notary seal. (I use the Diamonds bag for my jewelry.)

Video arcade classics

The success of video games like Space Invaders and Breakout led to an explosion of new games. Among the more popular were Centipede, Qyx, Choplifter, Defender, Tempest, and of course, PacMan. Each of these games spawned numerous shareware clones. Centipede had several Mac versions, one of the best of which is Bpeede.

The object is to spray insecticide at spiders, scorpions, and the centipede that invade your garden. The centipede has the distinctly unpleasant habit of breaking up into individual segments when you shoot it. Any one of these segments, or any of the other nasties will kill you if it hits you, so you must stay underneath it and fire bursts of bug killer upward. There are also mushrooms that the centipede has to crawl around. You can shoot the mushrooms for a few points each, but it's much better to work around them, since they block the centipede pieces from landing on you.

Qyx must have been what gave Marc Dutil the idea for a beautiful, and difficult, color game called Sparkz. The object of the game is to enclose 80 percent of the square. You do so by drawing blocks on the screen, which then fill with color. Meanwhile, you must avoid the Sparkz, which are little bubbles that move around the perimeter of the screen. If one hits you, the game ends. You must also avoid the fan-shaped thingie, which twirls back and forth around the unfilled area of the screen. If it touches you while you're drawing a box, you die. There are no second chances in this game. One false move and you're back to zero. Nevertheless, it's fun to play, mainly because the pastel-colored blocks make the screen look like a Mondrian painting. Figure 4-11 shows the game near the end of the first level.

Build a pair of peninsulas directly opposite each other, and then connect them. It's easiest if you build with small blocks, since your exposure to the rays is less.

Choplifter generated a whole series of games based on maneuvering a helicopter and shooting something below you.

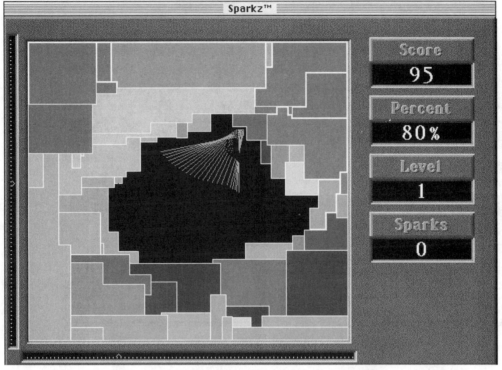

4-11 *You must fill 80 percent of the board in order to advance to the next level.*

In Armor Alley, your chopper must navigate its way through antiaircraft weapons to drop bombs on the enemy. You can add other forces as you advance.

Iraq Attack hit the bulletin boards about the same time that U.S. forces hit Saddam. You must shoot down MiGs and bomb oil wells in order to rescue some American "guests" from a dictator, and then land your plane safely on the carrier again. It's a color game that only runs on Mac II and later models. It's a challenging game to play, since the MiGs are shooting back at you. You only have three choppers. The game features good sound effects and a nice theme song, although the graphics, as shown in Fig. 4-12, are on the simple side.

SCORE: 4850

4-12 *The camels are a nice touch.*

Storm, a freeware creation from Finland, is an almost exact copy of the arcade game Tempest. In a Read Me file accompanying the game, author Juri Munkki states:

> The files that you have just unpacked are part of an evaluation release of Project STORM. What this means is that the product itself is not ready and should not be viewed as a fully debugged and working program. The game is also limited, but only because there hasn't been enough time to complete all the work . . .. Since going commercial appears to be more trouble than it's worth, STORM is going to be released as a free program, the way that it was originally intended . . .. Right now, none of the STORM programming team members have a lot of time available, so if you want to see this game completed, let us hear about you.

Even unfinished, the game is terrific. It's available on many bulletin boards and on several shareware CD-ROMs as Storm 0.9b1. The object of the game is simple. As you see in Fig. 4-13,

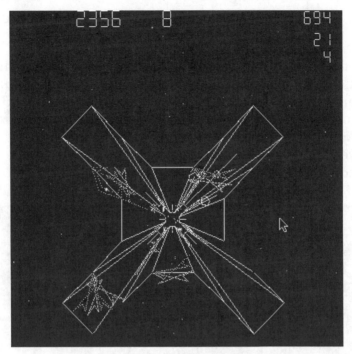

4-13 *This game moves fast!*

things fly up a grid. (What they are—alien spacecraft, bolts of electricity, antimatter—isn't important. Call them whatever you want.) You're waiting at the top. You must zap all the things coming at you before they hit you. When you zap everything on level 1, you advance to level 2, and so on. Use the mouse to move around the grid, or back and forth on it on later screens. It's a different shape at each level. Although there are bug warnings in the Read Me file, I found none while playing the game.

Little yellow dots

PacMan was probably the single most popular arcade game ever written. It launched everything from a cereal to a Saturday morning cartoon show, and generated quite a few copycat games, including Trashman, MacMan, and so on. The premise was the same in all of the games, and involved walking through a fairly simple maze, while being chased by some variety of bad guy. In the original game, the bad guys were a set of four ghosts.

There have been a number of PacMan games created for the Mac, including Ingemar Ragnemalm's black-and-white BachMan (with an interesting imitation-3D perspective); MacMan, also in black and white; and a color version of PacMan that comes from Japan and looks (and sounds) very much like the original. The latter version requires a 13-inch monitor and 256 colors. BachMan and MacMan are shown in Figs. 4-14 and 4-15.

| Score: 232 | Lives: 2 | Level: 3 |

4-14 *There are nine different levels in this version.*

 Blaze, from Softstream, is a very PacMan-like game. Instead of a little yellow guy who eats power pellets, you are a drop of water, running around putting out fires. Evil flames are eager to evaporate you, but you can re-power yourself at a hydrant and quench them. Figure 4-16 shows the Blaze screen.

Microcosm II, also by Softstream, looks similar, at least on the front of the box. But it's a fiendishly difficult variation on the same theme. You are in control of a tiny robot that can create

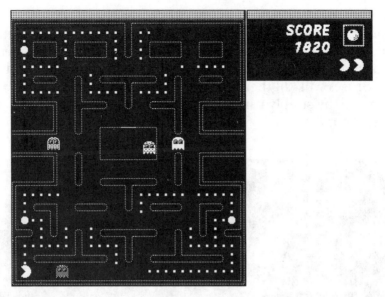

4-15 *MacMan is a black-and-white game that should play on any Mac.*

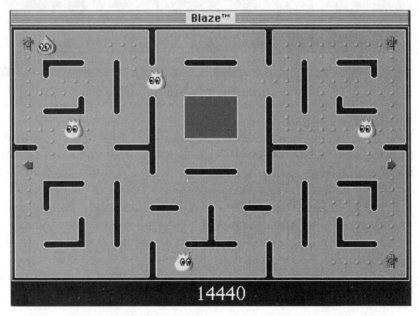

4-16 *The hydrants will help you extinguish the blazes.*

short strands of DNA. The "enemies" are viruses, which reproduce themselves. You must maneuver your robot through a PacMan-style maze. But, while doing so you must also determine and create the correct patterns of DNA so that the pills you fire at the viruses will kill them. You can pick up microchips that will help you, by simply running over them. Figure 4-17 shows the game board.

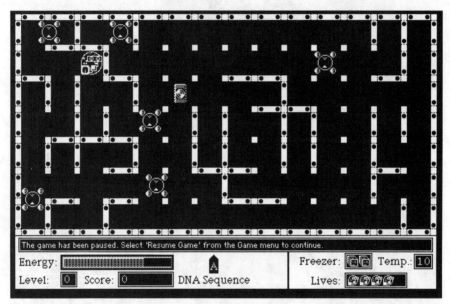

4-17 *This game is extremely difficult to play.*

You must also take care to avoid the "bad" robots that want to pull out your chips, or do other damage. Since viruses reproduce more slowly when they're cold, you can help them chill out by dropping ice cubes. The ice cubes also serve as a barrier, until they melt. This game can be played in black and white or color, and claims to be friendly to both System 6 and 7. However, it comes on two disks, and apparently needs both to function, but while one disk is an 800K disk that could be loaded into any machine, the other holds a file a little over 900K and requires a SuperDrive.

There's no printed documentation with the disks, but a manual in MacWrite II or Teach Text is included as a file. There's a built-in level editor, so you can create your own mazes. The game is even networkable, allowing you to play over an AppleTalk network, and to pass messages back and forth with another player as you play.

The PacMan concept has been taken in other directions, too. Maze games of all kinds abound. Some, like Gauntlet and Scarab of Ra, described in the previous chapter, have you looking for treasure in the maze while fighting off some sort of bad guys. Others are less adventure oriented.

S.C.OUT, from Inline Design, is an extremely clever variation on the theme. You've landed at an abandoned moon base. Your mission is to rid it of alien intruders, so that you can recolonize it. Your single-person vehicle can carry only one object at a time. Sometimes you'll need to carry rockets, sometimes keys, and sometimes bombs. Fortunately, everything you need is there, but it's not always right where you need it.

In the screen shown in Fig. 4-18, you need a battery. You can pick things up and drop them. To fire off one of the directional bombs, first be sure you have picked up one that's pointing in the direction you want it to fire, then just press the space bar. It will destroy everything within a three-square area, including you, if you're too close.

Rhodes is a clever little shareware game that sends you ricocheting through mazes. You are a Rhodes scholar at Oxford University, and you're visiting the legendary hedge maze. A piece of the maze is shown in Fig. 4-19. Trouble is, you're not very bright, or very patient, and you get lost a lot. You keep moving until you run into a hedge and then you bounce off in another direction. Bumping into the hedges lowers your patience. So does having a piece of hedge built or removed to make your path easier. But it's often necessary to help you reach the exit. Patience pills are sprinkled randomly throughout the maze. They'll make you feel better. The silver ones are the strongest. The top 10 Rhodes scholars get their names on the scholarship list. (And jobs

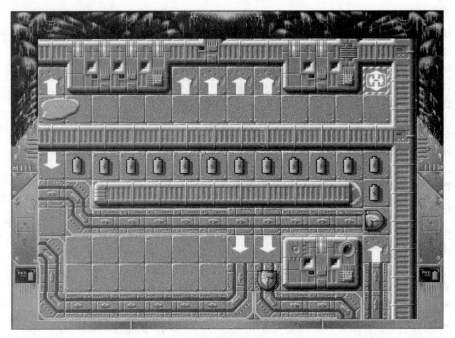

4-18 *Every S.C.OUT level is different, but most are fairly easy to figure out.*

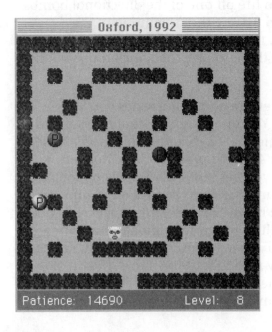

4-19 *Try not to bump into the hedges.*

in the Clinton administration?) The game also includes a maze editor, allowing you to create your own levels or to modify any of the 30 or so included.

Lode Runner has appeared in a number of formats including arcade and Macintosh. It's similar in concept to the PacMan-type game. You guide a critter of some sort through a playing field, which has treasures, traps, and quite often someone chasing you or waiting to ambush you. Your goal might be simply to amass as much loot as possible before getting killed, or to get through the series of screens in order to rescue the princess, get the ultimate treasure, or just get out alive.

Arcade games of this type include all of the variations on Donkey Kong and Mario Brothers. Donkey Doo is a pretty good shareware Mac clone of Donkey Kong, and Leprechaun, shown in Fig. 4-20 is a Mac adaptation of the SuperMario type of game. The major difference between Leprechaun and Mario Brothers, and other kinds of maze games, is that you can only see a small piece of the action at one time. Other than that, the goal is the same.

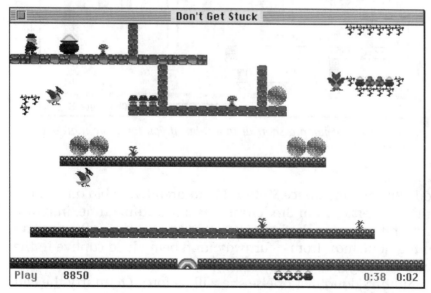

4-20 *Collect the pots of gold.*

Lode Runner is a less "cute" game with the same kind of action. Instead of a cartoon character, though, you're just an average citizen, stuck in some sort of subterranean passageway with lots of ladders and catwalks and bags of money lying around. The object once again is to pick up as many bags of loot as you can. You have to jump from some catwalks to others, and jumping too far can be fatal. There's a level editor so you can design your own levels. SpaceStation Pheta, shown in Fig. 4-21 is much like Lode Runner. There are keys you must pick up in order to open the doors to other levels.

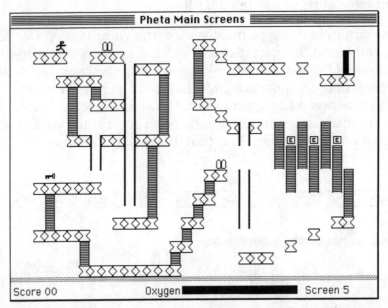

4-21 *You can jump a short distance, but if you fall more than one level you lose a life.*

Lode Runner and Space Station Pheta aren't very big on scenery. Prince of Persia, from Brøderbund, is a beautiful game, in black and white or color, that uses the same basic premise. You are a young nobleman from a faraway land being held captive in the Sultan's dungeons. You must escape and rescue your true love, the Sultan's daughter, or else she will be forced to marry the evil Vizier, Jaffar. You have only an hour in which to do it though.

You can jump from one level of the dungeon to another, if you're careful. If you miss, there are pits lined with razor-sharp swords waiting to impale you, and many other traps as well. Figure 4-22 shows an example.

4-22 *The jaws snap once per second. Can you scramble through while they're open?*

The Sultan's guards are also waiting with swords, and whenever you run into one, you'll have to fight. You'll fight better if you can manage to locate a sword. There are also potions that will increase your strength.

The graphics in this game, especially in color, tend to be rather . . . uh . . . graphic. If you're the kind of parent who tries to keep your kids from watching especially violent or bloody movies or TV programs, this game is probably not for you. The young nobleman dies many times, from being impaled on sword tips, being stabbed by the Sultan's guards, and so on. Each time, he bleeds all over the screen. Pressing any key restores him and restarts the game, but it also suggests that violent death is only temporary, a lesson you might not want your child to learn.

PG 13

Lemmings, from Psygnosis, is a clever and cartoon-like wrinkle on the Lode Runner model, and much less violent. Instead of one little guy, you've got lots of them—50 or more. And all they really want to do is get out of where they are. But, like all lemmings, they're not very bright. If their leader jumps off a cliff, the rest will follow. Your job is to get them safely through whatever obstacles they encounter. To do so, you have the ability to assign jobs to individual lemmings. You can tell some to become carpenters, building bridges where needed, as in Fig. 4-23. Make others stop traffic, forcing the rest to mill around and wait while a safe route is built. Some can climb rocks, while you can have others digging tunnels. You can even tell one or more to blow themselves up if they are in the way. You have a limited amount of time in which to save a certain percentage of the lemmings, in order to progress to the next level. The game has 120 different levels, and plays in both black and white and color.

4-23 *Lemmings are cute, but they're not very smart.*

You saw it at the movies

The video-gamer's dream came true in 1982, with the release of a movie called Tron, about a computer genius who suspects evil doings by a corporate executive. During his investigation, the bad guys zap him into another dimension and he finds himself a player in a gladiatorial video game. The film combined live action with superb animation from the Lisberger Studios, and was a box office success. Among other exiting adventures, the heroes of the film had to take part in an arena battle on high-tech motor bikes called LightCycles, which drew a solid wall of light behind them as they went along (at high speed). The game was played on "the grid": a perfectly flat surface along which the cycles could move quickly. The cycles could turn only at right angles. The goal was to cut off the other players in such a way as to force them to run into your light trail. As soon as they touched it, they were zapped.

There are at least two shareware Tron games for the Mac, both based on the light-cycle scene. Tron has simple graphics, but plays quite well in black and white or color, and lets you determine the starting points for each of the four cycles. As many as four people can play against each other, as long as they can each manage to get two fingers on the keyboard. The cycles are steered by pressing one key to go left, and another to go right. Up and down are left and right relative to the direction you're already going. (Three lefts make a right. Two wrongs don't.)

Cary Torkelson's LightCycle Duel is a great black-and-white shareware game in the same genre. It has a very well-planned, flexible interface for two-player use, and really nice digitized music. Unlike Tron, which has a plain, flat play field, LightCycle Duel can be configured with obstacles and mazes for the players to navigate through, adding to the challenge. A LightCycle maze is shown in Fig. 4-24.

BeamWars is a full-color professional-looking game, very similar to the two above. It requires 8-bit (256 colors or grays) video, and won't run on the original 12-inch LC monitor. Aside from that,

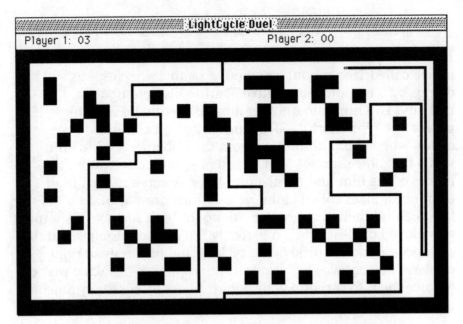

4-24 *Two players must share the keyboard to play LightCycle.*

and occasional crashes on the IIsi, it's a great game for up to four players, and the computer will play any or as many of the four as you wish. You can also determine the level at which the computer plays—novice or expert. It's tough to win at novice level and almost impossible to beat it consistently when the Mac is being an expert player.

The screen looks very much like Tron, although the premise is presented differently. You direct a beam of light instead of a light cycle. While you're trying not to run into the walls of the playing area or any of the other beams, you must force the other beams to do so. The round ends when three of the four beams have crashed. The survivor gets bonus points. The length of a game is determined by how much energy is expended in each round. As energy is used, the playing field begins to shrink. When it collapses in upon itself the game is over.

The various snake games appear to have a lot in common with Tron and BeamWars if you just look at them on the screen.

Instead of trying to run into each other, though, the snake game usually consists of a single snake trying to pick up something to eat, while also trying not to run into the scenery. Gobbler is typical of this type of game. You are Hedda Gobbler, a young snake with a hearty appetite. You cruise through your neighborhood, eating mushrooms and avoiding walking into the walls or the shrubbery. Everything you eat makes you grow. (Who says computer games aren't like real life?) When you use up all of your lives, the game is over.

Snakes Alive is a slightly different snake game. It's shown in Fig. 4-25. Like Hedda, you are a young snake munching your way around town, and trying not to bang your head against the stone walls. You can eat bugs, flowers, and eggs. Flowers make you grow, but don't give you any energy. Eggs and bugs increase your energy and give you points, as well as making you longer. If you run into yourself, you might accidentally eat part of your tail. It's not as good, energy-wise, as a bug or two, but it won't kill you.

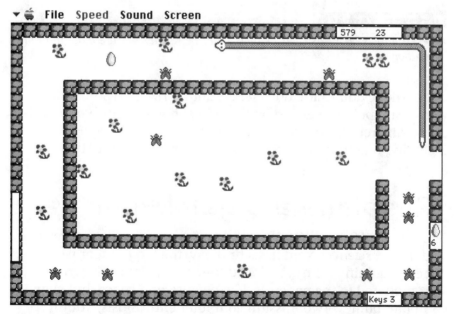

4-25 *There's a very large play area, but it remains the same from one game to the next so you can learn your way around.*

Mushrooms, on the other hand, will kill you if you eat too many of them. Your goal is to find all of the eggs in the garden. (There are supposedly 60 of them, according to the Help screen in Fig. 4-26.)

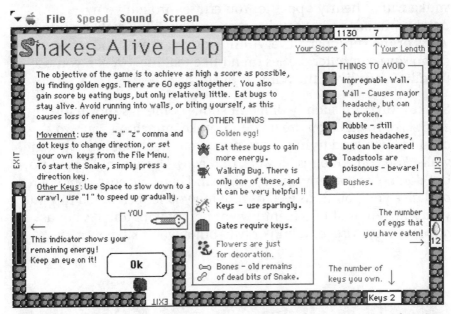

File   Speed   Sound   Screen

Snakes Alive Help

Your Score ↑   ↑ Your Length

1130   7

The objective of the game is to achieve as high a score as possible, by finding golden eggs. There are 60 eggs altogether. You also gain score by eating bugs, but only relatively little. Eat bugs to stay alive. Avoid running into walls, or biting yourself, as this causes loss of energy.

Movement: use the "a" "z" comma and dot keys to change direction, or set your own keys from the File Menu. To start the Snake, simply press a direction key.
Other Keys: Use Space to slow down to a crawl, use "1" to speed up gradually.

EXIT

┌── YOU ──┐

←

This indicator shows your remaining energy!
Keep an eye on it!

Ok

EXIT

┌─ OTHER THINGS ─┐
○ Golden egg!
✹ Eat these bugs to gain more energy.
🐛 Walking Bug. There is only one of these, and it can be very helpful !!
🔑 Keys - use sparingly.
🚪 Gates require keys.
🌺 Flowers are just for decoration.
💀 Bones - old remains of dead bits of Snake.

┌─ THINGS TO AVOID ─┐
◼ Impregnable Wall.
◼ Wall - Causes major headache, but can be broken.
◼ Rubble - still causes headaches, but can be cleared!
🍄 Toadstools are poisonous - beware!
🌳 Bushes.

The number of eggs that you have eaten!
→   12

The number of keys you own. ↓

Keys 2

4-26 *The rules aren't as clear as they might be . . . flowers are more than just decoration.*

Other snake games include Frenzy, Snake Tix, and SnakeBar, a very cosmopolitan version, with menus in your choice of a half-dozen different languages, and various kinds of wrigglers including one that apparently escaped from Sex Ed 101.

The Russians are gaming on us

Back in the '50s and '60s, Russia was "the enemy," or so we were told. In the sciences, and in technology, the biggest fear was "They're gaining on us . . .." And they were. Not only in areas that mattered to the generals, like defense and space, but even in computer games. Two Russian computer enthusiasts, Vadim Gerasimov and Alexey Pazhitnov, were responsible for the game that proved to the rest of the world that there was more to Russia than borscht and Perestroika.

Tetris took the basic concept of Space Invaders—things falling from the sky—but instead of shooting them, your task was to try to stack them neatly. The falling objects were variously shaped blocks, each composed of four cubes in one of seven possible combinations. You could rotate them and move them from side to side in order to fill rows, which would then disappear, scoring points for you. As your score rose, you reached a "higher level" of play . . . . The blocks fell faster, and the background screen changed from one picture postcard of life in Russia to another. The music, synthesized Russian folktunes, changed too. Tetris played in black and white, and even came with a desk-accessory version that was ideal for playing at work, since you could hide it quickly by clicking on the screen behind it.

Tetris led to Welltris, a sort of 3D version of the game, in which you dropped the blocks down the side of a well. A screen from Welltris is shown in Fig. 4-27. The graphics and music were

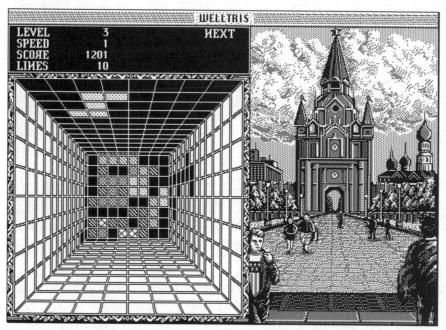

4-27 *Welltris added a third dimension to Tetris.*

similar, but the game was harder to play, and never became quite as popular.

Welltris, in turn gave us Faces, a somewhat different slant on dropping blocks. Instead of building horizontal lines, you assemble faces—chin and lips, nose, eyes, and finally hair or hat. Sounds easy—but you have to start the face over if you place the eyes where the nose should have gone, or otherwise get one out of order. Again the theme, and many of the faces, are Russian. You'll also find famous faces from the arts, literature, and even American history. Figure 4-28 shows how the game is played. As the pieces fall, you can move them left or right or swap them, but as soon as they touch a stack of pieces they stop. Perfect faces score more points than mixed-up ones.

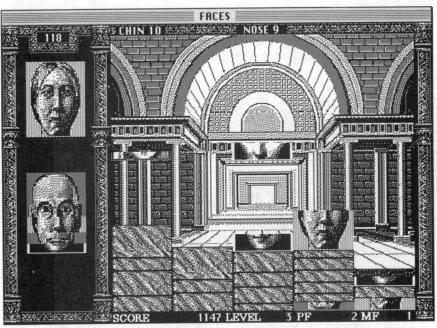

4-28 Many of the faces are famous.

Wordtris was the next game Spectrum Holobyte introduced in the Tris series. It makes the others look simple. Instead of merely piling up blocks, these have to make words, the longer the better.

It goes beyond difficult to darned near impossible, especially at higher levels, when the letters that drop seem to be mostly Z and F. Words can be spelled horizontally, vertically, or diagonally. The built-in dictionary knows literally thousands of different words, and it will sort them out and give you the points they're worth while you keep on dropping more letters. However, you can only score with a word once per game. As Fig. 4-29 shows, you can check the words you've made at the right of the screen.

4-29 *Wordtris gets harder as you go on. Letters fall faster, and there seem to be fewer useful vowels.*

As in the other Tris games, you can move the blocks from left to right and back again, depending on where you think you need them. Wild cards can be any letter you want. You can gain bonus points by spelling the word shown on the screen. It changes from game to game, or once you've spelled it.

The newest Tris game, as of this writing, is our old friend Tetris, reissued in color as Super Tetris, and dressed up with scenes from the Moscow Circus (see Fig. 4-30). A few other goodies have been

4-30 *Try to hit the bricks with symbols. They'll help your score.*

added, too, like bombs that will knock out some of the bricks, special bricks that remove the line they're in, and so on . . ... You can start at any level, but if you're going for a high score, start at the first level and work your way up. At higher levels, the pieces fall very quickly.

! With all of the Tris games, be sure you keep the manual in a safe, but convenient place. The earlier ones require that you look up and enter something from the manual every time you start the game. Super Tetris only asks you to do it once, when the game is first installed. (If you remove it and reinstall it again later, you'll have to go through this process, too.)

Because of its popularity, and probably because it was such an obvious concept once people thought about it, Tetris generated dozens of similar games. Some, of course, are better than others. One of the funnier ones was the version called Quayle's Tetris, which used only single, square blocks and dropped them very slowly. It was so simple even you-know-who could have played it.

Bikaka and Hextris are a pair of games that drop blocks composed of hexagonal shapes, rather than square ones. You can, of course, rotate the blocks for a better fit, and move them from side to side in the well as they fall. Figures 4-31 and 4-32 show screens from Hextris and Bikaka. Although they look similar, they play quite differently.

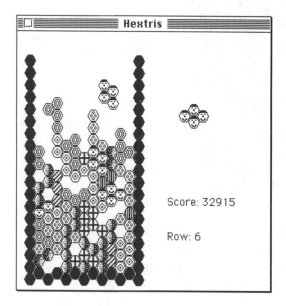

4-31 *Hextris, aside from its odd shapes, is much like Tetris.*

Hextris, like the original Tetris, has you racing the clock to complete horizontal lines of blocks. They fall faster as your score increases. Bikaka comes from Sweden, and its title—sort of a pun on the Swedish word for honey—refers to the honeycomb shapes the falling blocks make. It's a bit more difficult than Hextris. Not only do the blocks drift back and forth of their own accord, but whenever you complete a horizontal line, the remaining blocks shift one place to either side. So, you might have a gap that you're planning to fill in, but if the blocks shift before you get the piece you need to fill it, they could block your access.

Wesleyan Tetris is more or less like the original, with the addition of a sound track that insults you whenever you make a dumb

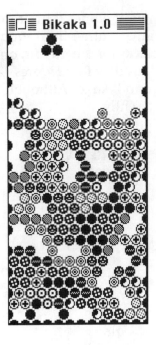

Score: 129
Level: 1
Lines: 6

4-32 *Bikaka is trickier. The rows shift sideways every time you complete one.*

move, and some interesting wrinkles including oddly shaped blocks that come up occasionally, and levels with blocks that move, appear, or disappear while you're playing, and various block shapes that you must work around on some levels. It's more of a challenge than regular Tetris, as you can see in Fig. 4-33.

There are some problems with the game's sound driver, though. You might need to play it quietly (i.e., with the sound turned off from the Control Panel) or else it will crash. You might choose to turn off the sound anyway, even if it's working well. It's a bit disconcerting, when you've accidentally dropped a block in the wrong spot, to hear, "You meant to do that, right?" or "Oh my gosh, that was the best move I've ever seen!"

Tetris Max is a (freeware!) basic Tetris game, with a nice soundtrack and elegant graphics. Tetronix is a French version of the game, with very strangely shaped blocks. Cumulonimbus, an almost freeware (the fee is a mere 50 cents) game uses the Tetris principle, but comes with a very entertaining explanation *why* you're dropping these oddly shaped blocks into a well. The

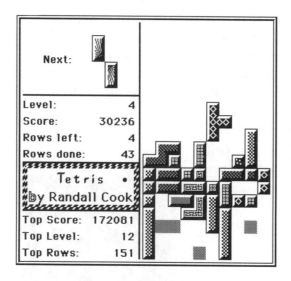

Level: 4
Score: 30236
Rows left: 4
Rows done: 43

Tetris •
by Randall Cook

Top Score: 172081
Top Level: 12
Top Rows: 151

4-33 There's a running commentary on your gaming ability as you play this one.

game's author, Mike Gleason, presents a scenario in which it's raining through a temperature inversion, so the rain is turning into ice crystals. He explains,

> . . . the ice is falling and accumulating in your well outside, which is bad, because the ice somehow clogs up the well and cuts off your water supply. But you happen to be a rich physicist specializing in aerodynamics and thermodynamics, and you rigged up a little gadget that heats the sides of the well. Anyway, you can melt a layer of ice if a layer of ice is completely solidified across and touches both sides of the well. With your incredible skill in aerodynamics you also rigged up a series of fans so you can move chunks of ice left and right, and even rotate them. The crystals will bond permanently the instant the bottom surface touches the bottom of the well or the top of another crystal, so the only way to get rid of them is to complete layers so you can melt them . . ..

The game itself plays like any other Tetris clone, except that you can designate the type of shapes to drop and the size and depth of the well.

Catch The Buzz adds an interesting wrinkle. As you can see in
Fig. 4-34, there's a little smiling face trapped in a gap inside the
blocks. That's the Buzz. To score points you need to trap him so
that he has no place to go. As soon as you trap one, a new one
will pop up somewhere else. This game plays in color or black
and white.

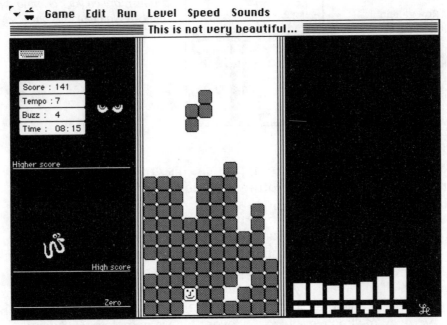

4-34 *As long as he can move to another square you haven't caught him.*

Dropper is a color-only shareware game that has you stacking
bars of different colors. The main difference is that you need to
make the piles four high or four wide, and they score differently
depending on whether the blocks run horizontal, vertical, or
diagonal. You must complete a certain number of stacks in order
to advance to the next level. Brickwell, shown in Fig. 4-35, does
much the same thing with patterns.

S'ydnar Squares is vaguely related to Tetris, in that blocks drop
down from above. But each block is comprised of colored cubes in
any of four different colors. You need to flip them around and

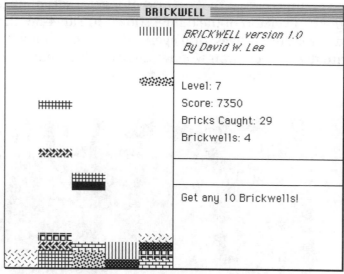

4-35 *Catch the patterned blocks and stack them carefully. If you let one fall, you lose it.*

stack them so that you make blocks of four same-colored cubes. These will disappear leaving you more board room in which to stack more cubes. It's a great-looking game, with two-track sounds in System 7, but the controls are awkward and don't follow the usual Mac interface. Your left hand moves blocks back and forth with the A and S keys, while your right hand rotates with the K and L keys. It works; but it would probably have been more user friendly to go with the Tetris J-K-L key map, as most Tetris-clones have done.

If there was a prize for the prettiest Mac game, Jewelbox would be a strong contender. Rodney and Brenda Jacks originally wrote it as a shareware game, but it was so well done and so popular as shareware that it was purchased by Varcon Systems. Some new gimmicks were added, and it was released commercially. Instead of boring geometric shapes, in Jewelbox you are playing with diamonds, rubies, sapphires, emeralds, and so on . . . .. You must stack them to make rows of three identical jewels horizontally, vertically, or diagonally. Every time you get three in a row, they'll disappear. Those above will fall down into the gap, so it's possible

to set up a chain reaction that gets rid of several sets at once. In
the commercial version of the game, shown in Fig. 4-36, there are
wild-card jewels, extra lives, and even some jewels that will zap
their entire row and column when matched. It's a beautiful and
highly addictive game.

4-36 *Jewelbox is beautiful, challenging, and fun.*

Columns II (included on the shareware disk) is another addictive
Tetris-like game. Like Jewelbox, you must stack up falling blocks
in sets of three: up and down, across, or on the diagonal. Unlike
Jewelbox, though, Columns can be played in black and white as

well as in color, as you can see in Fig. 4-37. You can determine how many different block patterns there are, from 4 to 12. Although most Columns blocks fall vertically, an occasional one lands horizontally, just to make matters difficult. There's also a black bomb that comes up once in a while, which changes the colors or patterns of the blocks on which it lands.

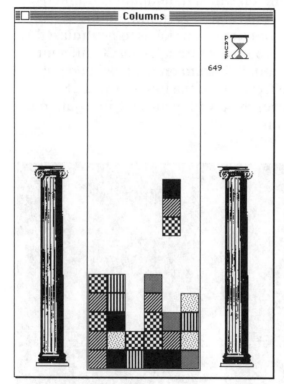

4-37 *You need to match three in any direction to get rid of them.*

Karate kids

In the past two years, the majority of arcade games have shifted from basic speed and skill games like Space Invaders or Galaxian, to what can best be described as martial arts games. Ninjas of all varieties, from Samurai Warriors to Turtles to Bart Simpson have been taking on all kinds of bad dudes. The ninja character can jump, kick, slash, or in the case of young Bart, swing his skateboard. Players must master strategy as well as speed, and learn what move best parries a particular attack.

FistFighter and MacNinja are a couple of good shareware martial arts games for the Mac. Operation Tsunami is a commercial Mac game featuring hand-to-hand combat. In it, you're a special agent sent to a remote island on which a madman is training an army of assassins, armored robots, and even mutant insects to take over the entire Asian continent. Your job is to neutralize this army, blasting and kicking your way through over 20 different kinds of bad guys, and eventually taking on the head bad guy himself. Awesome sound effects add to the fun. In Fig. 4-38, you've dispatched a couple of them with your machine gun, but you'd better look behind you.

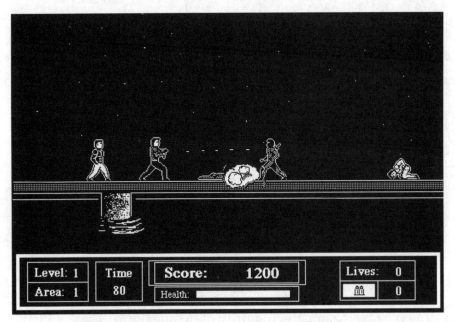

4-38 *There are lots of bad guys to fight off in this game.*

Thoroughly original ideas

We've traced the development of most of the popular arcade games from their probable inspiration. There are a few that are truly unique. These qualify as arcade games because they require speed and/or dexterity in order to earn points, not because they've ever been seen in an arcade.

Crystal Quest is one of my favorite games. It's played with a mouse, and the premise is very simple. You must pick up crystals, and avoid getting shot, zapped, or run into by a collection of nasties. You can shoot back, if you need to, but it's generally more effective to run. You do, however, have to avoid running into the traps that are placed in between the crystals, or running into any of the launching pads, either your own or those of the critters. Each round has a set number of crystals, plus some random bonuses. You get extra lives for scoring points. There are also bombs that will selectively kill off all the critters attacking you without shattering the crystals. The special bonus crystal can be shot or smashed by the bomb, so be careful.) Crystal Quest comes with a Critter Editor, which allows you to modify the existing group of nasties, and to create your own.

There is a trick to Crystal Quest, and it's that the mouse is velocity sensitive. A sudden motion will send your little crystal picker-upper scooting out of control across the screen, usually with fatal results. Practice very slow, subtle movements if you want to get high scores.

If you enjoy Crystal Quest, you'll love the brand-new sequel, Crystal Crazy. It's hard to see how something with no "story" can have a sequel, but here it is. More kinds of nasties to annihilate, but that's not all. Instead of just collecting crystals, you must erase pictures, smash glassware against the side of the screen, sink a run of pool balls in order, and assemble jigsaw puzzles, while grabbing for bonus points, enhanced shooting capability, armor, and of course, bombs. The sound effects are great, and the

game plays in black and white or color on any size screen. You
can even set a custom screen size, if you wish.

Plumb crazy

LucasFilms' PipeDream and AquaBlooperPiper from Casady &
Greene have a common premise. You're a plumber and you have
to stick assorted pieces of pipe together. PipeDream, shown in Fig.
4-39, rewards you for your efficiency. The more pieces you join,
the more points they are worth. Pieces fall from the chute and
you click the square to place them in. In later rounds you have to
start and end at a specific point. AquaBlooperPiper requires that
you actually complete a section of pipe so your customer can
take a shower. Pieces come along on a conveyor belt, and you
must select them and put them in position to end up with a solid
pipe from point A to point B, as shown in Fig. 4-40. Otherwise,
when the water comes on, your career will be all washed up.

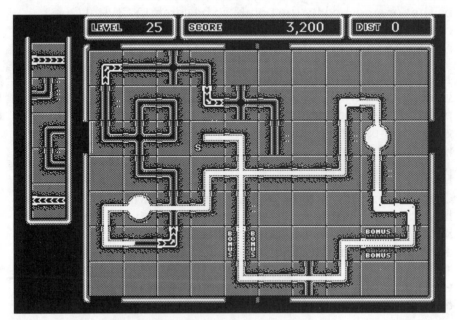

4-39 *Early screens just require you to build a certain length of pipe. Later ones
have start and stop points.*

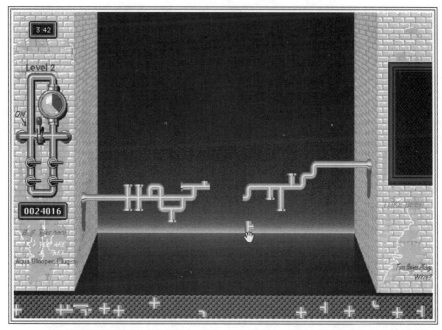

4-40 *Use the grabber hand to move pieces from the conveyor belt to the pipe.*

The ultimate mindless shoot 'em up

Can a game be pretentious? And if so, can it still be a terrific game in spite of it? Dynamix' Stellar 7 manages to be both pretentious and wonderful. It leads you through a long, involved (and probably unnecessary) plot, both on the screen and in the manual, before plunking you down in what's ultimately a shooting gallery. Ah, but what a shooting gallery! Seven different worlds, each with a hand-painted background . . . . Animation so fast it'll make your head spin . . . . And 14 different musical scores, plus incredible sound effects. This game needs color, of course, and headphones or stereo speakers would be a nice touch. The story line has to do with the usual evil overlord, in this case one Gir Draxon, who intends to conquer earth. It's up to you to stop him. You have a state-of-the-art fighting ship. Figure 4-41 shows the view from the cockpit. Your task is to find Draxon and destroy his flagship. Forget that. Shoot at anything that moves. The numbers on the right show your score.

4-41 *The radar screen shows what's coming up behind you.*

Game addiction can be hazardous to your health!

It's not uncommon to hear arcade games referred to as *twitch* games because, to play them, you use very subtle twitches of the mouse or joystick, or you twitch back and forth with a couple of keys on the keyboard. Twitch games, by their nature, tend to be extremely absorbing and even addictive. If you lose, you simply start over and keep playing.

Tetris is a good example of an addictive twitch game. Shortly after it first came out, one of the major medical journals had a piece on the diagnosis of a new musculo-skeletal ailment—a sort of bursitis—that was being called Tetris Shoulder. It was caused by holding the arm and shoulder in a tightly locked position for hours at a time, while moving only three fingers. Carpal Tunnel Syndrome, a numbness or tingling in the hand caused by compression of a nerve that runs through the bones in the wrist is another common game-player complaint.

What can you do to prevent game injuries? Aside from not playing games—which is *not* an option for most game addicts— you can teach yourself to take frequent breaks and to move around more while you're playing. Position the mouse or keyboard in a way that lets you rest your wrist or forearm on the desktop, or use an ergonomic wrist rest, available in computer and office-supply stores. You can also try using the Gravis GamePad instead of a mouse or keyboard controls. Since you can hold the game pad in your hand, it lets you lean back and sit comfortably while you zap aliens, run mazes, or stack blocks.

Visionary Software's LifeGuard is the ultimate solution for hardcore game addicts who need to be told when to quit. It interrupts your work, or play, at preset intervals to remind you to take a break. It even suggests activities, like stretching your arms, doing back and neck exercises, or taking a walk, to help keep you from stiffening up. This is an excellent gift for a Mac-aholic, and a good investment in your own health and sanity.

5

Let Mac put you in the driver's seat...

Have you ever wondered what it would feel like to fly a plane, schuss down the side of a mountain, or drive a racing car? You can experience these, and other pastimes right from the comfort of your Mac, with any of several dozen flying, driving, and sports simulations. If something goes wrong, unlike real life, the simulators let you keep on practicing until you get it right. That's a definite advantage, whether you're learning to fly a plane or sacking the opposing team's quarterback.

Flight simulators and driving simulators have been around for a long time . . . certainly long before the Mac came out. It was obviously easier, safer, and less expensive to train pilots in a simulator than in a real plane, especially when showing them how to handle safe crash landings and other emergencies.

During World War II, planes for training were in short supply, so most new pilots got most of their training on simulators, and never got into the pilot's seat until they were ready to solo. Early simulators used movies of scenery, and a realistic set of instruments that could be controlled by an instructor outside the simulator room.

Driving simulators were found in the arcades in the '40s, and consisted of a seat and steering wheel mechanically linked to a little toy car that could move from side to side in a window as you turned the steering wheel. Behind the car, a winding road revolved on a drum. You were supposed to keep the car centered on the road. It wasn't much like the real thing, but it was a beginning. Later models added the gas pedal, brake, and clutch, and a gear shift that controlled the speed of the scenery drum.

Computer flight simulators for the general public (as opposed to military and commercial flight training) were introduced in the PC platform in the early '80s and for the Macintosh in 1986. Microsoft brought us the first, and probably still the best flight simulator package. The current version, Flight Simulator 4.0, is so realistic that many amateur pilots use it for practice before landing at a new airport.

 The simulation includes 3D cockpit flight display, controls, and the necessary instruments for Visual Flight Rules (VFR) and Instrument Flight Rules (IFR) conditions as required by the Federal Aviation Agency (FAA). The graphics are as close as possible to a pilot's actual perspective. You can look ahead, as in Fig. 5-1, off to the side, or behind you, and you can also see what your plane looks like from the control tower or from a chase plane that follows you, as in Fig. 5-2.

As for planes, you have a choice of several different types. The Cessna 182 is recommended for beginners, since it's one commonly used by flying schools. It is a single-engine prop aircraft, with the kind of climbing performance and speed that keep the pilot busy adjusting the throttle and monitoring instruments, especially during take off and landing. The Gates Learjet is the "executive" plane. (Is it more than coincidence that

LET MAC PUT YOU IN THE DRIVER'S SEAT...

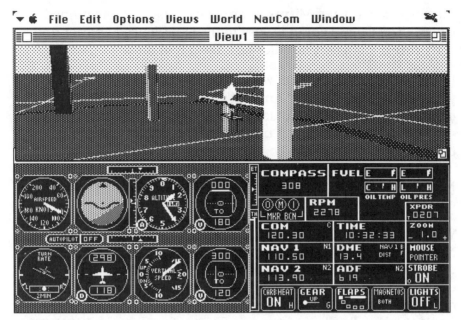

5-1 *We're flying over downtown Chicago. The instrument panel in our Cessna looks very much like a real one.*

5-2 *The plane you're flying is the one that's about to crash into the Sears Tower You're seeing the view from a chase plan.*

the chief executive of Microsoft happens to be a fellow named Gates?) The Gates Learjet is easy to fly. Experienced charter and corporate pilots say it handles just like a real one.

If you're the kind of person who admires vintage automobiles, you'll enjoy the Sopwith Camel. It's also Snoopy's favorite aircraft. Always wanted to design your own? Go ahead. Then fly a prototype, and see how it handles. If you crash, you can go back to the drawing board and try again. Want to see what unpowered flight feels like? There's a Schweizer sailplane in the Microsoft hangar. Try soaring on a thermal up in the mountains east of Seattle.

Where else can you go? Flight Simulator's "world" covers most of North America, including the continental United States, parts of Canada, Mexico, and the Caribbean. The populated world, in which you can see lots of identifiable landmarks, consists of 5 areas with a total of 125 airports. There are maps in the Flight Simulator handbook with the coordinates for all of the airports and maps of the major ones.

Like anything else, flying takes practice. You can expect to walk away from a lot of crashes before you actually get off the ground. One thing that will help is to use something that feels more like an airplane controller than a keyboard. Check out the Advanced Gravis MouseStick II. Like the Advanced Gravis GamePad described in the previous chapter, it plugs into the ADB port and gives you a heightened sense of reality when you play. Experts prefer to use two joysticks; one for ailerons and elevators, the other for the throttle and brakes or throttle and rudder. (The ADB connector is arranged so you can piggyback one into the other.) If you have only one joystick, the throttle and brakes are controlled from the keyboard.

If you're not ready to invest in a MouseStick, consider the Mouse Yoke, from Colorado Spectrum. It looks like a Cessna-style steering yoke, with two sort of horseshoe-shaped hand grips. The device clamps onto your desktop, and has an elastic strap to hold the mouse. The mouse ball rests over a slot in the fixture, and a shaft attached to the yoke rotates the mouse ball. Moving the yoke in and out controls up-and-down motion, and turning the yoke twists the shaft for left-right motion. It's simple, but effective. And it's a lot less expensive, at about half the price of a joystick. You could even (possibly) clamp it onto the edge of an airplane tray table, load Flight Simulator into your PowerBook, and fly yourself from Boston to LaGuardia duplicating the actions of your Delta shuttle flight.

Getting off the ground

Take offs and landings are the most difficult part of learning to fly. Once you're actually up there, holding the plane more or less level and at a more or less constant speed isn't difficult.

You will find the cockpits are similar, but not identical, in the different planes. The Learjet has a few gauges that are different from those on the Cessna, including the speed indicator ranges that are adjusted to show a vertical rate of climb up to 8,000 feet per minute, and an airspeed indicator that registers to Mach 1 (the speed of sound or 740 mph at sea level).

The sailplane cockpit is shown in Fig. 5-3. Since the aircraft has no motor, the instrument panel includes only the gyro compass, altimeter, and airspeed gauges, and the altitude indicator or artificial horizon.

To fly the sailplane in another part of the country, get there with the Cessna and then, when your speed is about 70 knots, switch to the sailplane.

Once you have mastered the basics of flying, start playing with experimental aircraft, crop dusting, formation flying, or even stunt flying. The Flight Simulator manual explains all of these. Here's what it says about the Immelmann:

> This maneuver was invented by a German ace, Max Immelmann, who used it as a tactical maneuver to evade other aircraft in a dogfight. The Immelmann is a half loop followed by a half roll, (as opposed to the "split S" which is a half roll followed by a half loop).

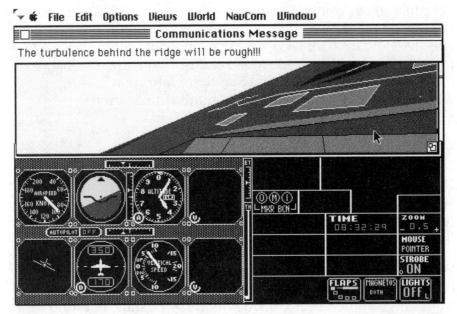

5-3 *The cockpit in the sailplane has no engine controls because a sailplane has no engine.*

The manual then goes on to explain exactly how to perform this move, with a diagram plus step-by-step instructions. Following the instructions guides you precisely through the turn. It's realistic enough that the book ought to come with one of those little white bags . . ..

Join the Air Force: ours, or theirs . . .

Learning to fly is certainly fun, but once you've mastered it, what else can you do? All of the action flight-simulation programs involve flying either historic aircraft like the Fokker Triplane or state-of-the-art warplanes like the Falcon F-16.

Falcon MC, from Spectrum Holobyte, lets you fly the plane that's been described as the backbone of the U.S. Air Force. Over 1,500 of these fast, agile planes are in service. During Operation Desert

Storm they logged more missions than any other aircraft, delivering laser-guided, and television-guided smart missiles on all-weather and long-range missions with a high degree of success. At the end of the hostilities, the 249 F-16s assigned to the area had flown over 13,500 miles, while keeping better than 95 percent of the aircraft in good flying condition.

Flying the Falcon feels a bit different from flying a Cessna, or even the Learjet. The main reason, of course, is that this isn't a pleasure craft, or even a commercial aircraft. It's a lean, mean fighting machine, and most of the controls are for the purpose of firing missiles of some sort at enemy targets, rather than keeping you in the air or monitoring the plane's performance.

The Falcon cockpit is designed for *situational awareness* (SA), very important when your survival depends on knowing not only how well your own plane is functioning, but who's creeping up behind you, who might start shooting at you from the ground, and how far you must go to "deliver the mail" or "dump your party favors," as combat pilots like to refer to bombing missions. The key to SA is the *head-up display* or HUD. It's the clear screen that's superimposed over the front cockpit window. It presents important flying and targeting information without blocking your view. The HUD functions in three different modes, depending on what you're doing. It varies for air-to-air and air-to-ground combat and gives a very different display for the Instrument Landing System. Some aspects of the HUD are always in view, and these are shown in Fig. 5-4.

The F-16 is a very fast plane. Speed is indicated on the airspeed scale in 100s of mph. The G-force indicators show your current G force (gravity) and the maximum you reach during the flight. This is most useful in real-world situations when an aircraft has sustained damage during a mission and the mechanics are attempting to determine the cause.

The Falcon manual teaches you how to fly the F-16, how to fire your missiles, and quite a lot about tactics and strategy. Once you're ready for combat, there are a series of missions to fly. You're an air force pilot in an imaginary country that is involved in a border conflict. If the enemy forces get out of hand, they will

5-4 *Fighter pilots don't have time to look down at the control panel, so plane designers found a way to move it up.*

overrun your air base and conquer the weaker country adjacent to you, whom you are protecting. To make the simulation even more real, in addition to flying your bombing runs, you also have to contend with supply shortages, aircraft load limits, and other military snafus.

The duty roster holds 10 pilots at a time. You select their names, photos, and call signs from the file of recruits supplied. You can retire pilots, and train new ones whenever necessary. Successful missions earn promotions. Uncompleted missions can result in a pilot being captured by the enemy, or being reported missing or killed in action. The latter two events always remove him (or her—Falcon MC is nonsexist!) from the duty roster.

The F-18, from Graphic Simulations, is the most state-of-the-art flight simulator yet. It's so far advanced that most of its instrument panels are computer screens rather than dials or gauges. At first, it seemed sort of strange seeing a computer screen simulating other computer screens, but as soon as I got the plane off the ground, un-reality took over, and I was too busy trying to keep it level and hit the target to think about the meta-computer image. This plane is very fast and very responsive. You've got to use a light touch on the stick, otherwise you'll see some spectacular crashes. If you remember to eject, you can parachute to safety and watch your plane go down. Otherwise, splat.

History buffs with an urge to fly will love the Fokker Triplane Flight Simulator, provided they can get it installed and make it function correctly. It is copy protected, and can be installed (a limited number of times) on a hard disk.

If you install it, plan to keep it, or be careful that you follow the instructions for removing it with the installer instead of just trashing it.

The Fokker cockpit in flight is shown in Fig. 5-5. It's an extremely simple plane to fly. Essentially, all you need to do is to center the

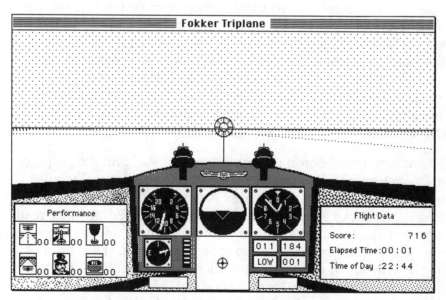

5-5 *That's not a hood emblem out there, it's your gunsight.*

rudder, press down on the throttle (6 on the keyboard), pull the nose up a little when the speed reaches 50 to 60 knots, and you're up. The manual also teaches you some 15 different acrobatic maneuvers including the Immelmann described earlier, the Whifferdill 8, and the 4-point Hesitation Roll.

A nice feature is that there's a panic button to level out the plane when it gets out of control. Just type Y (for Yikes!) to bring things back to an even keel.

The P-51 Mustang Flight Simulator also comes from Bullseye Software, creator of the Fokker FS. It uses the same *limited installation* method of copy protection. The P-51 is a World War II plane, capable of a top speed of 427 mph, and designed to strafe targets, dogfight, and even let you bail out. The "world" for this (and the Fokker described above) is France and Germany. You'll be able to recognize the Eiffel tower as you fly over Paris.

Red Baron, from Sierra/Dynamix, is another World War I Flight Simulator. You're not restricted to a single type of plane, though, or even to choosing one side of the war. There are both German and Allied planes available to you, and you can fight for either side. Create a career for yourself or fly a single mission. Dogfight a famous Ace if you dare . . . perhaps the Red Baron himself or young Herman Goering, or one of the top Allied flyers like Mick Mannock or Eddie Rickenbacker. Red Baron comes with its own joystick file for use with the Advanced Gravis MouseStick. The joystick is almost mandatory for successful flying in this game. You simply don't have eyes enough or fingers enough to watch the action, and work with a mouse and keyboard.

The action in Red Baron is remarkably realistic, and the graphics are beautiful in color. Figure 5-6 will give you a general idea of the view from your cockpit. Those dots in the distance are German planes, coming to shoot you down. Red Baron is more of a game than the other flight-simulator packages, but it's a good one. The manual will teach you some basic flying skills, but not in anywhere near the detail that Microsoft's Flight Simulator does. You will, however, learn a good deal about the fighting tactics and strategies developed during World War I.

5-6 Enemy planes ahead! Prepare for dogfight! (Where's Snoopy when you need him?)

Another interesting part of the Red Baron package is the ability to make and edit "movies" of your missions. If you make a fatal mistake, as we did in Fig. 5-7, you can see exactly what went wrong, and why. You can even edit on a new ending so you come out on top.

Hellcats Over the Pacific puts you in the cockpit of an F6F Hellcat, during World War II. First, you'll attend flight school near Carson City, Nevada, and learn to handle the Navy Model F6F Hellcat, a bigger, faster upgrade to the popular F4F Wildcat. Then you'll be transferred to the Solomon Islands, Guadalcanal area. You'll be based on fleet carriers and ground bases throughout the island chain. Figure 5-8 shows the view from the Hellcat's cockpit. Your machine gun is mounted in the nose. Use the crosshairs in the window to line up your target and fire with the space bar or mouse button. Hellcats comes with a copy of the actual pilot's handbook for the aircraft, complete with restrictions and warnings about letting it fall into enemy hands.

5-7 *Looks like I forgot to bail out.*

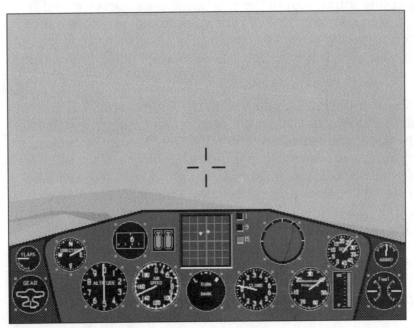

5-8 *There's another plane flying alongside you. Don't turn to the left!*

Hellcats Missions at Leyte Gulf is an add-on module, not a complete game. It requires Hellcats over the Pacific to run. But it includes eight more exciting battle scenarios, and retrofits your F6F with torpedoes instead of bombs, and adds rockets. For most of the action you're stationed onboard the carrier Intrepid, so you'll be taking off and landing on a moving vessel much of the time. Figure 5-9 shows what the carrier takeoff looks like from the pilot's point of view. The graphics aren't as detailed as in either Microsoft's Flight Simulator, or Falcon MC, but they're certainly adequate. If you like flying and shooting at things, Hellcats has plenty of action to keep you busy.

5-9 *Watch the carrier's tower whiz past, but remember to pull up as you reach the end of the deck.*

On the ground, looking up

You can get a different view of flying with a shareware game called Air Traffic Controller. You're up in the tower, with your radar screen and two-way radio. It's up to you to land the planes safely, without too many near misses, and obviously without a crash. Planes come up on the radar screen, as shown in Fig. 5-10, and you must keep track of them, keeping them far enough apart to avoid danger, and also getting them landed on time. It's definitely a challenge.

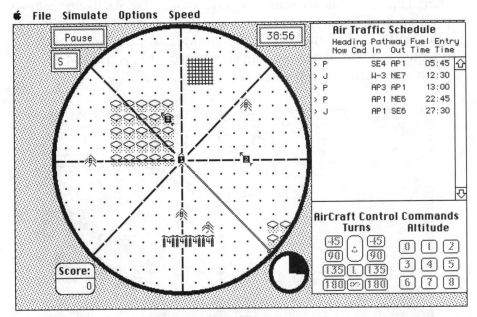

5-10 *There are more planes coming.*

Flying for fun

If flight simulators make you airsick, perhaps something a bit tamer is in order. John Calhoun's Glider might be just the right combination of flight and whimsey. Instead of flying an F-16, a Fokker, Messerschmidt, or Cessna, you're flying a paper airplane . . . the kind that, as kids, we turned our homework into. Glider was a shareware game that made good. It was purchased by Casady & Greene from author Calhoun, after a year of so of user group and bulletin board distribution. Early versions of Glider are still available for downloading on many boards, but the commercial version is well worth the price.

The premise is simple. You have a paper airplane. You launch it in the first room of the house. There are hot-air heating registers in the floor that cause updrafts that lift the glider. You can make it move forward and backward. Whenever you bring it over an updraft, it rises. Without the beneficial effects of the updraft, it sinks. You need to fly it from one room to the next, to get as far as possible through the house. But every time it crashes into something, or touches the floor, the glider is destroyed.

You have five gliders to start with. You can pick up additional ones in certain rooms in the house. (They look like pieces of folded paper.) You can also get a boost from a lit candle, which you'll occasionally find in a room. Of course, getting too close to a flame with a paper airplane can have disastrous consequences. Figure 5-11 shows a typical Glider room. The alarm clocks give you extra points, but the balloons and other things that come flying at you will knock the glider to the floor. Batteries, if you find any, will give your glider a boost. Rubberbands can be used

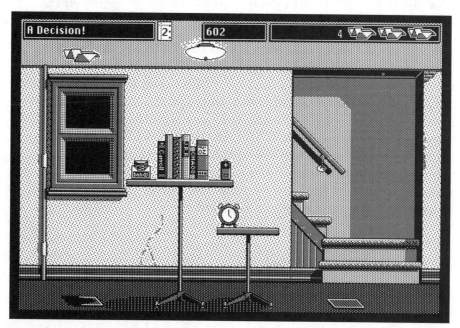

5-11 *From this point you can fly upstairs or continue into the next room downstairs.*

to shoot down balloons, helicopters, and other things that could hit you. There are also bonus points hidden in various places.

Glider can be played with the keyboard, mouse, or joystick. Since a maximum of four keys are used, the keyboard is sufficient, and probably easiest for a beginner, although it gives less control than the mouse. With two directional keys, for left and right, you're always going full speed in that direction. If you use a mouse, you can also control the velocity of your left and right movements, which is especially helpful later on in the game when the rooms get to be more difficult.

You can also create your own Glider houses. The Room editor is supplied with the program. Add furniture, hazards, and bonus points from the palette, and control the strength of the updrafts by dragging the line from the register to the maximum height you want the glider to be able to reach. Test fly a glider through your creation to be sure it's possible. You might find that you need to move an updraft, or adjust the size of a shelf or table in order to let the glider get past it. Rooms should be challenging but not impossible.

Other players' Glider house creations can be found on bulletin-board systems (BBS) and online services. If you create an interesting one, feel free to post it for other people to enjoy. Figure 5-12 shows a strange Glider room, that's part of a house I might finish some day. John Calhoun, the game's author, has published a second set of what he calls Mad Houses for Glider, under the name More Glider. (It won't function without the original program, though.) More Glider also contains a file of what Calhoun considers to be among the best player-generated Glider houses. Some are extremely imaginative.

Mac seat driver!

There aren't nearly as many driving simulators as there are flying simulators. This might be because most of the software companies are located in California, where driving isn't

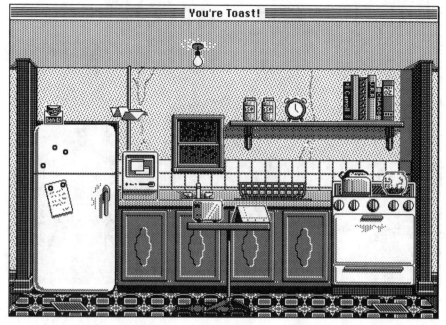

5-12 *Don't forget there's a reason why it's called a pop-up toaster.*

necessarily fun. Oddly enough, one of the two good driving simulators, Spectrum Holobyte's 'Vette, has California as its "world," specifically downtown San Francisco, and parts of the surrounding area. 'Vette is a very entertaining game, although somewhat difficult to play with a mouse. Colorado Spectrum has, however, produced a Mouse Wheel, similar to their Mouse Yoke for flight simulators, that looks and feels very much like a Corvette steering wheel. It clamps onto your desktop and holds the standard mouse in position against a drive shaft. Both Mouse Wheel and Mouse Yoke are available from many of the mail-order software companies, bundled with the appropriate application. I found the 'Vette and Mouse Wheel bundle for less than $50 in one catalog.

'Vette has two modes: racing and touring. The touring mode lets you drive through downtown San Francisco and visit some of the favorite tourist spots. Figure 5-13 shows the gate at the entrance to Chinatown. In racing mode, you're driving on one of four

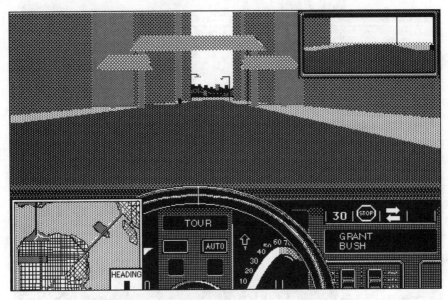

5-13 *The gate marks the entrance to Chinatown.*

racing courses over city streets between the Bay and Golden Gate Bridges, or from the Zoo to the Bridge, and so on. In Fig. 5-14, we're heading for the bridge. Notice the screen to the right of the dashboard that tells you where you are. Someday maybe all cars will have one of those.

Choose a stock Corvette or a souped-up model like the Sledgehammer. You'll be racing against a Porsche, Ferrari, or Lamborghini. If you have a modem and a friend who also has 'Vette, you can race against each other. You can also connect two Macs directly to each other or over an AppleTalk network to play the game, as long as each Mac has its own, registered copy of the game.

 Many games and other software applications, when used on a network, will check to make sure no other machine on the network has the same application with the same serial number. If an illegal copy is found on another machine, both will be disabled . . . sometimes disabling your system files, too. Software piracy isn't just illegal—it's hazardous to the health of your Mac!

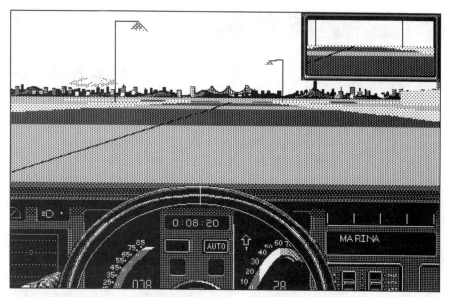

5-14 *Our opponent took a wrong turn. If we stay out of trouble, the race is ours.*

Ferrari Grand Prix is another auto racing game, similar to 'Vette, with five courses and a course editor that lets you design your own. The Ferrari is more difficult to control than the Corvette, and takes a good deal of time to master. Bill Elliott's NASCAR Challenge, from Konami, also has you driving on a track, one of eight official NASCAR tracks. The game was co-designed by Elliott, a Winston Cup champion and long-time stock car racer, and it's realistic enough that you can almost smell the burning rubber as they go around the far turn.

The Duel—Test Drive II, from Accolade, is an excellent road-racing simulation if you have an older Mac and can run it. Figure 5-15 shows a screen shot from the game, which unfortunately will not run reliably under System 7 or on any of the newer Macs. Accolade has no plans to update the game for Macintosh as of this writing, and an Accolade tech support person advised me that Accolade was "pretty much getting out of the Mac game business altogether."

5-15 *The Duel is a road race, so you've got to deal with traffic, too.*

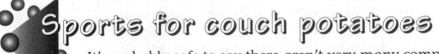

Sports for couch potatoes

It's probably safe to say there aren't very many computer people who are also great athletes. But many of us do admit to having secret dreams of coaching in the National Football League, shooting baskets with Alonzo Mourning or Shaq O'Neil, or even just breaking 100 on the golf course. The Mac can't make any of these things happen, but it can help you polish up your daydreams.

There are sports for all seasons—baseball, basketball, and football, of course, as well as hockey, skiing, boxing, and golf, both PGA-style and miniature.

So you wanna be a football hero? Try Brøderbund's Playmaker Football. Playmaker Football is a coaching simulation. You're the head coach, and you can design custom plays and strategies for your team, as well as work from the playbooks provided with the game. Then, your team hits the animated gridiron and tries out your ideas against an equally aggressive opponent. Play a full four quarters against another human-coached team or against the computer. Either way, it's a challenge.

Start, like all good coaches do, by studying your team roster. You've got a full squad of 11 offensive and 11 defensive players plus 8 specialists—kickers, and so on. Draft the players you want to add to your team, and cut those who haven't got the good statistics. Adjust the individual characteristics of each player on the squad to match your coaching style and your football philosophy, as shown in Fig. 5-16. Once you've got the team in shape, go to the chalkboard. It's shown in Fig. 5-17.

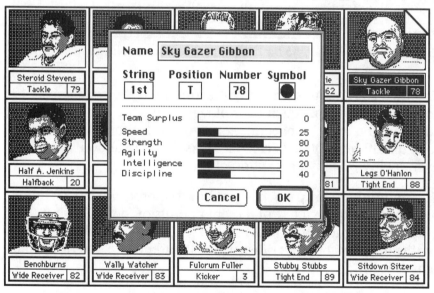

5-16 *Tackles need to be strong, but not necessarily smart.*

You can design plays from scratch or modify existing ones. Give each player detailed instructions, from a simple pass route to an elaborately detailed blocking scheme. There's a practice field, too, so you can refine your plays before the big game.

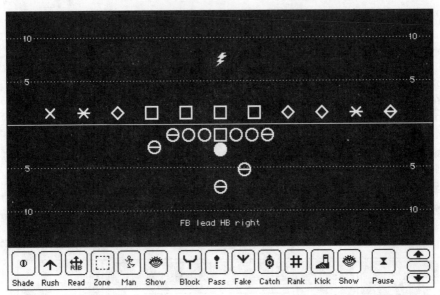

5-17 *The halfback swings to the right, and the quarterback hands him the ball.*

There's a coin flip to start the game, and then the two teams square off. Can you coach your players to a win? The clock is running, the crowd is cheering, and you've got to call a play. Will it be a halfback option? Screen left? As Fig. 5-18 shows, there's even a play-by-play description of the action.

The manual not only teaches you how the program works, but it also explains quite a few of the finer points of football: what qualifications are important for different positions, when to use particular plays or player instructions, and how to determine if a play is legal.

You can also find teams (and other people to play against) in the online services or BBS game libraries. A recent check of America Online showed 218 entries under the keyword PMFB.

The other well-known football simulation is NFL Challenge, from XOR. Unfortunately, it doesn't seem to run very happily under System 7. Too bad, because it was an interesting simulation that let you see how real teams from different years would have done against each other.

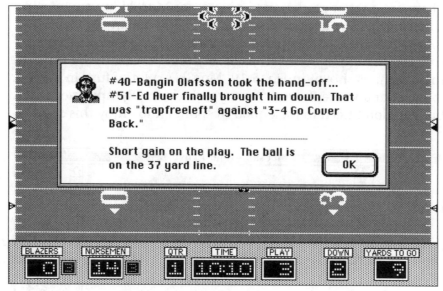

#40-Bangin Olafsson took the hand-off...
#51-Ed Auer finally brought him down. That
was "trapfreeleft" against "3-4 Go Cover
Back."

Short gain on the play. The ball is
on the 37 yard line.

OK

| BLAZERS | NORSEMEN | QTR | TIME | PLAY | DOWN | YARDS TO GO |

5-18 *You get the play-by-play after each down.*

Give your mouse a lift ticket

System 7 users will fare better with XOR's MacSki, which does
seem to be friendly with the current system. It's a mouse-driven
skiing game. You're racing downhill against the stopwatch.
Trouble is, it's a very crowded slope. There are trees, rocks,
photographers shooting models in abbreviated ski clothing, and
an unusual assortment of wildlife including rabbits, squirrels,
and penguins. Crashing into any of these, or any other hazard,
will make you fall down. You'll lose several seconds before you
manage to get back on your skis again. If you fall too often,
there's also a very large St. Bernard who'll come out to
administer first aid.

Skiing is done with the mouse, of course. Click at the top of the
hill to dig your poles in and go. Clicking a few more times will
get you enough pole action to build up some speed, so you can
go into the proper racing tuck. You can run over stopwatches that
will freeze the clock for a few seconds. If you run over a cake of
ski wax, you'll be able to go faster.

There are a set of predesigned courses for MacSki, plus a terrain editor that lets you create your own ski slopes complete with as much or as little scenery as you want to install. Decorate your course by dragging items from the scrolling menu at the right of the screen, as shown in Fig. 5-19. MacSki's a lot of fun, in color or in black and white. It won't turn you into an Olympic medalist, but you don't need to look good in spandex to enjoy this sport.

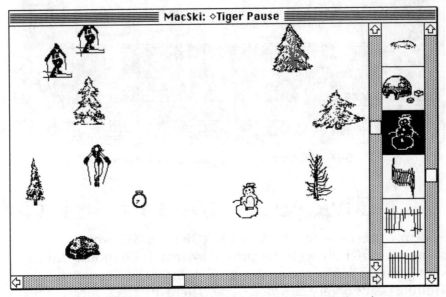

5-19 *Since it's winter, the grabber hand wears a mitten!*

There is a very clever freeware skiing game that functions much like MacSki, but lacks some of the fancier options. There are 10 different courses, and you and your friends may race as many as 12 different skiers in World Cup action. The mouse controls the skiers, and the action is fast. There are even sound effects. If you take the wrong side of a gate, you're disqualified, just like in a real race. There's also a course editor with this game, but the graphics aren't quite as fancy. This game is dedicated ". . . by the lousy Swedish skier Ingemar Ragnemalm to the great Swedish skier Ingemar Stenmark."

Indoor sports

When you go to a typical British pub, two things stand out: the beer, which is remarkably good, although usually served warm by American standards; and the activity around the dart board. Darts is an extremely popular game in the British Isles, and is catching on here, too. There's a shareware version for the Mac, which will at least teach you the fundamentals of playing and scoring dart games like Cricket, 501, and Around the Clock. Mac Darts are thrown with the mouse, and the technique is a bit tricky. Figure 5-20 shows a partially completed game of Cricket. In the variation, you must hit each of the highest numbers, plus the bullseye, three times to win. Darts can be played by one or two players.

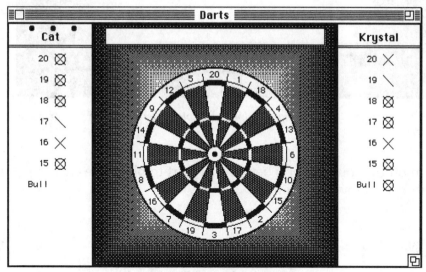

5-20 *This game is fairly close.*

Billiard Parlor, also a shareware offering, has a number of different pool and billiards games programmed in. The action is the same on all, but they score differently. Shooting pool with a mouse is similar to throwing darts with a mouse, but not much like using a pool cue. Center the pointer on the ball, click and drag to determine the strength of your shot. Release the button to shoot. You can even track the trajectory of your shot, to see where you went wrong or to study the physics of pool. Figure 5-21 shows an example.

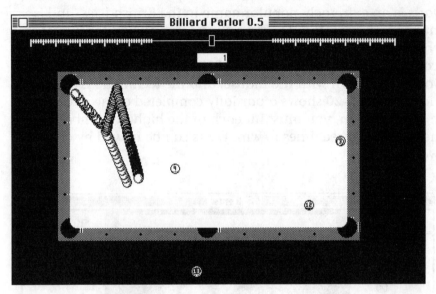

5-21 *When you're practicing, it helps to be able to see where the shot actually goes.*

Turn off the sound effects before you start to play. The clicking balls get annoying very fast.

For swingers only

"Golf isn't a hobby," or so say those who are addicted to it, "It's a way of life." Golfing is one of those sports people tend to get passionate about—you either love it or you hate it. Golf on the Mac is easy to love. It's pretty, especially in color, and it's easy to learn but hard to master. (Like the real game, perhaps?) The best feature of computer golf is that the weather, and the greens, are always perfect. You're not golfing in the rain, or in the snow. You're not slogging through the mud, risking heat stroke or frostbite. And there's never a wait for starting times. There have been several golf simulations produced for the Mac, but the all-time best comes from Electronic Arts. It's PGA Tour Golf, and as the name suggests, it's licensed by the Professional Golfers Association. The game is a cross between actual play, and watching a pro tournament on TV. There's nice use of animation throughout. When you approach a real-world hole you get a moving TV helicopter view around the green; then the view pulls all the way back to the tee.

You're playing on real-world golf courses, drawn from the actual PGA blueprints. Holes are shown complete with comments (text, not speech) from the smiling on-screen faces of the pros who play there. Figure 5-22 shows an example. The game comes with four different courses, and a separate disk holds three more including the famed Scottsdale Country Club. It also comes with a bunch of tough opponents for you—60 of the tour's leading players. Can you play in their league? Of course you can, if you spend some time at the driving range first. Remember, golf takes practice, whether you're playing out on the turf or inside on your Mac.

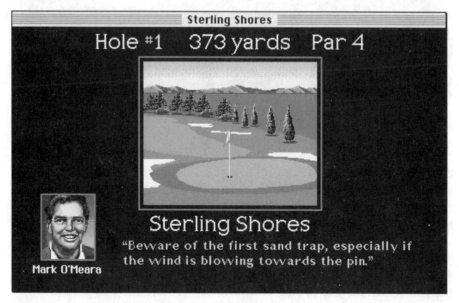

5-22 *The introductions to the courses will give you a few good tips about playing them.*

Experiment with both woods and irons. Learn to watch the wind, too. You're not playing in a vacuum, after all.

Once you've gotten the long game down, visit the putting green. PGA Tour Golf helps you learn how to read a green. When you select Putting Grid, you'll see a contour map of the practice hole's putting surface, like the one in Fig. 5-23. Practice long and short putts until you're stroking the ball into the cup easily. Now, as Fig. 5-24 shows, you're ready for some golf.

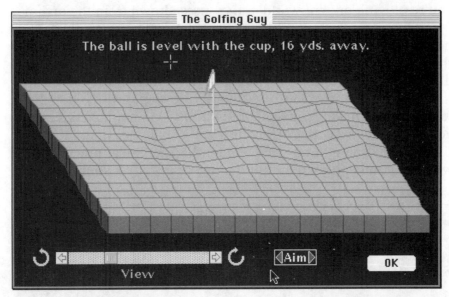

5-23 *Wouldn't it be nice if all putting greens were on a grid?*

For added realism, PGA Tour Golf includes sound effects— thowcks, bounces, random birds, splashunk when you land in a water hazard . . . even a polite round of applause when you sink a putt. Stop in the pro shop and make sure you've got the clubs you want. Visit the tour tent between rounds.

You can set up a tournament with one to four players. One (or more) of them can be PGA pros. In fact, if you set up for a single player, it can be the pro of your choice! Watch Tommy Armour, Larry Mize, Fuzzy Zoeller, or another of your favorite players play

5-24 *Choose your club, check the wind, and go for it.*

a round of golf, or set up a match with two top pros. You can sit back and watch them go for the big money, or compete against them. It's not quite as real as watching a pro match on TV, but at least there are no commercials.

Mac, ahoy!

There aren't any serious boating simulations for the Mac, other than those that turn it into a PT boat or other naval vessel. But there's a cute shareware game called Sail Away that lets you practice sailing a Sunfish on a large pond. As you can see in Fig. 5-25, it shows you the boat as you'd see if from alongside, as well as in relation to the wind and on a charted course. Adjust the sail and dagger board by dragging on the scroll bars. Clicking on the arrows will move your helmsperson from one side of the boat to the other, improving trim. You can even capsize it if you try! (Note: The Sailing Forum on CompuServe is the only place I've found this program. If you're interested in a particular sport, look for simulations in its online forum library.)

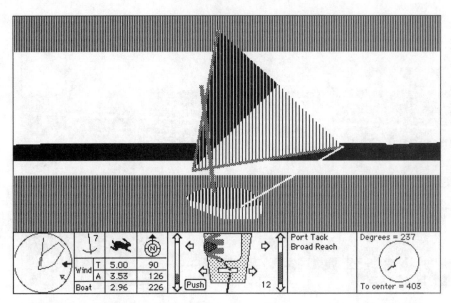

5-25 *You could actually learn quite a lot about sailing from this program.*

If you're planning to spend a lot of time at sea, you might want to download Ship's Code Blinker, available on most of the large services. It's a HyperCard stack that teaches Morse code with blinking lights, and random silly phrases. It isn't exactly a game, but it features a classy picture of a sailor by your humble author, and nifty programming by her husband.

Other good sports simulations include Hole-In-One Miniature Golf, HardBall II, 4D Boxing, Wayne Gretsky Hockey, and more. There are also shareware versions of baseball, basketball, golf, and other sports. Whatever your sport, if there isn't a simulation of it yet, just keep your eyes open at the software dealers and check the bulletin boards. There almost certainly will be one soon.

6

Simulated worlds

The people at Maxis must really understand human nature. Several years ago, they introduced a simple little black-and-white game for the Mac, called SimCity. It made you the mayor of a small city, with the ability to raise taxes and spend your constituents money on such necessities as police and fire protection, mass transit, housing, power plants, and even sports stadiums. Your city grew or failed, depending on how satisfied the local people were with your government, and whether you'd zoned enough industry to keep them working or too much, so the pollution made the city unlivable.

SimCity was extremely popular. It had elements of urban planning, politics, and economics—but it made them fun. It was the first example of a new kind of program called a *system simulation*. It appealed to many of us because we've always had the notion that we could do a better job of running things than the people who are in charge. System simulations give you three things: a situation, a set of rules, and a set of tools.

IT'S A MAD, MAD, MAD, MAD MAC

In SimCity, the situation is a growing city. Your challenge is to figure out how it works and take control of it. The rules provide the framework and limits based, in this particular example, on city planning and management factors. You have to learn to balance economic factors and human needs to keep the citizens happy, and to keep the city growth rate relatively stable. If something is rotten in SimCity, the people will move away, and your thriving megalopolis will turn into a ghost town. Figure 6-1 shows a happy city. The current version of SimCity is called SimCity Supreme. It adds color and a few other refinements to the basic program.

6-1 It might be time to lower the taxes.

Once players had mastered SimCity, they went in search of new worlds to conquer. Maxis obliged with SimEarth, which raised urban planning to the global scale. Now, instead of an unhappy group of citizens, you could have a whole planet mad at you. On the other hand, instead of merely being mayor, you had much more widespread influence.

SimEarth is based on James Lovelock's Gaia theory, which proposes looking at our planet and life on it as a whole entity, rather than as individual areas like ecology, economics, politics, and so on. It stresses the interconnectedness of systems. SimEarth treats the planet as a whole: life, climate, the atmosphere, and the physical makeup of the planet—from topsoil to molten core—all have an effect on each other.

SimEarth has two modes of operation. If you play it as a game, you are allotted an energy budget. You must try to develop, manage, and preserve your planet while staying within the predetermined budget. In experimental mode, you have unlimited energy. It's sort of the ultimate "what if . . .". You can set up a planet in any stage of development, introduce new factors, and watch the result. It's sort of a planetary spreadsheet, with "what ifs" built in.

When conditions are right for it, SimEarthlings will evolve. The one-celled variety come up first, and evolution proceeds more or less as we know it. The goal is to reach intelligent life, though that needn't mean humans or even mammals. Intelligent cetaceans, grasshoppers, or squid are equally possible if the conditions are right for them.

The basic building blocks of situation, rules, and tools are present, just as in SimCity. In SimEarth, the rules are based on global systems and management, including chemical and geological factors like atmospheric composition, climate, continental drift, and the effects of volcanoes, earthquakes, and other cataclysms, plus the biological and human factors related to evolution, food supply, and species distribution. Rules also reflect the positive and negative aspects of technology—wars, pollution and waste control, energy and food production—when a planet is far enough advanced for these to be factors.

Tools provide you with the ability to create, modify, and manage your planet; things you couldn't possibly do other than in a simulation. You can create a planet in any of four time scales, physically modify its landscape, trigger cataclysmic events to watch their effect, and plant various biomes and life-forms anywhere on your planet. You can choose to nurture a particular species to help it evolve intelligence by making sure that conditions are right for it. Your management tools include maps and graphs to help you see what's happening, plus windows that show reports and give you important messages. The Gaia Window lets you monitor the planet's mood by watching her facial expression. A cluster of SimEarth windows are shown in Fig. 6-2.

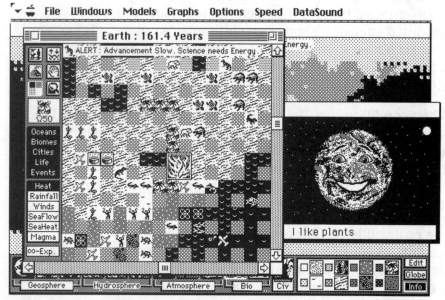

6-2 A clean planet is a happy planet.

The SimEarth User Manual is very comprehensive and will tell you a great deal about the game and also about planetary management. Parts of it are also quite funny.

 Be sure to read page 44, at the end of the tutorial section.

General SimAnt-ics

If you can make mountains out of molehills, what can you make out of anthills? If you were the game designers at Maxis, you'd make a game. Which they did . . .. It's called SimAnt, and while it does indeed follow in the footsteps of the previous simulations, it's also much more game-like. There are three modes: a brief game, in which you attempt to lead the black ants to victory over the red ants; a full game, in which you must not only defeat the red ants, but invade the house and avoid the evil human feet, lawnmowers, and pesticides; and an experimental mode for studying ant behavior, which is disconcertingly similar to human behavior. The ultimate goal of SimAnt is to take over the house and the backyard, and expand your colony by finding resources, mating, and taking over hostile colonies. With a few minor changes, they could have called it "SimBusiness."

SimAnt includes a tutorial function, in which messages appear on the screen and instruct you to try different options. Some of the disasters that can befall you are truly disgusting. For an example, see Fig. 6-3. Since this is interactive, it's possible to

6-3 *Spiders are even scarier when you're an ant.*

learn enough about the game this way to have an interesting (and successful) game without cracking the manual. Of course, the manual will tell you a lot more, including 100 pages or so about real yard-ant behavior. It's more than I ever wanted to know, but myrmecophiles will be gratified.

For population booms, set the nursing level high. Behaviors are set from the panel in Fig. 6-4. Eggs grow fastest if there is only one per square. Therefore, either move around when playing the queen, or play a worker and move the eggs. For more eggs, keep the queen well fed. To kill the spider, recruit at least 10 ants and lead them to the spider. Have them swarm around it by sitting next to it, and following when it runs.

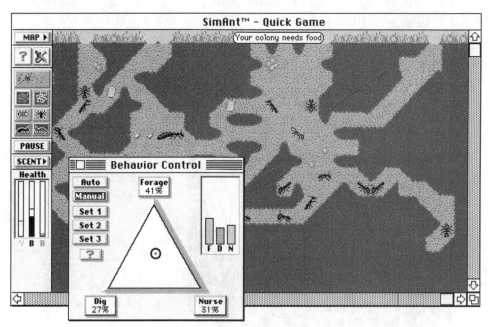

6-4 Behind the Behavior window is the map of your colony.

For a quick win, or just to keep the red population down, play a soldier ant, pick up a rock, and put it on top of the red ant hole. This then blocks them from taking food in or out, and the queen starves. Watch out for other holes that they build. Optionally, go into the hole, and block it from the inside with the rock. Then wait for the queen's health to go down, and eat some of their food. Attack the red queen when you are at full health, kill her, and win the game.

Sim Darwin?

In his wildest dreams, Charles Darwin might have imagined a biology laboratory like the one in SimLife—designed to simulate environments, ecosystems, evolution, and to create life. Yep—this one takes you a step further up the ladder. In SimCity, you are the mayor. In SimEarth, you are Mother Nature . . .. Now, you are the creator, making new plants and animals and populating worlds with them.

You can define a new species as we're doing in Fig. 6-5, and change its genetic makeup, as we have in Fig. 6-6. Then we place it in the world, and see what happens to it. Does it survive? Does it reach a peak of population and then die out again? We can change factors, one at a time, until we can understand the effects

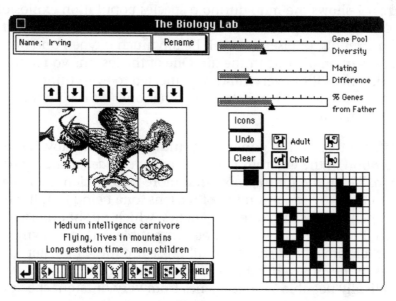

6-5 What's a nice creature like you doing on a planet like this?

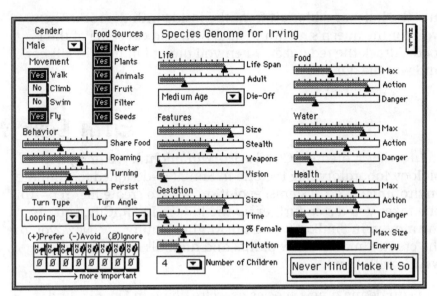

6-6 *He's more apt to survive if he can eat anything he finds.*

each has on our species, and then we can change the plant or animal to respond to the new conditions.

Figure 6-7 shows the map during a species population explosion. The corn plants are taking over. We need to develop some corn-eating animals, or else there will be too much oxygen and not enough carbon dioxide in the air. One of the lessons you learn with SimLife is that everything is connected to everything else. What one species does affects every other one. It's a valuable lesson for us all.

SimLife is more than a game, more than a computer toy, it's an exploration of the emerging field of *computer-aided modeling* or *artificial life*. In the future, more and more "real" science will be done in this way for a number of reasons, one being that it lets us experiment safely with altered genetics, which might otherwise give us life forms that wouldn't be compatible with our own . . . the sort of things that starred in all those Japanese monster movies in the '50s and '60s. Another is that, while it's theoretically possible to splice genes from very different species of animal or plant, we can't yet do it "for real."

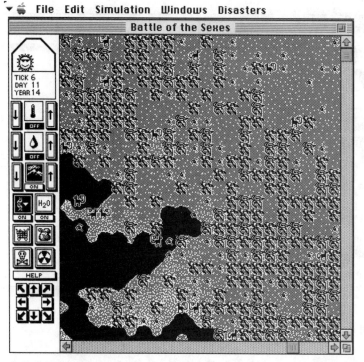

6-7 *We'd better create some corn-eating animals, before the corn plants get out of hand.*

Gene splicing is the subject of another intriguing simulation, G-Netix, from ISM. It's subtitled Recreate Mankind, and that is what you must do. The population of the earth has been destroyed by a deadly plague, and you, a biologist sent to an orbiting space station to run genetic engineering experiments, are the only survivor. You have all the equipment you need, and lots of human genetic material. You can bring it to life and recreate the human race, or you can unleash hideous mutations.

Your space station is equipped with the very latest equipment, including an artificial womb in which to raise an embryo, a gene sequencer to examine and rewrite genetic codes, and all kinds of testing apparatus. Figure 6-8 shows the embryo developing, and

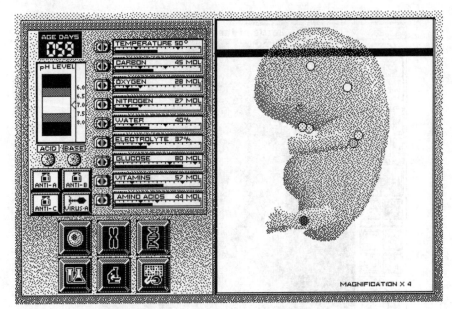

6-8 The dots indicate potential problems with the fetus. Looks like this one's developing flippers instead of feet.

Fig. 6-9 shows how a defective piece of DNA is "edited," by locating the sequence with the incorrect chromosome, and replacing it with a correct one from another sequence.

 G-Netix is not a game for the average person. It teaches genetics and biology at a fairly advanced and complicated level, and requires a good deal of time and effort to earn. By the way, it comes with an excellently written and illustrated textbook called Unwinding the Double Helix, which explains the fundamentals of genetics, and how DNA works. The book can be purchased separately for high school and college science courses. The game is appropriate for use in these courses, too, or for use by medical students or professionals needing a quick review. It's fascinating, if you already understand the basics of genetics, or if you truly want to learn. Personally, I found it extremely difficult, although my 14-year-old son (a science whiz) figured it out in an hour or so.

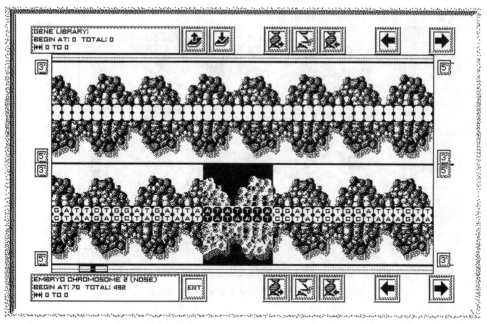

6-9 By splicing the right DNA sequences we can correct the problems while the embryo is still young enough to overcome them.

Is this any way to run a railroad?

A-Train, from Maxis, is superficially similar to SimCity, except that you're trying to make money for yourself, rather than keeping the citizens happy. It starts out as a railroad game, as in Fig. 6-10. You'll build train tracks and stations, buy rolling stock, and develop an effective system for transporting passengers and freight. Of course, you have to give people places to go, and there have to be factories to create a demand for freight service. So you'll start buying land and building offices, apartments, factories, golf courses, amusement parks and ski resorts, and whatever your city needs to keep it going. This, of course, takes money—more than you're likely to earn from a couple of train trips. So, you'll need to borrow from the bank to increase your real-estate holdings.

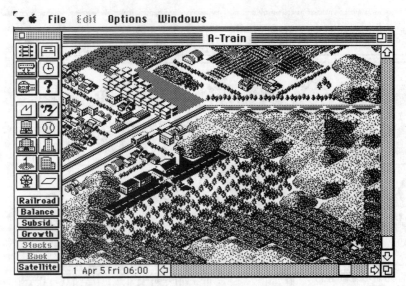

6-10 *This city could use some more development.*

Once there's money coming in, invest it in the stock market and build a financial empire like John D. Rockefeller. If your balance sheet starts to look like the one in Fig. 6-11, you might have forgotten to schedule the trains. That's what happened here. We built stations and laid track, but never got the trains running.

The ultimate goal is to make money, but there's more to A-Train than getting rich. Use it to explore the dynamics of city planning. See the effects of public transportation on the placement of recreational facilities, or on urban growth. Or, just lay tracks and play trains.

There are several shareware train sets that let you run trains around tracks, but the best variation on these is the one that came as a demonstration program with HyperCard 2.0. If you don't have it, you can probably download it from any of the usual sources. A busy train layout is shown in Fig. 6-12. Railroad Tycoon is another good commercial railroad game, quite similar to A-Train.

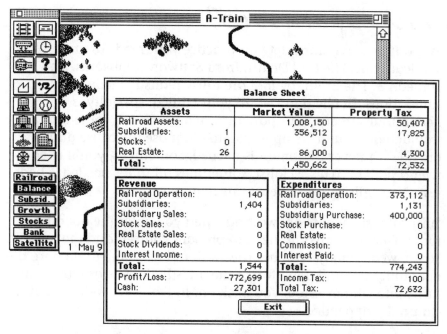

6-11 *The accountant says we're in trouble, and it looks like he's right.*

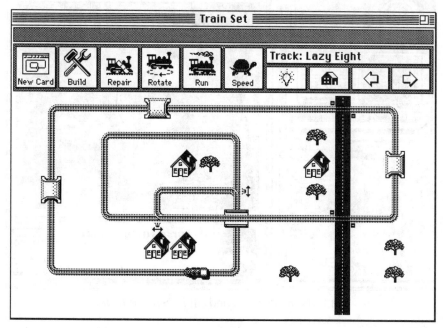

6-12 *Perhaps we should call this one B-Train.*

Smooth operators?

Two different programs let you practice your medical and surgical skills. Life and Death, from Software Toolworks, and Surgeon 3: The Brain, by ISM are fairly realistic medical simulations. In Life and Death, your clinical specialty is abdominal surgery. Your patients are all suffering some kind of stomach ache, and it's up to you to diagnose the cause and provide whatever treatment is needed. Sometimes, you'll need to refer a patient to a specialist, sometimes all that's needed is bed rest. Appendicitis and aneurysms require surgery.

Surgical instruments are waiting when you enter the operating room. First, though, you need to prepare yourself and the patient. Scrub, wear your gloves, use the swab full of iodine to prepare the operating site, and don't forget the anesthetic. The grabber hand turns into whatever tool you click on. In Fig. 6-13, we're about to clamp the appendix.

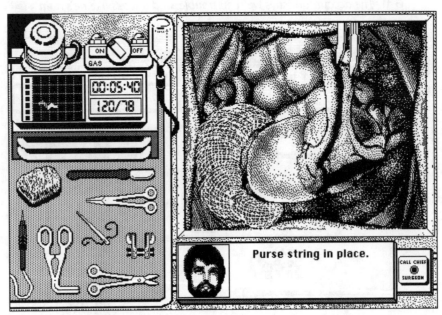

6-13 *Use two clamps and cut in between them.*

Your surgical assistants will help you out, at least until you've done a few operations and know your way around the belly. You will need to keep an eye on the patient's vital signs, and administer IV medications, if needed. Incorrect surgical techniques will send the Chief of Surgery in, and you might be sent back to medical school for a refresher course. After you've successfully completed an appendectomy, you can expect a series of patients with aneurysms. They're more difficult to diagnose and more complicated to operate on. Be sure to click on the "stuff" in the staff room for a giggle.

Surgeon 3 is a more advanced game, with the ghoulish advantage of coming in a full-color version. You'll be dealing with everything from migraine headaches and drug addiction to tumors, subdural hematoma, and cerebral aneurysm. This game will actually teach you quite bit about neuroanatomy and diagnostic tools. It hadn't occurred to me (until I lost a patient) that people with pacemakers couldn't be diagnosed with Magnetic Resonance Imaging (MRI).

The actual cutting is easier than in Life and Death, not because brain surgery is easier than belly surgery, but because the documentation is much better. In Life and Death, you're pretty much on your own. Operations aren't fully described anywhere, and when you get sent back to medical school you're told what you did wrong, but not really told how to do it differently. Surgeon 3 comes with an excellent guide to the nervous system, which explains the surgical processes in complete detail. It also supports System 7 balloon help, which is extremely convenient when you're fumbling for a particular instrument.

Figure 6-14 shows an operation in progress. We've opened the scalp flap and are in the process of drilling burr holes so that we can remove a piece of skull. Instruments, supplies, and drugs are located on tear-off menus and can be placed at the side of the operating table if desired. Figure 6-15 shows the surgical instruments and supplies available to you.

If you make a mistake, either in diagnosis or during surgery, you can expect to get a letter from the patient's malpractice lawyer.

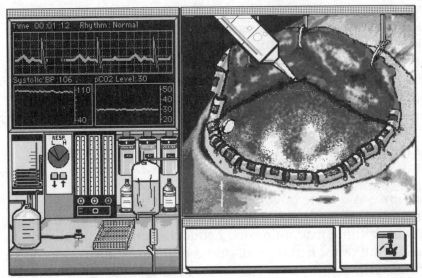

6-14 *Always drip water when you drill through bone.*

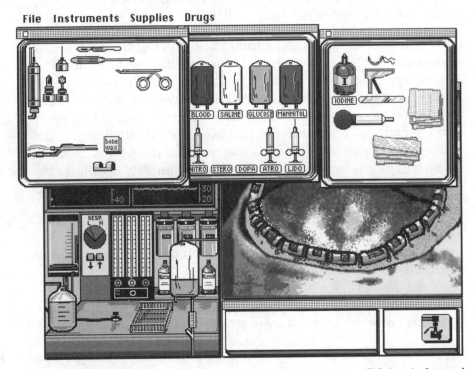

6-15 *Clicking on the EKG screen (under the instrument tray) will bring it forward when you need it.*

Read it carefully. It will tell you exactly what went wrong. If your operation fails, you can repeat it, or go on to another patient.

Simulated spending

"Your money or your life," the thief demanded, pointing a pistol at Jack Benny. Assuming his characteristic chin-in-hand pose, Benny hesitated and finally replied, "I'm thinking about it." He'd have enjoyed Capitalist Pig. This is a business simulation and, like the Maxis system simulations, it has an environment, plus tools and rules. You'll set up a business using start-up capital and work out your business plan, financial plan, and marketing plan. You'll be able to call on your advisors for help, and financial statements will tell you how well you're doing.

Figure 6-16 shows how the game is played. Scandals, which pop up occasionally during the game, can either help or hurt you. Your goal is to bring your company up to the top of the Pig Pen. Bankruptcy is failure. Of course, because this is a simulation your goal could be anything you want it to be. You can try to build a company with happy employees, rather than one that's as

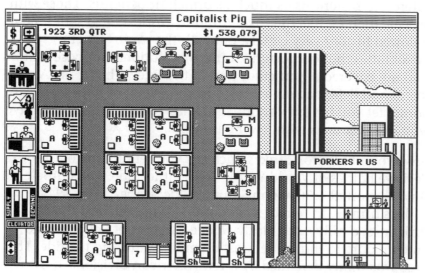

6-16 *Give yourself a raise . . . . You've earned it.*

profitable as possible. You can try for greater customer satisfaction, or even model the company you presently work for, and see if you could manage it better than your bosses do.

What you can't do, as the game's publishers warn you, is to use Capitalist Pig as a decision tool for a real business. Although its computer modeling is accurate based on real statistics, it's not meant to be a crystal ball for real-world situations. Nor can you use it to test a product for salability. It takes your word for what you've created, and doesn't know, as the manual carefully states, "the difference between basketballs and beefsteaks." (Remind me never to eat dinner with those people.) Still, if you're interested in business, economics, or the stock market, this is a game you'll really get into.

War is heck

My generation came of age in the '60s, believing that, as the late artist Corita Kent aptly put it, "War is not healthy for children and other living things." Perhaps, if war simulations could someday replace "real" wars, our leaders would be content to rattle joysticks instead of sabers. As it is, war simulations are of interest to historians as much as armchair generals. Those with specific themes, like the Civil War and World War II series, have followed history very closely, but with the same "what if" possibilities that characterize other simulations. Suppose Patton had not covered a particular part of the line. What if the Axis forces had defended a particular town instead of losing it? War games let you try out various strategies, to see if you could have won in fewer days with fewer casualties.

Brøderbund's Patton Strikes Back lets you refight one of the decisive battles of World War II, from either side. The Battle of the Bulge began at 5:30 AM on Saturday, December 16th, 1944. Hitler's armies, in retreat since summer, had selected the Ardennes, a hilly and thickly wooded section of Belgium and Luxembourg to make their last attempt at turning the tide. The area was thinly defended by a few American divisions, grown careless after the victories of the past few months. German forces, represented by arrows on the map in Fig. 6-17, attacked. The Allies, represented by circles with shields, were caught off guard. You're in charge. What will you do?

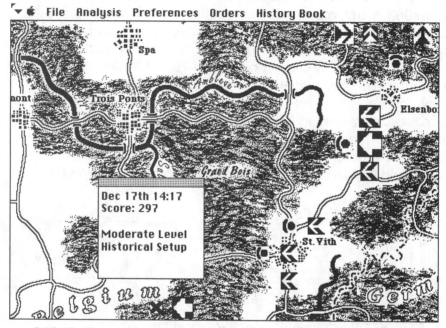

6-17 *The German forces are well spread out. You'll need reinforcements.*

If you're playing as an American, you must hold onto as much territory as possible while waiting for Patton's troops to move up. Essentially, you must stand firm until you're about to get clobbered, and then retrench. If you are playing as a German, you'll order your divisions to attack and destroy the Allied units, and to capture as much territory as possible, including the bridges across the Meuse River. Assess the combat readiness of your units, and order your troops into battle. Tell them where to deploy and when to attack.

Patton Strikes Back includes an on-screen history-book menu that gives you detailed, in-depth background about the people, weapons, and major events in the game, as well as animated news clips, and anecdotes that will pop up on your screen occasionally, about people and events in the game.

Never let yourself get attacked from the rear. If your troops are being attacked on both flanks, bug out! The V for Victory series from 360 Pacific consists of three different battle scenarios: Utah Beach, Velikiye Luki, and Market Garden. More might be forthcoming, as this battle series is deservedly popular. The V for Victory games are more complex than Patton Strikes Back. There are more variables to deal with, and more options, as you can probably determine from the game shown in Fig. 6-18. You can, of course, play from either side, and can choose factors that work in your favor or against you, as well as the historically accurate version. Suppose, for example, that a particular battle had gone on during bad weather instead of good weather. Bad weather

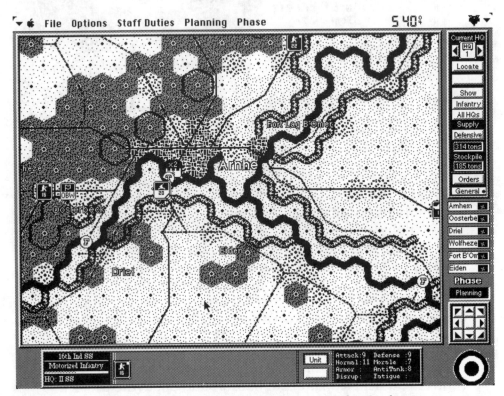

6-18 *This scenario shows the fighting at Market Garden.*

would have meant that there was little or no air or naval support available, and the results might have been quite different.

The Battle of Britain, from Deadly Games, uses the plotting map used by RAF Fighter Command in the summer of 1940 to track incoming raids, and the same tote-board system to track the Hurricaine and Spitfire squadrons sent to intercept those raids. This game runs under HyperCard, and comes with a copy, if you don't already have it installed. It will run in black and white or color, on any Mac from a Plus on up. The graphics, as shown in Fig. 6-19, are based on the scanned map. At the end of each day you'll get a copy of the newspaper, as in Fig. 6-20. You'll need it to see how you're doing, and to watch the weather forecast for the following day.

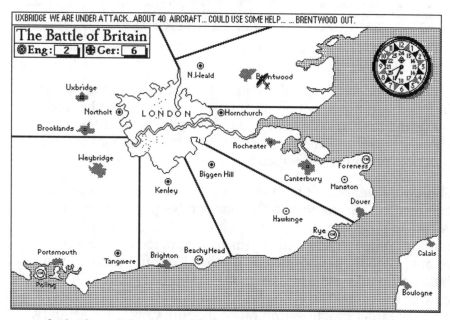

6-19 If you click on an air base, you'll be able to check on its planes.

Play war

There are really two kinds of war games: those that follow historical scenarios, and those that are essentially fantasy. The

6-20 *You can even print out a copy of the paper for easier reading.*

latter type of game doesn't attempt to refight a previous war, and in fact might not be set on this planet. The difference between these and the "zap the alien" space wars discussed in an earlier chapter is simple. These are games of strategy, rather than target practice. You must plan ahead in order to win.

Shareware war games tend to be a lot less elaborate than their commercial counterparts. Still, they can be quite exciting to play. A case in point is a game called Midway. The graphics are crude, but the game is lively and engrossing. Also, look for Covert Action, Global Thermonuclear War, and Empire Master on bulletin-board systems (BBS) and shareware collections. These are among the more interesting war simulations. Additionally, artillery target-practice simulators abound. Check out Artillery, Cannon Fodder, Mac Gunner, and Ballistics.

War at sea

Harpoon is a highly technical battle simulation, the first "unclassified" simulator that shows how to conduct a naval

battle under modern warfare conditions. You are a Side
Commander in charge of both naval and air units for one side of
a scenario. You have a full range of naval vessels, plus
submarines and aircraft at your disposal. Your task varies,
depending on the scenario. You might be escorting a convoy of
supply ships in the North Sea, keeping an eye on escalating
hostilities in the Mediterranean, or monitoring satellite
reconnaissance and guarding the strategic Straits of Malacca or
the Persian Gulf. The Scenarios Editor also lets you invent your
own situations, or modify existing ones.

Harpoon is difficult, more so than most games, mainly because
there are so many variables, but also because the interface
appears to have been designed with the PC in mind and then
translated to the Mac platform. Figure 6-21 shows a typical
screen from the game. Technically, however, it is far superior to
other games. Tom Clancy, author of *The Hunt for Red October*,
claims to have gotten most of the technical data on submarines
from the Harpoon ship specification database.

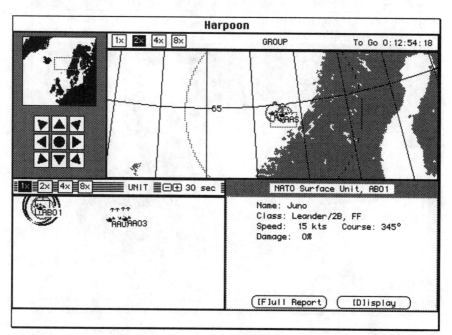

6-21 *There's a convoy off the coast of Norway that we're keeping an eye on.*

Strategic Conquest is a fairly simple game, but one that it's possible to spend many hours playing since it's never the same twice. Your goal is to capture the world, and to fight off your attackers. You have armies, navies, and an air force with which to do this. So do the other guys, and they have, alas, the same goal. The game is played on a large map. When you begin, very little of the territory is showing. You'll have one city and one army to start with. You'll be able to capture a second city as soon as you find one, and the game spreads outward from that point.

In Fig. 6-22, we're quite a few turns in, and our cities are building ships and planes as well as training armies. An inland city can build planes and recruit armies. If it is a port city, it can also build ships. Different kinds of ships and planes require different numbers of days to build. The more powerful ones—battleships and bombers, for instance—take much longer. As you are building outward, your adversary is doing the same. Fairly soon

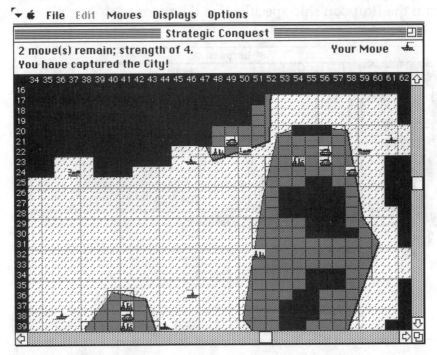

6-22 *The black squares are unexplored territory. Send a plane or a ship over them to explore.*

you'll meet him, most likely in a naval battle, but possibly on land. Enemy cities look different. They are dark colored and require much more force to capture than the neutral cities you conquered first.

One of the many reasons I like this game is the packaging. Delta Tao is a company with an "attitude," and part of that attitude is to be earth-friendly. The game is minimally packaged, with the disk and reply card stuck into the manual (which is printed on 100-percent recycled paper). The manual is, as reviewers say, "a good read." The game is easy enough to play without ever reading about it, but you'd miss a lot, including the recommended reading list: *Calvin and Hobbes*, *The Tao of Pooh*, etc. If you like the manual, be sure to send in the registration card because it will put you on the mailing list for Delta Tao's occasional newsletter, *The Changing Path*, which is another "good read."

The Ancient Art of War and the Ancient Art of War at Sea were a terrific pair of battle simulators, which are unfortunately obsolete under System 7. Brøderbund has no plans to update these, but if you are running System 6 on a compact Mac, and come across the games anywhere, they're well worth a look.

New worlds to conquer

After you have achieved control of your own planet, what's next? Space conquest is an obvious choice for simulations, since, at this point in history, we're not quite ready to do it for real. In fact, we have no way of knowing whether there's anything worth conquering out there, never mind whether or not it's possible. Space conquest games, therefore, are strictly fantasy.

Spaceward Ho!, from Delta Tao, starts you out on a single, wonderfully equipped and heavily populated planet. You'll use it as a home base to explore the rest of its galaxy. You are looking for star systems like your own, on which to build colonies. When you find one, you will send a colony ship to carry the necessary people and materials to establish a colony there. You can terraform the planet to make it friendlier to your colonists, who will mine all the metals from it and use it as a base for further exploration, Eventually, it will grow large enough to be profitable for you. More money means that you can afford more space ships, and more expansion. Some of your money should also be spent on technology research, so you can build better ships. Eventually, your space hopping will bring you in contact with somebody else who has the same idea, and you'll have to battle for supremacy. You can defend yourself by building defense satellites at your colonies, and by building fleets of fighters and counterattacking. If you'd rather avoid fighting, you can choose to befriend some of the aliens instead.

To help you keep track of where you are and what you're doing, the game uses three windows. The largest one, in Fig. 6-23, shows the star map, and your current budget, planet, and fleet data. The scrolling message window keeps a history of what's going on in your game. It gives you messages about the planets you're colonizing, and the results of any battles you might engage in. If you click on an old message, the game will give you further

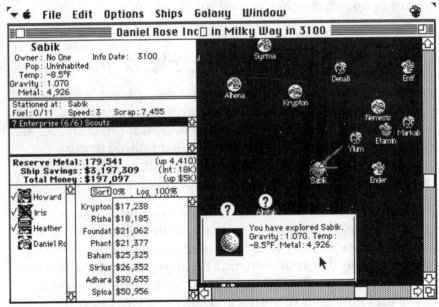

6-23 *Pick a planet to colonize, and send a team to explore it.*

information about it. When you click on a message about a planet, the map will scroll to that planet and it will be selected. If you click on a battle, you'll be able to see a replay of it. To build ships, use the ship menu. You'll get a dialog box like the one in Fig. 6-24 that lets you select the type of ship to build, and tells you what it will cost.

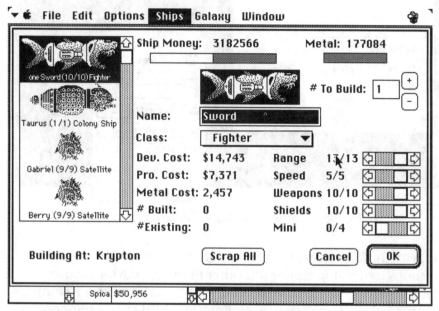

6-24 *Choose ships carefully. You need a few scouts, and some to carry colonists to your new planets.*

Galactic Frontiers, from Softstream, is similar to Strategic Conquest in format. There's a map, shown in Fig. 6-25, only it contains planets rather than cities. Send out your ships from your home planet to explore and conquer adjacent ones. After you control them, enhance them with industry, fortifications, and radar. As many as four people can play, or the computer can play as one or more of the four possible empires.

Pax Imperia, published by Changeling Software, is an even more complicated galactic empire simulation. As emperor of your home planet, you can decide whether it's most important to you

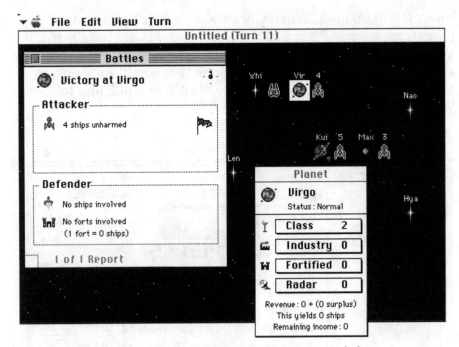

6-25 *You appear to have attacked an unoccupied planet.*

to get rich, to explore, to design new weapons and ships, or perhaps to develop trade with other planets. Like all modern heads of state, you'll have a cabinet of expert advisors in matters of protocol, defense, science, exploration, and even espionage. You're playing against anywhere from 1 to 15 other players, who might be human or computer, or any combination. To set up the game, enter the number of people who'll be playing, and then the number of computer opponents. Your live co-players will have to be able to reach the keyboard, though. At least, as of this writing, the game isn't networkable, although future versions probably will be.

As the game begins, you have three fleets of spacecraft and a treasury of money and materials. You'll begin by sending one of your space fleets to explore another solar system. The large map shows the likely stars that are within traveling distance. You're searching for planets that will be relatively hospitable to your species, and contain mineral resources that your people can mine and refine to build cities, spaceships, and weapons for defense and conquest. The more like your home planet another one is, the easier it will be for your miners to get at its resources. The game can be played on four different levels, from beginner to expert. At the expert level you'll be designing your own weapons and spacecraft, engaging in diplomatic negotiations with other planets, and managing your finances.

The graphics, as shown in Fig. 6-26, feature multiple windows and maps that let you scroll around and zoom in and out. There's music, too. This game isn't just punctuated with synthesized sounds and mindless bits of tune, it's actually scored for what sounds like a full symphony orchestra! The opening theme is especially nice. It's these little details that show how much thought was put into designing this game.

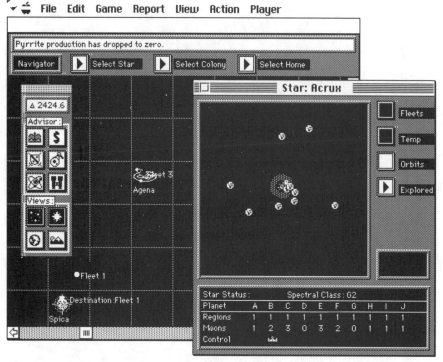

6-26 Pax Imperia *is a complex, but fascinating simulation.*

IT'S A MAD, MAD, MAD, MAD MAC

Pax Imperia is regarded by many players as the very best of all space-colony simulations. As many as 16 different empires can play, although the game will move much faster if you limit it to 3 or 4. This game can be played on several levels, making it suitable for beginners and advanced players as well. As you get familiar with the game, you'll be able to choose your own cabinet advisors, and even custom design the species of the "people" on your home planet. Pax Imperia is a game you won't outgrow in a few days. There's enough here to keep the average game player busy for months.

7
Puzzles & more puzzles

The very first game most of us played on a Macintosh was the number puzzle. Apple realized, back with the first 128K Mac, that people's real-world desk accessories included toys as well as notepads and other functional stuff. They looked for a game or toy that would show off the Mac's graphic abilities, and would require familiarity with the mouse.

Mice were still a fairly new concept for computer users, and the human interface group at Apple, if there was such a thing back then, would have been thinking about ways to make users mouse-friendly. It would be an important step in making the Mac user-friendly. The puzzle was ideal. It was relatively easy to program. You had 15 active sections on a 4-by-4 grid. When they finally came together, you were rewarded with a chime. (Now you hear "Ta-dah!")

Did you know that you can change the puzzle? The System 7 version comes with an Apple logo instead of the numbers. To revert to the original numbers, select the puzzle and type command+X to remove the picture. Or copy any PICT from the scrapbook, clipboard, or clip-art file, or draw your own in any graphics program that saves in the PICT format. Select the puzzle and paste in your new art. Figure 7-1 shows some puzzles we created. It works best if the PICT is square and not too finely detailed, since it reduces to fit.

7-1 *The clown, bear, and tiger were "borrowed" from Super Tetris. The dog lives here.*

Cliff Johnson—the Puzzle Master

There's something intriguing about puzzles. Even people who don't like most computer games tend to enjoy the ones that are based on some kind of puzzle. Perhaps it's that puzzles typically require solutions, rather than luck, to complete. They are an intellectual challenge. Among the most challenging of all are the puzzle collections by Cliff Johnson. Two of these, Fool's Errand and At the Carnival, are regrettably out of print, although rumors persist that Johnson is working on an updated, full-color version of Fool's Errand. The third, 3 in Three, is one of Inline Design's most popular games.

Fool's Errand was based on the Tarot deck. It tells the story of the Fool, who must travel throughout four strange lands belonging to the Pentacles, Cups, Wands, and Swords. You help him in his journey by solving puzzles. Some are simple. Others are very difficult. Most require considerable thought and a few need manual dexterity. Figure 7-2 shows one of the more common type of puzzle. You must enter the correct letters in the boxes. There are also word searches, trick mazes, 3-by-3 letter shuffles, a card game with no obvious rules, and even more.

7-2 *The key to solving this lies in starting at the beginning.*

Some of these puzzles don't come with instructions, so part of the problem is figuring out how to solve them. Each puzzle you solve also gives you a piece of the final puzzle, which is a map of the Fool's travels. If you can reassemble the map, you will be able to use it to solve the final problem, which is to find the 14 treasures hidden in the map. Fool's Errand is a thoroughly absorbing game.

At the Carnival was Cliff Johnson's second title. Unlike Fool's Errand, there wasn't really a plot. You visited a carnival and solved the puzzles you encountered there. Each puzzle told you a little bit more about the amusement park. Some relied on rather gross, juvenile humor: You could ride the Loop-O-Puke, the Roto Vomit, or the Alpine Upchuck. But the puzzles were as intriguing as those in Fool's Errand and players loved the color (on a Mac II) and the sound effects and spoken dialog that popped up frequently.

 With 3 in Three, Cliff Johnson has gone back to something close to his original storytelling format. The plot is clever, if a bit fantastic. Thanks to a power surge, the number 3 has fallen out of a spreadsheet and gotten lost in the innards of a computer. You must help her find her way back by solving the puzzles. Again, some are easy, while others will make you think.

This time there are some new puzzle formats, too. One of the simpler ones involves a set of platforms that raise and lower themselves according to the numbers at their bases. (See Fig. 7-3.) The 3 can hop from one platform to the next, as long as they're at the same level. The trick is to get it from the left side of the screen to the right. But if the platform on the left comes level with

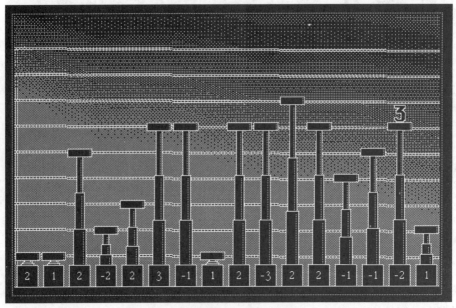

7-3 *The 3 can only move to another platform at the same level.*

the one it's on, it'll hop backward. . .. In the earlier rounds the platforms move independently of each other. Later on, they move in some relationship to each other. For instance, if you raise a platform one step, the one that's to the left of it might go up three steps, and some other one might drop a step.

Another type of puzzle uses scrambled letters. The letters move along predetermined paths each time you click on one. You must figure out what the paths are, and how to rearrange the letters to make the three-word combinations required. Figure 7-4 shows an example. In this puzzle, we must try to make the letters spell "yes," "no," and "maybe." But the paths aren't logical. The letters from the top jump to the bottom, while the letters in the center of the bottom row shift left or right. It can be done, but it takes a good deal of trial and error to solve these.

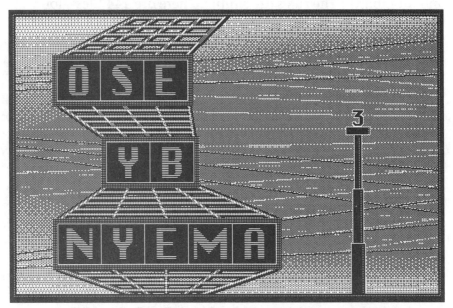

7-4 *Trial and error is the only way to solve many of these puzzles.*

3 in Three is full of clever sound effects, outrageous puns, and animated sequences. You'll see a new scene every time you solve a puzzle, and as in Fool's Errand, each puzzle solved adds a piece

to the final puzzle. 3 in Three runs in color or black and white on all Macs from a Plus on up. It is comfortable with either System 6 or 7, and takes relatively little disk space—less than 1M.

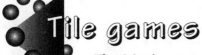

Tile games

The Mac's own number puzzle is a tile puzzle. You move squares around to achieve a particular pattern. That principle has been adapted to a number of different kinds of games. In typical tile games you place or remove tiles according to specific rules, or rearrange them into particular patterns.

Shanghai II, published by Activision, is the latest commercial version of a game that's been equally popular as shareware for a number of years. (Two popular shareware versions are Gunshy and Mombasa.) The rules are simple. There are 144 tiles—four each of 36 designs. Tiles are stacked in a particular pattern, with some on top of others. You must find and remove pairs of tiles. But you can only remove tiles from the top or outside of the stack. There are 12 different layouts or "boards," and an editor that lets you design your own. The game is harder than it sounds. Figure 7-5 shows the beginning of a game.

A second game, called Dragon's Eye, is also included in Shanghai II. It's played with the same tile set, but with very different rules. Dragon's Eye requires two players, one of whom might be the Mac. One player is the Dragon Master, and the other is the Dragon Slayer. The Master tries to bring the Dragon to life by adding tiles to complete the dragon layout, as shown in Fig. 7-6.

The Slayer tries to match tiles from the six in his hand to remove them, keeping the dragon from coming to life. Players take turns. If the Slayer cannot remove a pair of tiles, he must add one to the board, and draw another to fill his hand. The Dragon Master must fill in vital parts of the Dragon if they become uncovered during play, and must add a tile each turn until there are no more, or until the dragon is fully built.

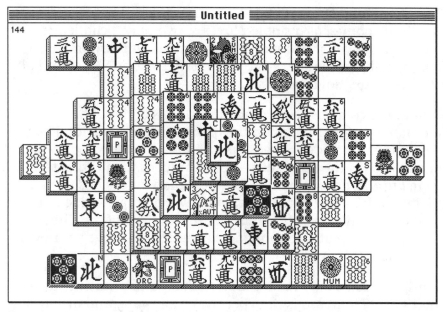

7-5 *This is the standard Mah Jongg tile set. Others include national flags, Dungeon and Dragons figures, and animals.*

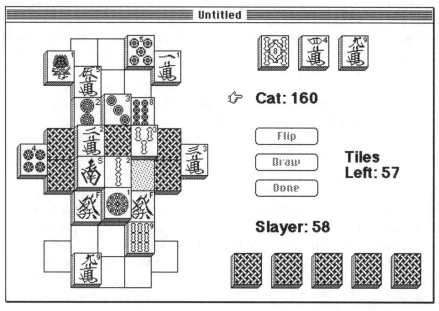

7-6 *The slayer can take away as many pairs of tiles at once as he (or she) can find.*

Shanghai II and Dragon's Eye also can be played in several ways: as solitaire games, as a single-player or two-player challenge, or as a single-player or two-player tournament. In tournament form, you'll play Dragon's Eye as both Master and Slayer and all 12 of the Shanghai II boards.

Shanghai II comes with several different sets of tiles. The traditional design is based on the game of Mah Jongg, and has tiles representing flowers, seasons, dragons, and winds, as well as nine in each of the three suits—dots, bamboos, and characters. There are also flags, alphabet blocks, hanafuda designs from a traditional Japanese card game, and several others—nine in all. It comes with tile layouts for each of the 12 signs of the Chinese zodiac, plus an editor so that you can design and save your own custom layouts.

 Gunshy contains only the basic Shanghai game with one layout, but it's free. Mombasa is (inexpensive) shareware, and includes several layouts, plus an easy-to-use editor that lets you create your own. It's shown in Fig. 7-7 with a tricky 3D layout. Some tiles that appear to be covering others, actually aren't—so you have to experiment to see which ones are stuck and which can be moved. Mombasa comes with several alternative sets of tiles. The default pattern has African designs, which probably explains the origin of the name of the game.

Tesserae, from Inline Software, is a beautiful and intriguing game. There are nine differently shaped layouts called mosaics. At the beginning of the game the mosaic is covered in tiles— bright colors on a color screen or marked with distinctive symbols in black and white. Tiles might be colored either primary (red: circle; yellow: cross; blue: square); secondary (orange: cross in circle; green: cross in square; purple: square in circle); or tertiary (black: all three symbols). The opening of one of the upper levels of the game is shown in Fig. 7-8. Your objective is to clear the board, leaving only one tile, and to do so in the fewest moves possible. You can get rid of the tiles by jumping them over each other.

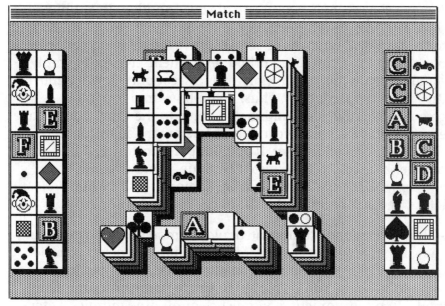

7-7 *Mombasa is played just like Shanghai II. Remove tiles in pairs.*

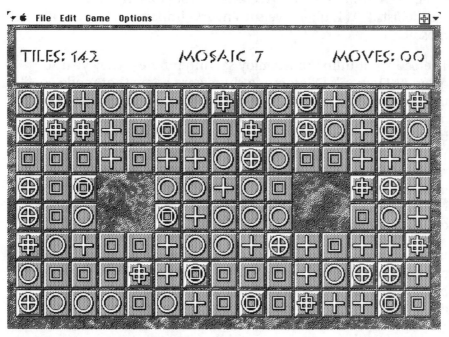

7-8 *Tesserae can be highly addictive. The game has a great sound track, too.*

A move consists of jumping one tile over another. If you have three reds in a row, for instance, jumping the first over the second to the third will remove the second and third, leaving you with one red tile. You can jump primaries to themselves or to empty squares. If you jump a primary over a secondary, it will remove itself from the secondary. Thus, if you have in a row, blue—green—blue, and you jump the first blue to the third, you'll leave empty—yellow—blue. Secondary colors are made by landing one primary on top of another. If you jump, for instance, a blue over another blue to a yellow, instead of blue—blue—yellow, you'd end up with blank—blank—green. Tertiaries result when you land a secondary on a different one, e.g., green on purple.

Although it sounds complicated, play is made easier by selecting Show Legal Moves from the Options menu. Whenever you click on a tile, black dots will flash on all the tiles you could legally jump to. Tesserae can be played in single-game or tournament mode. In a tournament, you must clear all nine mosaics. Later boards have more tiles and more combinations. The advanced level, according to the Help screens, is for "experts and masochists." At higher levels it's nearly impossible to clear the mosaic.

The people at Inline must enjoy solving puzzles. They've also given us Darwin's Dilemma, a shareware game that made good. Originally called IconQuest, it was a fairly simple shareware game created by Canadian programmer André Ouimet. The board contained a bunch of icons, some of which were identical. You shoved them against each other. If they matched, they merged. When you merged the right number, they'd "evolve" into another icon. The goal was to merge them all into one. Figure 7-9 shows the IconQuest screen. It was a clever game, but after a few rounds it got boring.

Inline Software picked up the game, and helped Ouimet expand on it. The result was Darwin's Dilemma, a multilevel puzzle that begins with amoebas and paramecia and takes you up the evolutionary ladder to man. There are 20 different levels in

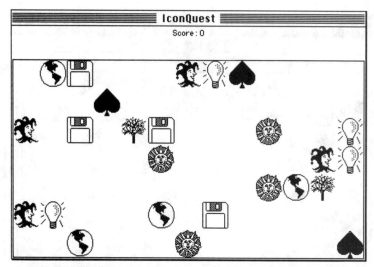

7-9 *When you bang the icons together they merge. If you merge the right number, they'll evolve into a different icon.*

Darwin, plus an editor that lets you create your own worlds and determine the evolution of them.

Figure 7-10 shows one of the middle levels. Use the mouse to move Darwin around. When he's next to an icon you want to merge, click it and he'll kick it. It will move as far as it can, until it runs into another one. Icons will wrap around, as will Darwin's foot. If you kick something at the right edge of the board, it will appear at the left.

Something to think about

Cogito, ergo sum. I think, therefore I am. With those few words, the philosopher summed up the entire reason for Man's existence. (No cheering please, lest I be accused of putting Descartes before the hoarse.) Cogito is a game that will make you think. It also comes, at least in the United States, from our friends at Inline, but it's actually a French import. Cogito is a set of puzzles based on the same principle that made the Rubik's cube

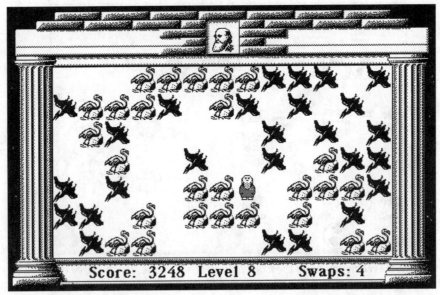

7-10 *The icons in Darwin's Dilemma are beautifully drawn, especially in color.*

intriguing. Instead of a cube, though, you're dealing with a flat board, covered with 72 tiles.

When the puzzle is correctly assembled, the nine central tiles make a square with a different pattern from the surrounding tiles. When it's jumbled, you have a sort of checkerboard effect. The tiles can be slid horizontally and vertically. But whatever you do to one, you do to the whole row or column. There are many levels, and at the start of each the tiles are shuffled around. You must unshuffle them to restore the pattern in order to advance to the next level.

It's easy in the early rounds when the tiles move with an obvious logic. As you reach higher levels, the logic becomes harder and harder to follow. If you push one row, you might find that the row that actually moves is the mirror image of it, moving in the opposite direction; or that the row that moves is two away and moves three squares for each one you push, and so on. It becomes a real challenge.

To resume a level without playing all the ones that came before it, keep a list of the passwords that you are given at the end of each round.

Cubic puzzlers

The best known cube puzzle of all is Rubik's Cube, a 3-by-3 cube with six differently colored sides. (After you've played with it for a while you have six multicolored sides.) Many people have tried to duplicate the Rubik's Cube in software, but it really doesn't work very well. The Mac's point-and-click interface doesn't lend itself to a grab-and-twist motion, and when you can look at only three sides of the cube at once, it's too hard to remember what's on the side you can't see. There are other cube-type puzzles that do work on a Mac, though. An incredibly difficult version called Rubik's Wrap is played on a flat surface with rotating tiles. It's worth looking for.

Kaleidocubes is an intriguing puzzle, and a good game whether played solitaire, or against the computer or another live player. It runs in black and white, with patterned blocks as shown in Fig. 7-11, or in 16-color mode. The premise is simple. The board starts with a single block, and subsequent blocks are played one at a time. You must place them so that edges that touch, match. You can rotate the blocks in either direction. You have 30 seconds to find a place for the block.

Sounds simple? Early in the game it is. As the board fills up it gets progressively harder to find a space where the block will match on all adjacent sides. Eventually, you'll go over the time limit, which you can set for anything from 5 seconds to 1 minute. The first time that happens you simply go on to the next piece. The second time, the game ends. Or, you can choose to pass an impossible block without waiting for the time-is-up signal. But if you pass twice, the game's still over.

It's challenging and fun, especially when you play a two-player game against the computer, and give yourself a short time limit.

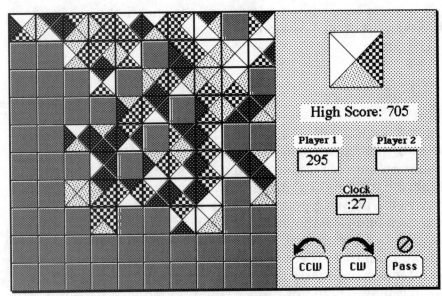

7-11 *Kaleidocubes is fun for all ages.*

In solitaire mode it's more of a puzzle, though you can race the clock. You can also design custom boards, perhaps with some of the squares filled in, or in some shape other than square. The Board Editor is very easy to use. Click on a square to fill it, or click on a filled square to restore it. Be careful not to make your boards too difficult. If winning is impossible, the game stops being fun.

Stories in stones

Ishido, subtitled The Way of Stones, is a very Zen-like game. It's simple to learn, but extremely difficult to master. At its most basic level, the game simply consists of a board and a set of tiles, called stones. There are two each of six colors and six patterns for a total of 72 stones. The board is 8-squares high by 12 wide, for a total of 96 squares. The perimeter is set with dark squares. Stones placed on dark squares don't score.

To begin the game, six stones are placed on the board, one at each corner and two in the middle, with corners touching. At each turn, the computer draws a stone at random and places it on the oval at the upper right. You must find a place on the board for it next to a matching color or symbol.

When a stone touches two others, it must match the color of one and the pattern of the other. To match three, it must share one attribute (color or pattern) with two of the adjacent stones, and the other attribute with the third stone. Figure 7-12 shows a nearly completed game. Four-way matches are also possible, and score extra points. You're placing a stone in a "hole" made by four others. Two stones must match one of the attributes of the center stone, and the other two must match the other attribute.

7-12 *Continue placing tiles until you run out of tiles or places to add them.*

To master the game, you must learn to make four-way matches. Doing so also lets you consult the Oracle to get a question answered. You need not do so, but if you wish you can select Oracle from the Options menu and enter a question in the box. If you make a four-way match, the combination of stones that does so and their locations on the board, along with the precise time you did it, are factored together to produce a numerical value corresponding to a hexagram in the I-Ching, or Book of Changes, an ancient Chinese book of auguries. These are often cryptic and open to interpretation, but those who follow the way of the stones believe that these auguries simply bring to the surface that which we already know on the subconscious level. Figure 7-13 shows one such finding.

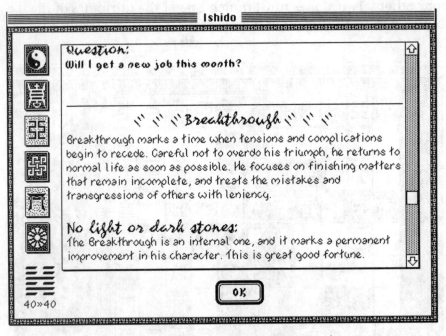

7-13 *These answers are open to interpretation.*

By the way, if you want the wisdom of the I-Ching without playing Ishido, there are many sources. The best translation in print is by Richard Wilhelm, published by the Princeton University Press, Bollingen Series XIX, 1967. Computerized versions include several shareware stacks, and Synchronicity, a beautiful program from Visionary Software, described in chapter 9.

Ishido, whether or not you choose to use it as a decision-making tool, is a pretty and relaxing game that can be played on any Mac from a Plus on up. Color, although rewarding, isn't necessary to enjoy the game. It's equally hypnotizing in black and white. There's a limited, deluxe edition that comes in a handmade walnut case, suitable for your jewelry, steak knives, or anything else that can be kept in a shallow box. Only a thousand of these were made, and each box is numbered. The game book is also numbered and signed by designer Michael Feinberg, programmer Ian Gilman, and producer Brad Fregger. It's a work of art.

Earthly delights with a heavenly goal

Heaven and Earth is a brain game of a different sort. It comes, surprisingly, from Buena Vista Software, part of the Disney empire. But there's nothing cartoonish about it. Like Ishido, it was created by Michael Feinberg, and is based on myth and legend. Specifically, Heaven and Earth takes you on a pilgrimage to the mythical kingdom of Shambhala in ancient Tibet.

Within the framework of the game there are three separate pieces: a card game, a set of intricate puzzles, and what the game's creators call a "toy"—a pendulum that swings back and forth across your screen. You must master all three of these pieces before you can get anywhere with the game itself. These different kinds of activities all require that you develop what Feinberg calls a "meditative strategy." The solutions to problems don't come from banging your head against them, but from looking inward and discovering the answers you already know, much like interpreting the auguries of the I-Ching in Ishido.

In the card game, which is loosely based on a Japanese rummy game called Hanafuda, you learn to carefully consider moves, and to look for the "elegant" solution rather than the quick one. The cards themselves are works of art, with sound effects and dazzling animation. There are four landscapes, four seasons, and four elements represented in the deck. Each of the cards combines these, and also has a month assigned. Cards are dealt four at a time in the first of four rounds, and you must choose one of the four cards dealt each time, giving you a hand of 12 cards. These are combined into tricks based on their characteristics. Different kinds of tricks have different point values. A trick might have two, three, or four cards.

There are also celestial phenomena that occur randomly, just as they do in the real world. These might multiply the point value of a trick. Certain combinations of phenomena will multiply points in a negative way, so you must learn to avoid them. When the points are scored, those cards are retired. In the second round (shown in Fig. 7-14), three cards are dealt; in the third, two cards. In the fourth round, the remaining 12 cards are your hand. It's sometimes wise to save particular cards for the last hand, instead of selecting them in early rounds. Your chances of combining higher-scoring celestial phenomena increase as the game goes on, since new phenomena can appear in later rounds.

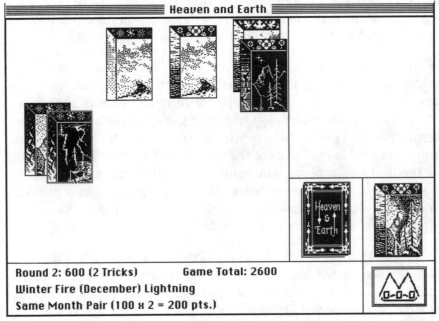

7-14 *Clicking on a card tells you its month, element, and season.*

The puzzles, which in Heaven and Earth are called Illusions, teach you to think flexibly, to suspend your beliefs, and to see beyond what's there. There are different kinds of puzzles. Some, like the example shown in Fig. 7-15, require you to flip tiles to create certain patterns, some have you assembling jigsaw puzzle pieces into flat or 3D shapes, and some have you running mazes. Some can be solved by just mousing around, while others require deep concentration. Generally speaking, the puzzle sets are in an ascending order of difficulty, but if one proves to be a stumbling block, bypass it and go on to the next.

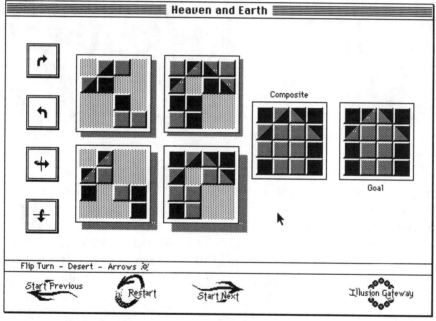

7-15 *This one is almost solved. One more flip might do it.*

The pendulum is the most Zen-like of the three activities. It simulates a real, weighted pendulum that swings back and forth on your screen over a bowl. Within the bowl are energy wells that exert a gravitational pull on the pendulum. There are also negative energy wells that will try to pull it away or kick it in the wrong direction. The goal of the game is to make the point of the pendulum touch certain highlighted parts of the bowl. In Fig. 7-16, the target is that round "water drop" near the top of the screen.

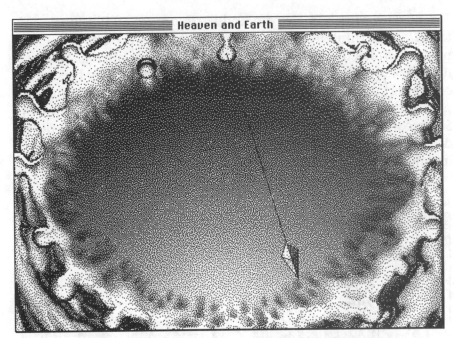

7-16 *The pendulum takes a lot of practice, but after a while your hand learns what to do to move it in the right direction.*

To use the pendulum successfully, you must learn to relax and swing with it. Once you surrender to it, you can gently steer it in the direction you want it to go. If you try to move it too quickly, or too aggressively, you will lose control. In this sense, the pendulum is the opposite of a traditional arcade game, in which you must be quick to score points. The best way to achieve success with the pendulum is simply to play with it, not caring about the outcome. When you find yourself becoming connected to it, you'll be able to move it wherever you want, more by thinking it there than by pushing it there. The most successful players use barely perceptible mouse twitches. As with any form of meditation, practice makes perfect.

The Journey is the final part of Heaven and Earth. Although you don't need to master the three activities before you begin your journey, you'll certainly find the path easier if you are familiar with them. The puzzles, pendulums, and card games you'll encounter are similar to those you've already seen, but not the same. You will need to use the skills you've learned in order to solve them. Unlike the Illusions that can be solved in any order, the journey must be completed one step at a time. There are 108 steps. Along the way you'll find the Tantra, "free" steps on your pilgrimage. They are a series of aphorisms, verses, and quotations to inspire and entertain you. Heaven and Earth is more than a game, it's an experience.

What's yours is mines...

Crossing a minefield carelessly will put you on the road to the hereafter just as readily as embarking on a pilgrimage to Shambhala. Fortunately, the minefields in question are actually a game. There are many mine variations as shareware games, and a new one from Inline Design has been released as a commercial game, too. The principle is the same for all of them. You have a minefield, marked off into squares. Any square might have a mine buried under it. If you click on a mine, you're dead; just as if you'd stepped on a real one. If there's nothing under the square, you're free to click again. If a square has a number on it, that tells you how many of the squares touching it contain mines. If you are lucky, and if you think about what the numbers mean, you can map the entire minefield without stepping on any mines.

Inline's Super Mines is a more forgiving game than any of the shareware versions I've tried. You get several mine sweepers per minefield, rather than just one. The graphics are neat, too. Figure 7-17 shows a Super Mines minefield.

Shareware mine games include Saddam's Revenge, Mines, Minesweep, and Minesweeper. They are all more or less the same. Some let you configure the size of the board and the number of mines on it. Saddam's Revenge, shown in Fig. 7-18, turns the Reset button into his face whenever you lose, but at least you get the pleasure of clicking on it.

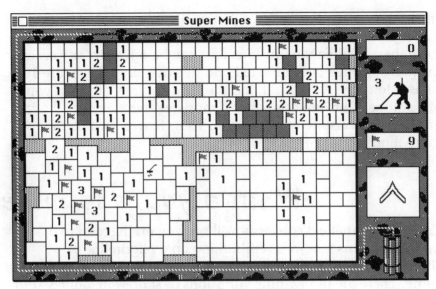

7-17 *Be careful where you step!*

7-18 *You can determine the size of the board. This one is the beginner level.*

 Hex Ya!, which you'll find on the disk in the back of the book, as well as on various bulletin-board systems (BBS) and shareware collections, takes the concept of minefields and goes a step further with it. The playing board, shown in Fig. 7-19, has

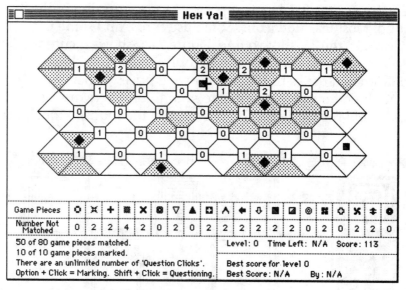

7-19 *There's another matched pair.*

triangular pieces set into hexagons with numbers inside them. The numbers mean exactly what they do in an ordinary mine game—there are X number of mines touching the numbered block. Anything touching a zero block is safe to click on. But here's the difference. When you click on a block, if it's not a mine (which is called a headache in Hex Ya! terms) you'll see a symbol of some sort. Your job is to match up all the symbols, as in a game of Concentration, while avoiding the mines. Programmer John Decker has put together a very tricky game.

You can figure out and mark the location of most of the mines just by studying the numbers. But there are some cases where you won't be able to tell for certain, specifically when there's only one headache indicated on one of the outer hexagons. It could be in any of several blocks. In such a circumstance, it would be helpful to be able to peek. Beginners can play the game without a time limit, and with unlimited "peeks" or Question clicks. As you gain proficiency, add the time limit. The number of Question clicks available to you will shrink as you go to shorter time limits, making the game even more of a challenge.

There are quite a few less-complicated Concentration games around. Most use Mac icons. Some use cards, and some use "prizes" like the TV show game. Figure 7-20 shows a cute version called On the Contrary, for two to four players. It includes sounds and animated boxes that open to reveal prizes. When you match two, their dollar value is added to your total. There are 12 rounds, and the winner is the player with the highest final score.

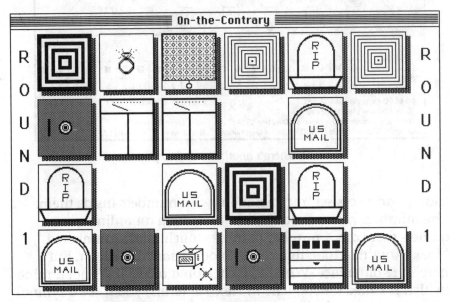

7-20 *Not a match, and the board goes back . . . .*

Jigsaw puzzles

There have been times when I have considered turning the Mac's screen into a jigsaw puzzle—mostly after a system crash when putting my fist, or other solid object through it was a great temptation. But it would have been too hard to reassemble. "Real" jigsaw puzzles, although they exist for the Mac, honestly aren't quite as much fun as the cardboard kind. Since all of the pieces need to appear on the screen, you're effectively limited to a reasonable number—perhaps 25 or so. The serious jigsaw puzzle builder scoffs at anything with less than 1,000 pieces. Still, they're fun for kids, and do serve to teach a beginner how to click and drag pieces with a mouse.

There are several shareware or freeware jigsaw puzzle games. Some let you bring in your own PICT files from your favorite graphics program to make your own puzzles. Figure 7-21 shows Duane Blehm's Puzz'l program, with a jigsaw puzzle I created from a scanned pencil sketch. This program works only in black and white, but there are others that offer color as well.

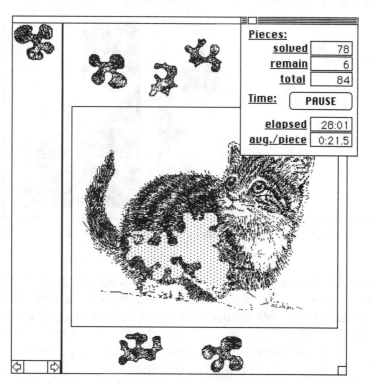

7-21 *Use any kind of picture you like for a puzzle, but remember that the details might be hard to distinguish.*

Tangrams and similar types of puzzles in which you must combine specific pieces to make certain shapes are abundant in the shareware and freeware libraries. Tangrams have been popular for several hundred years. They are believed to have originated in China, and were brought to Europe and America by sailors who purchased sets of tangram pieces in laquerware or ivory as gifts for their wives and children. Tangrams use seven pieces and a combination of triangles and quadrilaterals to form other shapes. The mathematician and puzzlemaker Sam Loyd published over 600 different tangram designs. Figure 7-22 shows a tangram stack in HyperCard.

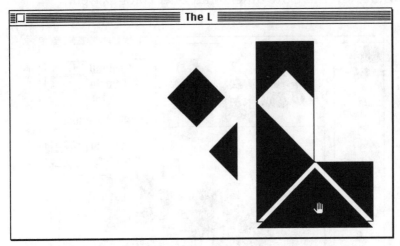

7-22 *Some tangram shapes need a lot of imagination.*

Polyominoes is a game based on fitting shapes together. Each shape in the set of 12 pieces is comprised of five squares, and they fit onto an 8-by-8 square board. It's theoretically possible to fit them all onto the board, although few people ever succeed in doing so. You can play Polyominoes alone, solving various puzzles, or play against the Mac, the object being to place pieces in such a way that your opponent can't put down another piece. It's a difficult game, but intriguing.

Peg o' my heart

Peg puzzles have been around for a long time. One story attributes the first to a prisoner in the Bastille, before or during the French revolution, who made the game from splinters of wood stuck into the dirt floor of his cell. Another states that a Frenchman traveling in America in the late 1700s observed Native Americans (Indians, to him) playing the game with arrows stuck into holes in a board. The commonest forms are a triangle or hexagon of holes with pegs in all but one. The triangular board is attributed to mathematician/philosopher Blasé Pascal.

The usual game is to remove all but one peg. To remove a peg you must first jump over it with another. One such game is called Pegged, with the hexagonal board that this game calls the French board. Pegged comes with more than 12 differently shaped boards and setups, including a cross, hourglass, rectangle, and several variations on the hexagon puzzle, plus a menu of game variations for each board. You could play this game for a long time without playing the same board twice.

Figure 7-23 shows another very simple, but elegant peg game using the triangle board. This particular game is called Tee-Oh, and was written by Marc Dutil, author of Sparkz and a half dozen other good games. Unlike most games and puzzles, this one actually rewards you for your efforts to find a solution with "a few words of Oriental wisdom" when you succeed.

The words are different each time you solve it.

The ultimate peg puzzle is Master Mind. It consists of set of colored pegs and a board with many sets of holes. There can be as many as eight pegs or as few as four or five. (Using more than one peg of the same color is optional.) One player, or the Mac, sets up the pegs in a particular order. The other player has to guess the correct order. Each guess gets a response, according to how many of the guesses are fully correct (a black peg: right color, right position) or half correct (color used in a different position). From these responses, the player can deduce the correct order of the pegs. Figure 7-24 shows a finished game, from a shareware version of the game called Test of Minds, by Marc Dutil. The black pegs indicate guesses that were completely right, and the white ones guesses that were half right. Part of the

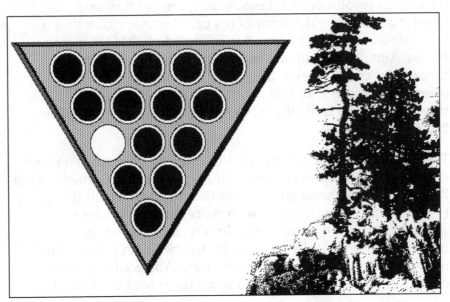

7-23 *With this board setup, you can only make diagonal jumps.*

7-24 *If you take too long guessing, the alien drums his fingers on the table and rolls his eyes.*

difficulty with this game comes from not knowing which peg the right guess refers to. The wrong guesses help you eliminate colors that aren't used.

Mathematical puzzlers

Mathematicians love to create puzzles. That's been known for hundreds of years. Some of the best have been created by top mathematicians of their day. Computer programmers also have to be pretty good at math, so it's little wonder than many are intrigued with puzzles and have created computer versions of many of their favorites. These aren't the sort of thing one might find commercially, but there are dozens of good math puzzles on shareware and freeware disks and CDs and in the online service and BBS libraries. Look in educational forum libraries as well as in entertainment or game libraries, since many are posted by and for math teachers to use with their students.

Towers of Hanoi is a classic puzzle, credited to a French mathematician, Prof. Edouard Lucas. The premise is simple. You have a set of disks in different sizes, stacked from largest on the bottom to smallest on top, on the left one of three platforms. You want to move them to the right platform. You must move them one at a time and not resting a larger disk on top of a smaller one.

The opening setup from a version called Faulty Towers of Hanoi is shown in Fig. 7-25. You can configure the puzzle with as many disks as you want up to a maximum of 15. There's always a solution to this puzzle, but it involves a lot of disk swaps and requires a good deal of patience to work through it yourself. You can also let the Mac solve it for you. With nine disks in the set, as shown here, it takes 511 moves. With 15 disks to move, it took 32,767 moves and about 20 minutes for a 68040-based Mac Centris 610 to solve the puzzle, working at top speed.

Sliding tile puzzles are always popular, although most are a good deal harder than the 15-tile square that is the Mac's desk-accessory puzzle. That one, by the way, was created by Sam Loyd,

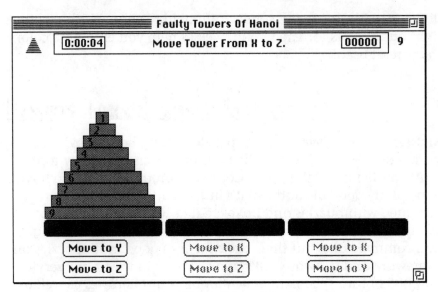

7-25 *You can't put a large disk on top of a smaller one.*

who also brought us Loyd's Lunacy, a different kind of sliding-tile puzzle. The object of Lunacy is to move the large square from the right side of the puzzle to the left side. Sure, it sounds easy enough. But take a look at the layout of the puzzle in Fig. 7-26. It's possible to solve it, if you apply enough patience.

 André Ouimet's 10 Tile Puzzle in Fig. 7-27 is similar, but easier since it has two pairs of small blocks. By the way, this puzzle achieved notoriety a few years ago when a prankster copied the puzzle, embedded a virus in it, and uploaded the result on the InterNet. Several thousand unwary Mac users downloaded it before the virus was discovered. You can't be reminded too often—*always* check new files with an anti-virus program before you run them!

Puzzling words

Word puzzles are the other major category of puzzle that can work well on the computer. Centron Software's Puzzle Master includes 50 of the toughest *New York Times* Sunday crossword

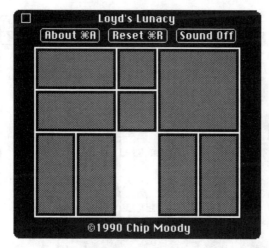

7-26 *Believe it or not, it can be done (but not by me).*

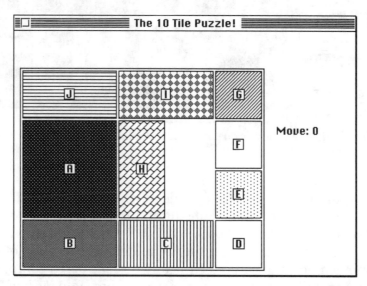

7-27 *André Ouimet's version is easier, but still nearly impossible.*

puzzles and 200 of the daily puzzles—enough to keep any puzzle lover busy for almost three quarters of a year. Follow up with Crossword Creator to build your own puzzles. Type in the words, and the program does the rest. A similar program, called Cross Master, is shown in Fig. 7-28. It can be used to play existing puzzles as shown here, or to create your own.

IT'S A MAD, MAD, MAD, MAD MAC

Famous Pairs

#	Clue
41	Romeo and —
3	Linus and —
5	Smith and —
7	Jan and —
9	Abbott and —
11	Mickey and —
12	Black and —
15	Simon and —
16	Sigfried and —
18	Kidder and —
21	Adam and —
22	Bert and —
23	Laverne and —
24	Castor and —
25	Sonny and —
28	Rogers and —
30	Bausch and —
32	Bang and —
33	David and —
34	Johnson and —
36	Siskel and —
37	Sampson and —
39	Bartles and —
41	Romeo and —
44	Romulus and —
45	Bob and —
46	Orville and —
47	Burns and —

Puzzle answers shown in grid: LUCY, WESSON, DEAN, COSTELLO, MINNIE, DECKER, SCHUSTER, ROY, PEABODY, ERNIE, EYE, SHIRLEY, POLLUX, CHER, HAMMERSTEIN, LOMB, OLUFSEN, GOLIATH, JOHNSON, EBERT, DELILAH, JAYMES, JULIET

7-28 *The puzzle shown here is one of the samples that come with Cross Master. You can also create your own.*

A cryptogram is a simple cipher code in which one letter has been substituted for another. Substitution might be at random or according to a pattern such as A = Z, B = Y, C = X, and so on. Cryptograms are a natural for the computer. In fact, some of the earliest machines that could technically be considered computers were used to decipher codes. There are programs to generate cryptograms for you to solve, and there are other programs that will attempt to solve cryptograms that you type into them. Figures 7-29 and 7-30 show a pair of cryptogram programs. The first, which runs in HyperCard, is called Cryptogram 4.5; the second is Cryptosolve. Both come with some cryptograms to solve, and let you create your own, too.

7-29 *Cryptograms have practical applications, too.*

7-30 *Most cryptograms seem to be "noble thoughts" like this one, perhaps because their creators read Bartlett for inspiration.*

IT'S A MAD, MAD, MAD, MAD MAC

There are many programs that will generate word searches, those pages of assorted letters much beloved by teachers of vocabulary. Others serve as limerick generators, Mad-libs story files, and even Hangman games. There are enough different kinds of puzzles to keep you and your Mac thoroughly baffled.

8

Traditional games

Frankly, it didn't seem to make much sense to use a computer that cost several thousand dollars to play a game that could be played with a 50-cent deck of cards . . . until I tried it. There are lots of reasons why most board and card games are actually more fun on the Mac. One reason is that you don't need to find an opponent. The computer is always willing to play, and (usually) gives you a fair deal and wins or loses gracefully. Playing against a computer is also a great way to learn a game or to improve your skills as a player. Familiar games take on new attraction when they're presented with sound effects and nifty graphics. Many even include animation.

The game of kings

An ancient Sanskrit proverb says, "Chess is a sea in which a mosquito may drink and an elephant may bathe." There's a universal appeal to the game. The basic moves are easy enough for a fairly young child to learn, and the strategy involved will keep even the most experienced adult players engrossed for hours at a time. People even pay money to watch superstar players like Anatoly Karpov meditate over a chess board.

Chess is a natural for computerized play. The moves are easy to describe in computer terms, and a computerized opponent can be as easy or difficult as you wish. There are several commercial chess games on the market. Sargon 4 and Checkmate both play a pretty decent game of chess. Many serious players prefer Checkmate, finding the interface a bit easier to use. Checkmate runs on anything from a Mac Plus on up, and can be played by modem against another live player. (Since it also runs on a PC, Atari, and Amiga, your chances of finding an opponent are excellent.)

Checkmate's author, by the way, is a master-level chess player. Checkmate has consistently beaten Sargon 4, and Chessmaster 2000, as well as several PC chess programs in head-to-head play, making it an exceptionally powerful program, and a worthy opponent for anyone up to master or grand-master level.

Battle Chess, now available on CD-ROM as well as disk, goes beyond "normal" chess. The players come to animated life on your screen. The queen doesn't just capture a pawn, first she knocks him unconscious by zapping him—á la Wonder Woman. The bishops zap with their scepters. The rook turns into a monster, moves, and turns to stone again. Each piece has its own animated sequences complete with sound effects. Figure 8-1 shows the screen during a game. The pieces actually have personalities.

Unfortunately, there's no way to get a screen shot of the animation, but it's a riot to watch, and a good way to get kids interested in chess. Battle Chess is also playable by modem, and has a basic telecommunications program built in. You can switch back and forth between the 3D view that lets you enjoy the animation, and a more traditional diagram view, as shown in Fig. 8-2. The diagram makes it a bit easier to visualize the board and select a move, but doesn't let you watch the battle.

8-1 *The knights in Battle Chess are on foot, not on horseback.*

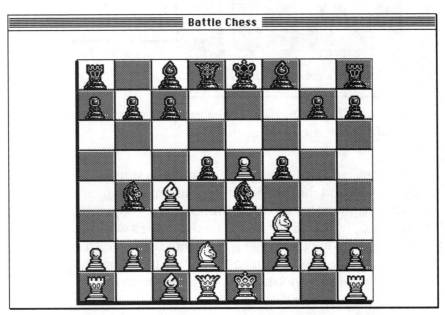

8-2 *It's often easier to devise a strategy in the more familiar view.*

Among the handful of shareware chess programs available for downloading, there's one clear standout: GNUChess, from the Free Software Foundation. It was originally written for a mainframe, and the Mac interface has been carefully and neatly done, as Fig. 8-3 illustrates. The program also keeps a list of moves in algebraic notation. This is not quite as easy to read as the more traditional chess notation, but e2e4 is the same as P-K4. GNUChess has no shareware fee, and comes with all kinds of documentation, including explanations of how the program "thinks."

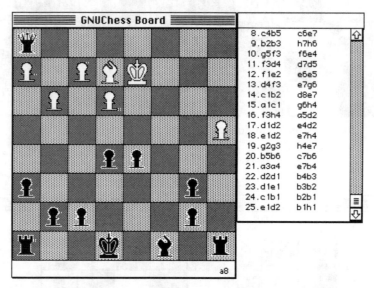

8-3 *GNUChess is freeware, and as powerful as any commercial program.*

These will interest both chess players and programmers, as might the concept behind the Free Software Foundation, which in brief is that effective programs can be communally or cooperatively written by many people, thus improving on each other's work and adding to the general body of knowledge; and that the free distribution of these programs will serve as a catalyst to inspire more cooperation and more knowledge sharing. A good thing, all in all.

Checkers and Backgammon

Both Backgammon and Checkers are old favorites, and it's rather surprising that neither has been released in a commercial game format. Nevertheless, there are shareware versions of both, and they'll keep you, or your kids entertained for many hours of play. Brad Quick's Checkers is a deceptively simple-looking game. It has four levels of play, and the upper two are extremely hard to beat.

Checkermania, in Fig. 8-4, is a fancier, full-color game that adds a couple of variations to the standard Checkers game. One of these is a Return-the-Flag mode. If you can get across the board, capture your opponent's flag with one of your kings, and return it to the bottom row on your side, you win automatically. This prevents games from ending in a draw or deadlock of some sort with each player having only one or two pieces left, chasing each other around the board indefinitely. The other addition is called Magic Spells. Special squares appear on the board. If your

8-4 Checkermania has nice 3D graphics.

checker lands on one you can pick it up. Some can be used to protect your own pieces, others to remove one of your opponent's checkers. It puts an element of luck into the game, making it possible for a less-skilled player to win.

3D Checkers, another shareware game, has a nice looking board and several play levels, but didn't seem to run very happily under System 7.1.

 There's a very good freeware Backgammon game available from the usual sources, and included on the disk in the back of this book. You can play against a smart computer opponent or another player. The rules are exactly as they are when you play with a board and checkers. You can double by clicking on the doubling cube. If you're playing against the Mac, it'll double whenever it thinks it can win. You might decline the double, and resign the game, if you agree that the Mac is winning, or accept and play it out. Figure 8-5 shows a game in progress.

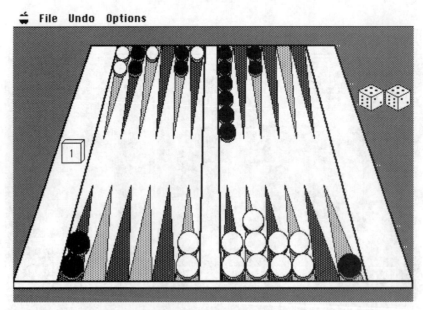

8-5 Sometimes I suspect that the Mac cheats. It always seems to roll doubles when it needs them.

Earlier versions of this game allowed you to cheat . . .. The Mac would beep when you tried, but you could put the pieces anywhere you wanted them. In the current release, that "bug" has been fixed. When you make an illegal move, the piece moves back as soon as you release it.

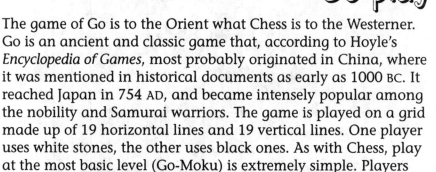

Go play Go

The game of Go is to the Orient what Chess is to the Westerner. Go is an ancient and classic game that, according to Hoyle's *Encyclopedia of Games*, most probably originated in China, where it was mentioned in historical documents as early as 1000 BC. It reached Japan in 754 AD, and became intensely popular among the nobility and Samurai warriors. The game is played on a grid made up of 19 horizontal lines and 19 vertical lines. One player uses white stones, the other uses black ones. As with Chess, play at the most basic level (Go-Moku) is extremely simple. Players take turns placing stones on the board. The first player to get five in a row—diagonally, horizontally, or vertically—is the winner.

Go, in the United States, became popular when released as a board game called Pente. The rules are essentially the same, the board is the same, and the stones, in the board-game version, are plastic jewels in bright colors. The only difference between Pente and Go-Moku is that Pente allows players to capture each other's stones under certain circumstances. Pente attracted a great many new players, some of whom became intrigued with the concept and learned the more complicated game of Go. There are a couple of shareware versions of Pente. A particularly elegant one is called Five Stones. It's shown in Fig. 8-6.

Connect Four is vaguely similar to Pente, except that you must line up four counters rather than five. You drop them into stacks from above on a board that's a sort of gravity-fed 8-by-8 grid. As you try to line up your own four, you must also block your opponent. It's really quite a lot of fun. There's a little tiny version of the game that takes up only 8K of disk space and seems to run

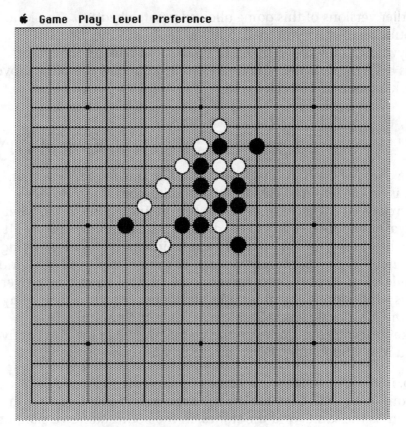

8-6 *White has five in a row, and wins the game.*

on any Mac. It's ideal for the PowerBook since there's no disk access needed once you open the game. It's shown in Fig. 8-7.

The more complex version of Go, which is also called I-Go or Wei-ch'i, is also played on the 19-by-19 board by two players. Players again take turns placing stones on the board, but their goal is to connect stones to form horizontal or vertical units of two or more adjacent stones that will control territory on the board. It's possible to capture your opponent's units by surrounding them. A unit "lives" as long as it has an open "breathing" space at one end of the unit. When an enemy stone is placed on the last breathing space, the unit dies and is removed from the board, all stones being prisoners of the enemy.

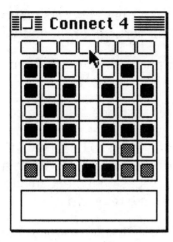

8-7 The gray tiles are barriers the game places at higher levels. I'm playing white and am about to win this one.

There are other equally complex rules, involving the way in which territory is defined and how points are counted at the end of the game. One of the best ways to learn the game is to purchase Nemesis Go Junior, an excellent commercial game that teaches the basics of Go. Once you have mastered Go Junior, you could move up to Nemesis Go Master, the equivalent to a grandmaster level in Chess.

Reversi—Othello

Reversi first appeared in London in about 1888. Its inventor, Louis Waterman, published a series of articles on strategies for winning the game in a magazine called *The Queen*, devoted to "affairs of interest to ladies." Reversi is a fairly complex game, and one would have to conclude that the ladies of the day were better educated than we might have believed, or at least didn't suffer from math anxiety.

The game was published in the United State as Othello and is played on a checkerboard or on any 8-by-8 grid, the alternating colors being unnecessary. Each player has 32 counters, similar to checkers, only double-sided, with a different color on each face. The board is set up with four counters in the center, two of each

color, and players alternately put down their counters adjacent to
similarly colored ones in a horizontal, vertical, or diagonal line.

The rules of play are extremely complicated. To quote from
Hoyle's Rules for Reversi:

> The piece must lie on a line with another piece of its own color so
> as to enclose without break one or more pieces of opposite color.
> The enclosed pieces are then reversed and so become of the
> same color as the enclosing pieces. If a piece is played so as to
> complete the enclosure of adverse pieces on more than one line,
> the enclosed pieces on all such lines are reversed.

Clear as mud, huh? That's why Reversi/Othello is such a natural
for the computer. It's very easy for the Mac to watch the play and
flip all the pieces in the proper direction.

There are at least a half dozen different shareware games in the
Reversi/Othello family. One of the most interesting is called TAO,
for This Ain't Othello. It's shown in Fig. 8-8. What makes the
game so much fun is that it talks back while it's playing, much
like a real opponent. When the Mac wins, it gloats. When you

File Edit Game

TAO

● Macintosh   26

○ Dead Meat!   32

Take that, humanoid!!

8-8 *If you have MacinTalk in the system folder, the game will insult you out
loud, not just in print.*

win, it makes a lame excuse, like "I must be plugged into a faulty outlet." It plays very happily on older Macs, and will run on a color Mac if you set the monitors to black and white and turn off 32-bit addressing.

Many older games, especially the shareware and freeware variety, are not 32-bit clean. If you can't open a game, or if you keep on getting system crashes or unexpected error messages, try turning off 32-bit addressing and color.

Advance to go

In 1930, Charles Darrow invented a game that he called Monopoly. He brought it to a game publisher up in Salem, Massachusetts run by two elderly Yankee brothers. Parker Brothers management looked at the game, and gave its creator 25 good reasons why it would never sell. It took too much arithmetic. The game lasted too long, and so on, and on . . . . The most important reason, though, was that people were still in shock from the stock market crash a few months earlier. A game that let's you lose money by investing in real estate, railroads, and utilities hit too close to the nerve for most people.

But Darrow believed in his game and finally scraped up enough money to have the boards, cards, and boxes printed up himself. He sold the game to stores in New York City and Boston. A few years later the wife of one of the same Parker executives who'd refused the game happened to play it while vacationing with friends. She came home raving about the game, and convinced her husband that Parker Brothers owed it a second look.

By this time the economy had begun to recover. They decided to try it, after dressing up the graphics and adding the caricature of Rich Uncle Pennybags. In 1935, Parker Brothers released Monopoly. It was an instant hit. Monopoly became the most famous proprietary board game in the world. There are licensed editions in 33 different countries, most featuring streets in a local town, much as Darrow's original game used street names from the coastal resort of Atlantic City, New Jersey. (Monopoly's popularity might well have helped Atlantic City turn into the gambling center of the East . . .. Prior to the game, it was known only for saltwater taffy and bathing beauties.)

Today, Monopoly is published in 23 languages, plus a half dozen different computer formats. Human Wave Technology/Digital Eclipse brought the game to the Mac. It's published by Virgin Games. A partially finished game is shown in Fig. 8-9.

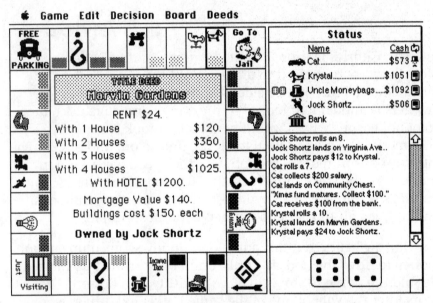

8-9 *Mac Monopoly plays like the board game, but it's much easier to set up.*

Monopoly plays just like the board game, with a few exceptions. One of the advantages to computer play is that you needn't go flipping through your property cards each time someone moves to see what the rent is, or to whom it's paid. The computer handles the banking and bookkeeping automatically, and without mistakes (although the Chance card: Bank Error in Your Favor—Collect $200 is still in the pack).

You can keep track of who owns each property by simply typing Command+L or selecting Show Owners from the Board menu. This marks each owned property with the symbol for the owner's token—car, hat, etc.—as you can see in Fig. 8-10. The board reverts to normal when you click on the dice again. You can also elect to show your own properties or those of another player as shaded blocks, making it easier to remember who's getting close to a monopoly on real estate or railroads.

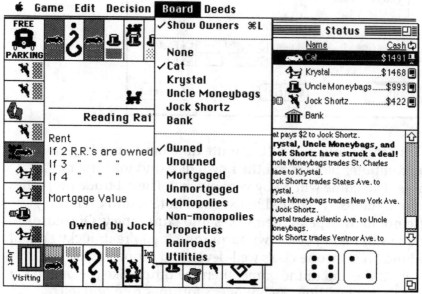

8-10 *There are fewer arguments about who owns what when the Mac is the banker.*

Most people who play the board version of the game adopt a few optional rules to help keep the game interesting, and to make sure it doesn't last forever. Among the familiar options are time limits, and the idea of paying fines to the Free Parking area so that whoever lands there collects the money. The computer game also offers these, and other options. You can apply them from the Options box shown in Fig. 8-11. Just click on the options you want to apply. You can do this at any time during the game.

```
┌─────────────────────────────────────────────────────┐
│▤▤▤▤▤▤▤▤▤▤▤▤▤▤▤▤ Options ▤▤▤▤▤▤▤▤▤▤▤▤▤▤▤▤│
│ Game Options:                                         │
│   ☐ Landing on "Go" doubles salary                    │
│   ☒ Free Parking collects fines        Ante: $ [500]  │
│   ☐ No auctions                                       │
│   ☐ No trading allowed                                │
│   ☒ Time limit game          [10] minutes remaining   │
│ Program Options:                                      │
│   ☒ Computer players roll for themselves              │
│   ☐ No computer trade proposals                       │
│   ☐ Cash invisible                                    │
│   ☐ Set up mode                                       │
│ Program Variables:                                    │
│   Marker Speed:      Slower  ◁▦▦[  ]▦▦▷  Faster       │
│   Card Auto-Close:   Off      ◁▦▦[  ]▦▦▷  Faster       │
│                                                       │
│  ( OK )          ( Official )          ( Cancel )     │
└─────────────────────────────────────────────────────┘
```

8-11 *Customize the game the way your family likes to play it.*

If it's getting late, put a 10-minute time limit on things and let the computer players roll their own dice and take their own turns. The game will go by very quickly. They'll trade properties among themselves, build houses and hotels, and eventually attempt to overspend themselves into bankruptcy. Of course, you're still taking your own turns, and if you're unlucky enough to land on someone else's well-developed property, you could lose it all. At the end of the game, there's a graph like the one in Fig. 8-12 that shows how each player's fortunes rose and fell.

Other board games have been converted to Mac formats, including Risk and Scrabble, both from Virgin Games. Like Monopoly, they are accurate and successful copies that take advantage of the Mac interface to make the game more enjoyable. TV game shows have also been responsible for more than a few computer games. Jeopardy, Wheel of Fortune, and Family Feud are some of the games that exist in commercial and/or shareware form.

Figure 8-13 shows a shareware version of Wheel of Fortune that many players say is far superior to the commercial version. PhrazeCraze has been around almost as long as the TV game,

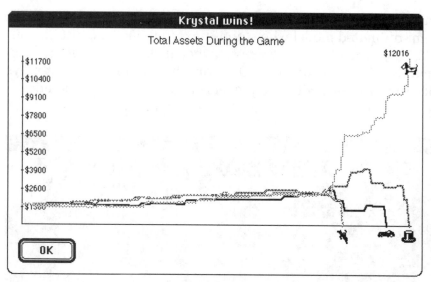

8-12 *Unfair . . . Krystal always wins!*

8-13 *You can add your own phrases, too.*

but it still seems to run reliably under System 7. It even features a semi-animated model who stands next to the letters, just like on TV. The Family Feud program spawned a clever shareware imitation called That's Your Opinion, shown in Fig. 8-14. It plays like the TV game, with two players or teams, and the audience responses are just as weird as those of a real audience.

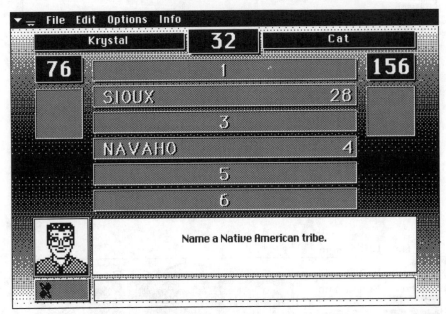

8-14 Perhaps I should try Cleveland?

Lexi-Cross is advertised as "the 21st-Century TV game show that's beyond words." While I don't know if I'd go quite that far, it *is* a clever game and one I thoroughly enjoyed playing. Like Wheel of Fortune, you spin for points and guess letters in a puzzle, but first you have to uncover the letter tiles on a large board, which also holds "lose-a-turn" squares, points (to gain or lose), and wildcards to let you enter a vowel or reveal a row of tiles. After you've filled in enough of the crosswords, you try to guess what word they all apply to. Figure 8-15 shows a game in progress.

8-15 *The answer is "gold."*

It's the pits . . .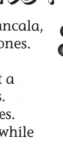

There's a very interesting and very ancient game called Mancala, or Ka'lah that is played by two people with a handful of stones. Some say it originated in India, others credit Africa. In the original form it was played in the dirt. Participants dug out a series of shallow pits and collected a fistful of small pebbles. Later, boards were made with hollow wells to hold the stones. Kings and chieftains played it with jewels or gold nuggets, while poor people played with grains of dry corn, olive pits, or whatever they had. It's still fascinating today, and the Mac makes an excellent opponent.

Mancala, shown in Fig. 8-16, is a shareware game. Each player has a row of small pits and one larger one. Each small pit has three, four, or five stones in it to start the game. The object is to end up with more stones in your large pit than your opponent has in his. To play, you take the stones from any of your pits and distribute them to the right, one per pit, including the large pit. If

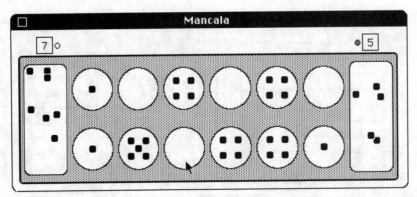

8-16 *There are ways to force a win. Watch the way the Mac plays and learn from its success.*

you have more, continue around to your opponent's side of the board. If the last pebble ends in the large pit, play again. If it lands in an empty pit, capture your opponents stones from the opposite pit and put them in yours. Playing against the Mac is extremely challenging. Since the game is based on math, the computer has a definite advantage. Another version of this game, called Killer Kalah, is almost impossible to beat.

Among the other board games for which you can find shareware clones are Mille Bornes, based on the French card game Parcheesi; Battleship; Operation; and even the former vice president's favorite game, Mr. Potato Head. Look for these and more on bulletin boards, online services' games forums, and on shareware distribution disks and CD-ROMs.

Dice are nice

Dice games are easy to write programs for. Most programming languages have some kind of random number generator built in, so there are quite a few good dice games in circulation. Among them are several variations on Yahtzee, a sort of poker dice game that became popular in the '50s and '60s. The game is played by rolling five dice, and scoring them on a list that includes full house, three of a kind, four of a kind, and so on.

The scoring chart of a partially completed game of a variation called Triple Yahtzee is shown in Fig. 8-17. Each roll of the dice can only be scored one way. You can re-roll any or all of your dice twice more, if you don't like the numbers you got on the first attempt. Players take turns, and the high score wins. Triple Yahtzee is essentially the same game, but three rounds are played and scored at the same time and the cumulative score added up. Thus, if you get a full house more than once, you don't need to waste it by taking it as a lesser scoring hand. There are at least a dozen different versions of Yahtzee in shareware form.

Scoreboard	Pete			Roger		
Ones	2			2		
Twos	4			6		
Threes	12			9		
Fours	4			12		
Fives	15			10		
Sixes	12	12		18		
Total	49	12		57		
Bonus						
Upper Total	49	12		57		
3 of a Kind	23			14		
4 of a Kind	12			6	7	
Full House	25			25	25	
Small Straight	30			30		
Large Straight	40	40		40		
Yahtzee	50			50		
Chance	26	18		25		
Lower Total	206	58		190	32	
Yahtzee Bonus						
Combined Total	255	70		247	32	
Triple Yahtzee	255	140		247	64	
Grand Total	395			311		

Roll

2 more

8-17 *Triple Yahtzee lets you play three hands at once and make the best use of high-scoring dice.*

A better mousetrap

Remember a game called Mousetrap? It was a sort of 3D board game, in which you had to assemble a sort of Rube Goldberg-ish contraption to try to catch a little plastic mouse. Sierra On-Line has just introduced a wonderful new game that takes that concept a step further. The Incredible Machine is one you build on the screen out of parts you drag from a box. Sometimes your goal is to get a basketball through a hoop. Sometimes it's to free the mouse and send him home. It changes from one level to the next. The parts you can use include animated conveyor belts (powered by gerbils running inside wheels), gears, ramps, bowling balls, stepladders, pipes, and so on. The right pieces to solve each problem in the set are always supplied, but it's up to you to put them in the right order. (There might be parts left over, too.) It's lots of fun for all ages, and will probably teach you a good deal about applied physics in the process of playing.

It's in the cards

A deck of cards turns any gathering into a party. Whether your game is Bridge, Seven Card Stud, or Go Fish, as long as you've got someone to play against, it's guaranteed fun. But you can't always pick up a fourth for Bridge, or a table of high rollers for a little casino action. That's where the Mac comes in. You can play the games you enjoy whenever you want. You don't need to wait for the Thursday-night bridge club, and you don't need to go jetting off to Vegas or Atlantic City. More to the point, you can emerge from a game with your bank balance intact, even if you have a run of bad luck. (Of course, you won't get rich from gambling on your Mac, either.)

Bridge is still the most popular card game of all. In 1980 it was estimated that 60 million people in all parts of the world play Bridge. Thanks to Artworx, their Macs can play too. Bridge 7.0 is the latest in a series of Bridge-playing programs published by Artworx. The author is a nationally ranked player, and a Mac user. This game lets you play either Contract or Duplicate Bridge, or Whist. Bidding is done by simply clicking on the bid you want to make, as shown in Fig. 8-18. If you aren't sure, ask for a hint. It will tell you what to do, and why. You can modify your partner's bidding to be conservative, normal, or aggressive. Normal follows the Goren point-count requirements. Conservative looks for more high-card points for a particular bid, and aggressive settles for fewer.

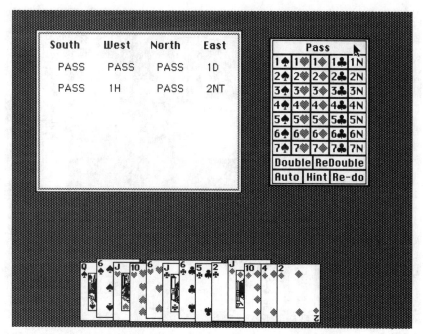

South	West	North	East
PASS	PASS	PASS	1D
PASS	1H	PASS	2NT

Pass
1♠ 1♥ 1♦ 1♣ 1N
2♠ 2♥ 2♦ 2♣ 2N
3♠ 3♥ 3♦ 3♣ 3N
4♠ 4♥ 4♦ 4♣ 4N
5♠ 5♥ 5♦ 5♣ 5N
6♠ 6♥ 6♦ 6♣ 6N
7♠ 7♥ 7♦ 7♣ 7N
Double ReDouble
Auto Hint Re-do

8-18 If you're not sure what to do, click Hint.

The game has digitized sound during the bidding round. Turn it off from the Preferences box. (It does nothing to enhance the game, and sounds as if it was recorded in a wind tunnel.)

Play follows logically. The table is shown in Fig. 8-19. Click on your cards to play them, and click on the dummy's hand, when your partner is the dummy, to play those. The score is kept as a running count on the Menu bar, and the score is totaled at the end of the hand. You can also cheat and look at your opponents' hands by selecting them from a pull-down menu. This can be very helpful if you're using the program to teach yourself Bridge or to improve your bidding skills. You can tell the program to bid for you automatically, and to play out the hand automatically, so you can watch what it does. You can also replay hands, save them, and print them out for reference.

There's one spot in the accompanying manual that could be confusing. The reference to the "open Apple" key comes,

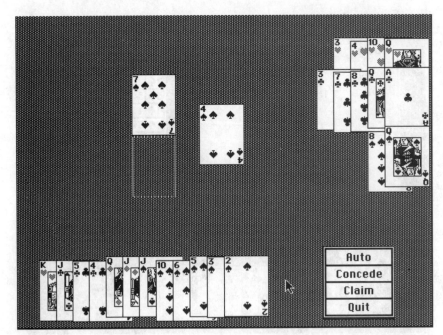

8-19 *Play the hand out yourself, or click one of the boxes at right to make the game go quicker.*

according to an Artworx spokesman, from their programmer. Most of us know it as the command key.

 Softstream publishes a computerized card-game collection called Classic Trilogy that includes Cribbage, Whist, and Hearts. If you like any one of these games, it's a good investment. If you like all three, you're really in luck. Classic Trilogy, by the way, is great for a PowerBook, since it doesn't ask much from the CPU and is compatible with virtually any Mac and both Systems 6 and 7. You can use Classic Trilogy as a game-playing partner or as a tutor to teach yourself the games.

 If you need help figuring out a game, turn on the on-screen Help. Every time you play the wrong card, the Hint screen will pop up, as in Fig. 8-20, to suggest a better choice. You can, of course, play it your way, or take back your card and consider the suggestion. If you don't need playing hints, leave them turned off. You can

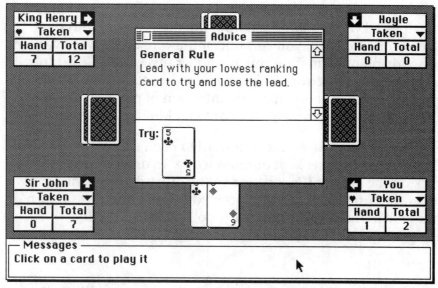

8-20 This is a great way to learn these games.

adjust your computer opponents' playing skills to match yours under the Options menu, and even change their names.

According to Hoyle

Edmond Hoyle was a middle-aged English barrister, fond of coffeehouses, and the friendly pursuits that went on there. In 1742 he managed to combine his vocation and avocation by collecting the "laws" of the game of Whist, to which he was admittedly addicted. He published a slender volume called *A Short Treatise on the Game of Whist* that immediately became a great success, and was reprinted many times over, eventually with the addition of other games of skill and chance.

For 250 years Hoyle has been the authority on card games. So, a computer program that calls itself Hoyle's Book of Games had better be pretty darn good. Sierra On-Line has brought out two volumes of Hoyle's Games. Volume I focuses on classic games like Gin Rummy, Hearts, and Cribbage, while Volume II offers 28 different solitaire variations. Are they worthy of Hoyle? I'm not convinced. Even though the games are nicely done, with on-screen rules for each, you can find shareware or freeware versions of nearly all of them for a much smaller investment. The other advantage to shareware is that you don't need to keep games on your hard disk that you have no intention of playing. If you're a Cribbage player, do you really want Old Maid or Crazy 8s?

 Figure 8-21 shows a simple, but hard to beat, shareware game of Gin Rummy. Score is kept automatically. To draw a card, either click on the deck or the top card in the discard pile. To discard, select the card to throw away from your hand and press return. If you look in the various shareware collections you'll find everything from Bezique to War, Pinochle, and Poker.

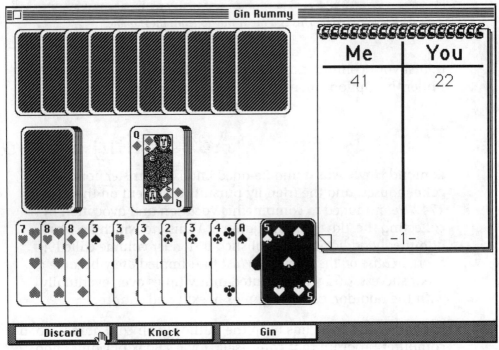

8-21 *Sure, he's ahead now, but you can still win.*

Casino gambling

Here again, there are both shareware and commercial games to let you test your luck or improve your skill at such games as Poker, Blackjack, and even the slot machines. Among the commercial games, Varcon's Aces with Tens is a standout. It's Blackjack, but with a couple of features that make it ideal for the beginner. It plays casino-style Blackjack, with seven players at the table, plus the dealer. The layout is shown in Fig. 8-22. Play goes from right to left. You enter a bet for each player, or let some sit out a hand. You can review all kinds of statistics including the current shoe, the count table, and the current odds of drawing any particular card in the deck. You can even look to see what point count won most often, and how often the dealer busted.

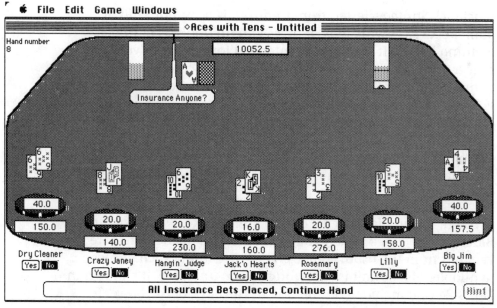

8-22 *You can adjust each player's betting strategy.*

Figure 8-23 shows the kind of statistical analysis that the program gives you. This game, like Varcon's other games, comes in a reusable velvet bag instead of a cardboard box—a nice

				Game Summary					

Aces with Tens Game Results Summary - Untitled - After 8 Hands.

Player Name	Hands Played	Won	Lost	Bust	Push	Surrender	BJs	Insurance Won	Lost
Big Jim	9	3	5	1	1	0	0	0	1
Lilly	7	4	3	1	0	0	0	0	0
Rosemary	9	4	5	1	0	0	0	0	1
Jack'o Hearts	5	2	3	1	0	0	0	0	0
Hangin' Judge	5	3	2	2	0	0	0	0	0
Crazy Janey	6	2	3	0	1	0	0	0	2
Dry Cleaner	7	3	3	2	1	0	0	0	0
Dealer	48	24	21	13	3	0	0	0	0

8-23 *After an evening of Blackjack these statistics will show how good a player you really are.*

feature. The bag, by the way, is the right size to hold a deck of cards, for non-Mac gaming.

Blackjack Strategy Tester, from Centron, is a similar kind of game. Like Aces with Tens, it gives you an analysis of the winning hands. It seems to be intended for a more advanced player, though. Capstone's Trump Castle is a cute set of casino games including Blackjack, Craps, Roulette, Baccarat, Video Poker, and the ever popular "one-armed bandit." It's great for casual players, but the animation and digitized photos might prove annoying if you were working out a serious strategy. Centron's Casino Master is another good compilation of your favorite casino games, with fewer distractions than the Trump Castle game.

If you're looking for specific casino games, like a slot machine, Blackjack, or Video Poker, you're sure to find good shareware versions from the usual sources. There are many such games available. MacBandit is fun, and runs on any Mac. It's shown in Fig. 8-24 and included on the disk at the back of the book. To play, you simply select a sum of money to bet and use the mouse to pull the handle. The payoffs are shown on the chart. Naturally, the best payoff of all occurs when the machine shows three Macs.

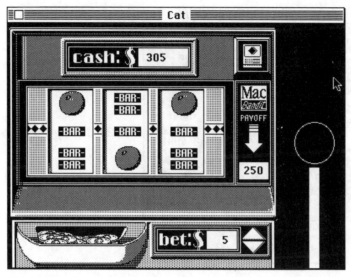

8-24 *There's something hypnotic about pulling down that lever, even when you do it with the mouse.*

ColorJack, shown in Fig. 8-25, is a simple two-player Blackjack. Despite the name, it also plays in black and white. Video Poker, in Fig. 8-26, plays like the coin-operated ones. Select the cards you want to keep and draw to replace those you don't want. This game shows the payoff of various hands. An excellent Craps program (written by a Las Vegas resident!) is shown in Fig. 8-27. Mouse Craps is great if you already know how to play the casino game. If not, you'll be floundering until you figure out the game.

Riverboat Poker is a well-done version of a favorite casino game called Texas Hold 'Em. As you play, the game keeps a careful statistical analysis of your hands and how well you've played them. Figure 8-28 shows an example. This is a game that can teach you a lot, if you're into the math enough to understand what's displayed on the screen. If you're not, ignore it and play by the seat of your pants as most of us do. The tiny animated hand that deals the cards is a cute touch, too.

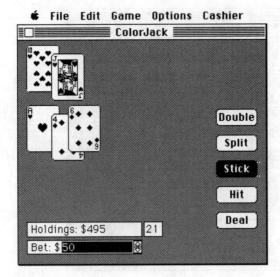

8-25 *Twenty-one beats twenty!*

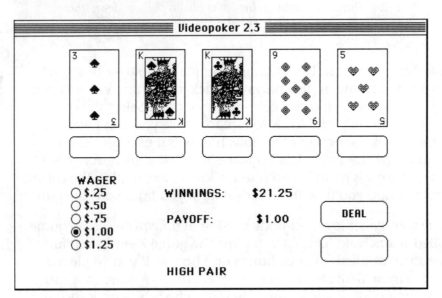

8-26 *Click the buttons under the cards to deal new ones.*

Solitary pursuits

You could argue that any game that can be played by one player against the computer is a form of solitaire. But there are many

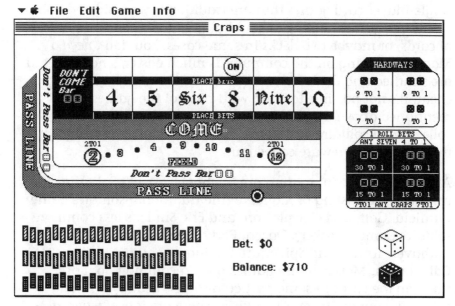

8-27 *You don't have to go to Vegas, or Atlantic City. Just go to your Mac.*

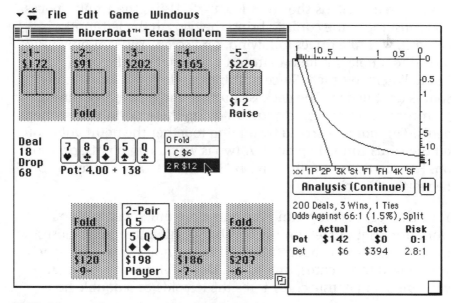

8-28 *If you understand statistical analysis, this game can turn you into a poker whiz.*

single-player card games that are traditionally considered to be "solitaire" games. Sure, you could play any of them with a deck of cards, or maybe two decks in some cases. You don't *need* a Mac. But playing on the computer is much easier, since the cards are shuffled and dealt for you. And even if you are tempted to cheat, it's not possible to do so with most of the games. As mentioned above, Hoyle's Book of Games Volume II, is a collection of solitaire variations. You can find just as many or more in any shareware collection.

Among the more interesting are Michael Casteel's Solitaire collection, consisting of Klondike (the traditional solitaire game), Canfield, Golf, and Calculation; and Eric Snider's less common solitaire games—Baker's Dozen, Forty Thieves, and Montana. Seahaven Towers and Spider are fascinating games, as is Calculation. Most solitaire games have a common goal of stacking the cards in some particular order, usually building in suit and sequence from ace to king. There are lots of ways of accomplishing this task, though.

In Montana, the entire deck of cards is dealt, face up, and the aces are removed, as shown in Fig. 8-29. Using the empty spaces, you must move the cards to bring the twos to the left-most column, with the threes following, and so on. You can only move a card to a hole if it follows in suit and sequence the card immediately to its left. Since nothing can follow a king, those spaces are filled in. The deck is shuffled and dealt three times, with cards in their correct places staying there during subsequent deals. This game is scored by adding together the point value of all the cards correctly placed. A two is worth two points, and so on. Face cards are worth 10 each. So, completing the game would be worth 336 points.

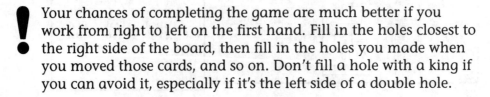

Your chances of completing the game are much better if you work from right to left on the first hand. Fill in the holes closest to the right side of the board, then fill in the holes you made when you moved those cards, and so on. Don't fill a hole with a king if you can avoid it, especially if it's the left side of a double hole.

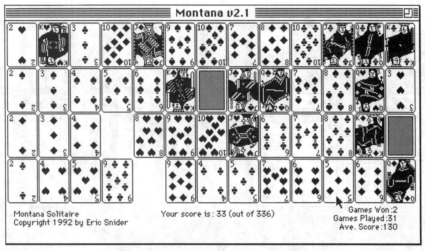

8-29 *This version keeps score as you play.*

Just ignore these. Often you'll end up moving the queen elsewhere instead.

Seahaven Towers is complicated to explain, but its beautiful graphics make it a pleasure to play. The game layout, as shown in Fig. 8-30, has four spaces to hold the four suits. As soon as an ace becomes available it must be played to one of these four spaces. There are also four "tower" spaces at the top of the layout. The cards are dealt in 10 rows, each row consisting of five cards, overlapped upon each other. The two left-over cards are placed in two of the tower spaces. Only the top card of each row, and the four cards in the tower spaces are available to be moved. Any aces thus exposed go immediately to the suit spaces. The cards are built on these aces in ascending order. Cards may be built upon those of the same suit in descending order in the layout, as long as you only take them one at a time from the rows.

You can use the empty tower spaces to hold cards as you are moving them from one row to another. In the example shown, we can place the Jack of Diamonds in the tower while we move the queen on top of the king, and then move the jack back onto the queen in the new row. By making these moves, and with luck,

8-30 It's not easy, but it's intriguing, especially fairytale told in the About . . . box.

we should be able to uncover the aces, twos, threes, and so on for all four suits. Cards that can move to the suit spaces will do so automatically.

Gallery is an unusual solitaire game, the object of which is to assemble a "picture gallery" of jacks, queens, and kings. The layout is shown in Fig. 8-31. One of the unusual features of this game is that after you play a hand, the Mac plays the same cards and tries to beat your total. It also keeps statistics on how you and the Mac do—the number of games won, lost, and drawn, and the difference in the number of cards you and the computer leave. It's quite fascinating to watch the computer play a hand, especially when you beat it.

SpoydWorks solitaire is a collection of games—26 in all— including the ones described above as well as many others. Figure 8-32 shows the layout for a game called Spiderette. The documentation is excellent. Solitaire Help appears under the

8-31 *The black bar on top of a card means there's a place it can be moved to.*

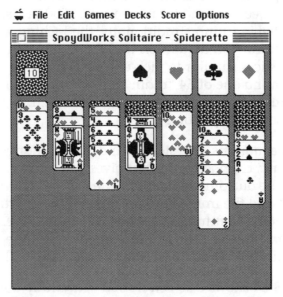

8-32 *SpoydWorks includes many solitaire variations.*

Balloon Help menu. There are many different deck designs and you can even add your own using ResEdit. You can play games individually or play them all as a sort of solitaire tournament. The game also keeps statistics so you can see how many times you've actually won a particular game.

Fortune tellers

Some people believe quite firmly in the notion that the future is predictable. Others think it's nonsense. Most of us don't quite believe it, unless we get a particularly auspicious or flattering report. Nevertheless, astrologers, numerologists, and fortune tellers of all kinds abound, even on the computer. If there's any science at all involved, a computer-generated fortune might be more reliable than a human one, since the outcome isn't influenced by external factors like what you're wearing when you consult the soothsayer.

One of the oldest known methods of divining the future is the I-Ching, or Book of Changes, a mathematically based system that has been around for more than 2,500 years, and which originated in China. Traditionally, the I-Ching was "cast" by concentrating on a question and flipping a coin or tossing yarrow sticks (similar to pick-up sticks) to arrive at a number representing one of 64 "main" hexagrams or symbols. For each hexagram, there's a text passage in the I-Ching that gives a response to the question asked.

Some hexagrams are "stable" and do not change. Others have a secondary, changed form that gives you another hexagram that affects the outcome of the first. The first hexagram concerns the present and the immediate outcome of the question, the second relates it to the future. There are, as you might expect, several programs that cast the I-Ching and give you the text responses from the book. Figure 8-33 shows a freeware I-Ching program.

Figure 8-34 shows a screen from a beautifully done commercial program called Synchronicity, from Visionary Software. The term

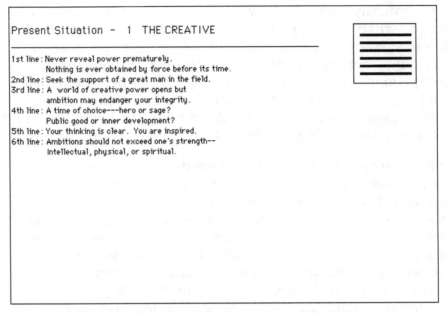

Present Situation - 1 THE CREATIVE

1st line : Never reveal power prematurely.
            Nothing is ever obtained by force before its time.
2nd line : Seek the support of a great man in the field.
3rd line : A world of creative power opens but
            ambition may endanger your integrity.
4th line : A time of choice---hero or sage?
            Public good or inner development?
5th line : Your thinking is clear. You are inspired.
6th line : Ambitions should not exceed one's strength--
            Intellectual, physical, or spiritual.

8-33 *This program runs as a HyperCard stack.*

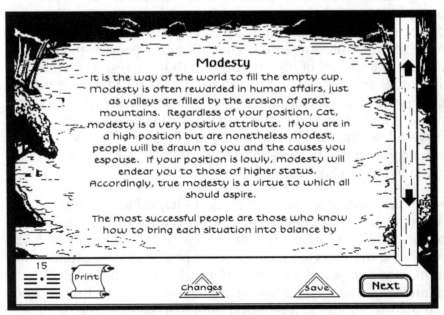

Modesty

It is the way of the world to fill the empty cup.
Modesty is often rewarded in human affairs, just
as valleys are filled by the erosion of great
mountains. Regardless of your position, Cat,
modesty is a very positive attribute. If you are in
a high position but are nonetheless modest,
people will be drawn to you and the causes you
espouse. If your position is lowly, modesty will
endear you to those of higher status.
Accordingly, true modesty is a virtue to which all
should aspire.

The most successful people are those who know
how to bring each situation into balance by

15

Print   Changes   Save   Next

8-34 *Synchronicity has beautiful color graphics.*

"synchronicity" was coined by psychologist Carl Jung to explain the patterns of meaningful coincidence or how things tend to go together; how people and events coincide in time and space by something more than chance. Jung's theories are based on an interpretation of the I-Ching, and suggest that when confronted with a question or a need to make a decision, we know subconsciously what we ought to do, but need an external event, like casting an I-Ching, to bring it to the conscious level.

When you open Synchronicity you are transported to an Oriental garden, complete with the sounds of a gentle stream and frogs chirping. After a relaxing break, you are invited to enter your question and to focus on it mentally. You are then given as much time as you need to relax and prepare, and finally you're asked to press some keys at random, three times. This is where the element of "meaningful chance" enters into the equation. Your keystrokes are transformed into one of the 64 hexagrams, then "changed" if indicated, and the response is displayed on the screen.

The meaning of the hexagram is explained, but it's up to you to interpret it in the light of your own question or situation. Answers can be saved or printed. If a meaning is unclear, you can ask for more information. Amazingly enough, many people who are ordinarily skeptical of such things find that the responses from Synchronicity are "right on." Perhaps it's just that they are good at applying ambiguous statements to their own circumstances, or perhaps there's more to it than we know. Synchronicity is powerful. If you ask silly questions, you'll get silly answers, but if you approach it with sincerity, you might be surprised and delighted with what you learn.

 Since computers deal with numbers, it's logical to create a numerology program to run on one. Plato and Pythagoras both considered that numbers had meanings and that letters could be reduced to numbers according to their position in the alphabet. In his work *Timaeus*, Plato set forth an elaborate theory of numerology, founded on numerical relationships, metaphor, and symbolism. Prime, an interesting numerology program, applies these theories, does the necessary calculations, and gives you a reading based on a combination of your name, and date and time of birth. An example is shown in Fig. 8-35.

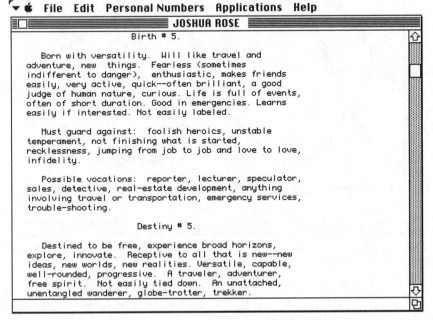

File Edit Personal Numbers Applications Help

JOSHUA ROSE

Birth # 5.

Born with versatility. Will like travel and adventure, new things. Fearless (sometimes indifferent to danger), enthusiastic, makes friends easily, very active, quick--often brilliant, a good judge of human nature, curious. Life is full of events, often of short duration. Good in emergencies. Learns easily if interested. Not easily labeled.

Must guard against: foolish heroics, unstable temperament, not finishing what is started, recklessness, jumping from job to job and love to love, infidelity.

Possible vocations: reporter, lecturer, speculator, sales, detective, real-estate development, anything involving travel or transportation, emergency services, trouble-shooting.

Destiny # 5.

Destined to be free, experience broad horizons, explore, innovate. Receptive to all that is new--new ideas, new worlds, new realities. Versatile, capable, well-rounded, progressive. A traveler, adventurer, free spirit. Not easily tied down. An unattached, unentangled wanderer, globe-trotter, trekker.

8-35 This description fits him perfectly!

Biorhythms are a semi-scientific, or pseudo-scientific—depending on who you ask—way of understanding the human body's natural cycles. There are three cycles: mental, physical, and emotional. The mental cycle goes from peak to peak every 33 days, the emotional cycle every 28 days, and the physical cycle every 23 days. Supposedly, it's best to plan activities that require you to be at your physical best for the days when you're at the top of your physical cycle, mental activities for positive mental days, and so on. The critical days each month are the ones on which one or more of the cycles cross the midpoint from positive to negative on the graph. Figure 8-36 shows a typical biorhythm chart. The 8th of the month is destined to be a bad day, according to this chart. All three cycles intersect at the mid-point

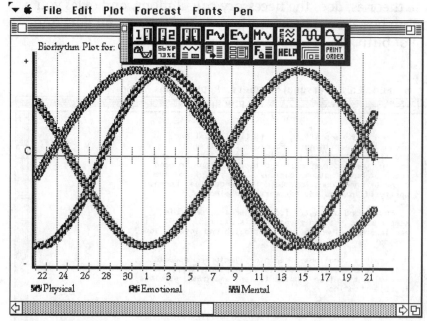

8-36 *If your partner's biorhythms intersect with yours, the critical days could be even more critical.*

on that day, a triple critical. Since biorhythms must be calculated from the date of your birth, the computer does them much more easily that anyone working with pen and graph paper possibly could.

The simplest fortune teller of all is a little program called Rosarium that generates a motto for each day. It's shown in Fig. 8-37. If your fortune indicates the sudden acquisition of great wealth, check some of the many lottery number pickers. The one shown in Fig. 8-38 is specifically tailored for the Massachusetts Megabucks drawing, but you can find lottery number pickers for many other states, too, as well as a couple of universal number choosers that ask you to enter the number of numbers to pick, and the range from which to pick them.

There's no guarantee that you'll win using the number selector, but there's no guarantee you won't. It's absolutely as good as any other way of picking your numbers. Statistically, each day is a

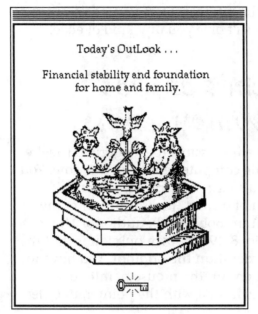

8-37 *This program seems to give only good news.*

8-38 *Some say the only way to win is not to bet. Then, you're a dollar ahead.*

fresh start. So knowing what the numbers were yesterday, or every day for the past five years, doesn't give you any kind of edge.

Games you wouldn't expect to find on a computer

There are a few games that are impossible to categorize. They're not your run-of-the-mill arcade computer game, at any rate. You could possibly consider Jacks a sports simulation, but only if the playground game is your idea of a sport. Jacks is one of many wonderful shareware games from Bob Grubb, author of That's Your Opinion. It's shown in Fig. 8-39. My own opinion is that the computer version is much harder than the original. You have to click to throw the jacks and then run the mouse pointer over them *and* catch the ball by touching it with the pointer, in order to advance.

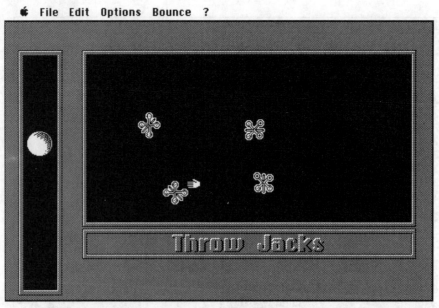

8-39 *This game would probably be easier to play on an older, slower Mac.*

Recycle is a politically correct game that has you sorting trash on a conveyor belt, snipping six-pack rings apart to protect the wildlife, and planting daisies. It's shown in Fig. 8-40. It's not an arcade game, since you're doing something socially useful instead of shooting at some kind of monster. The belt gets faster, and the game gets harder as your score increases. It's a lot of fun, and reminds you that recycling is important. One thing I learned from this game that hadn't ever occurred to me is that paint cans, even empty ones, are considered toxic waste.

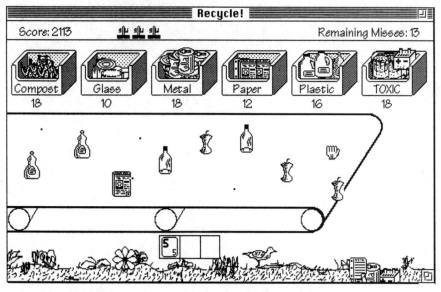

8-40 Move the gloved hand over the piece of trash and drag it to the correct bin to score a point.

Finally, something weirder still . . . Russian Roulette for the computer. The screen contains a field of mirrors, all set at an angle. Around the perimeter of the field are barrels. One of these barrels is full of dynamite. Shooting it will set off a massive explosion, ending the game. Of course, you have no idea which barrel it is, but you must shoot and destroy all of the others without hitting the target one. You can set the game to give you a warning tone when you hit within three squares of the dynamite box. You can also set the number of barrels to hit per game, and number of mirrors for the Mac to place at random within the playing field. It's not always possible to win or lose, depending on how the game has set itself up. Sometimes there are two barrels opposite each other, so you can't shoot either one. It's fun, without being totally mindless. What more can anyone ask?

9

Educational games

Every parent with a computer at home knows that there's no way
to keep the kids away from it. Even the youngest ones are
fascinated by what happens on the screen, whether it's typing
words, drawing pictures, shooting space aliens, or simply
watching grass grow on the screen saver. The computer can be a
wonderful toy and a terrific teaching tool, with the right software.
Some parental input and supervision is required, of course,
especially for younger children who might do some inadvertent
damage or get frustrated when things don't seem to work as they
should. Older kids need supervision, too—mostly to make sure
that the homework gets done before they become too engrossed
in the latest game of Intergalactic Gerbil Warriors or
SpaceLazerMazer.

Child-proofing the computer

The fact is, children are less likely to do actual physical damage to the computer or its peripheral parts than adults. But you do need to go over a few basic rules before you let children of any age start using the mouse and keyboard. Teach them to:

Be gentle. Mice and keyboards are not designed for throwing or banging—or chewing on.

Never unplug anything while the machine is turned on. (And don't unplug anything when it's off, unless you know what you're doing.)

Turn the computer off by using Shut Down. Don't just push the switch (on machines that have one).

Never, ever, open files that aren't yours. It's an invasion of someone else's privacy at best, and you could accidentally lose important papers, at worst.

It's a very good idea to install Apple's At Ease desktop if you'll have kids using your Mac. It lets you designate specific applications or files that young or novice users may open, while hiding and protecting everything else on your hard drive. Your checkbook, correspondence, and other important files can't be viewed, erased, or played with.

Edmark's KidDesk does much the same thing, but appeals to younger kids even more, since it looks like an actual desk, complete with a pencil holder, clock, and calculator. There's even a nameplate, and a frame for a digitized picture of the child. Parents can place whatever software they want the child to use on the desk, and know that everything else is protected.

Many parents suggest using a keyboard shield to keep cookie crumbs, spilled juice, and other substances out of the Mac keyboard. It's an excellent idea for adults who like to drink coffee or soda while working, too. Several manufacturers make molded transparent covers from thin plastic material. They're made to sit over the keys on standard Mac and third-party keyboards, and come in various sizes to fit precisely on each model. Your local computer store will probably have at least one brand. These keyboard shields are so flexible you will hardly know there's anything there, but your keyboard will be completely protected from dust, pet hair, crumbs, and all kinds of liquids.

Having the right hardware is important, too. The standard Mac mouse is made to fit the adult hand. It might be too big for a child to hold comfortably. Kidz Mouse is a brightly colored plastic mouse designed for the younger set. It looks, naturally, like a mouse, complete with big round ears that act as mouse buttons. Kids love them, and do seem to find that the Kidz Mouse is easier to control.

Appoint is bringing out a Mouse Crayon, similar to their excellent Mouse Pen, that looks and handles like a marker or fat ballpoint pen, and plugs into the ADB. The Mouse Pen has a pair of buttons conveniently located under the tip of your index finger. One clicks, the other clicks and locks. The Mouse Crayon will presumably have the same buttons. It should be in stores by the time this book reaches the shelves. It comes in your choice of four Crayola colors, and should make drawing much easier for kids or for anyone else. (I can't wait to plug one into my PowerBook.)

Selecting software

Once you've protected your Mac from kid damage, what are you going to put on it for kid software? That depends mostly on the age of the kid in question, and whether you're looking toward entertainment, education, or some combination of the two. Many of the games teach as the child plays. Some, like the Reader Rabbit or Math Blaster series, are clearly aimed at teaching particular skills, although they do so in an entertaining way. Others, notably Spelunx and the Caves of Mr. Seudo, Kid Pix, and the Castle of Dr. Brain, let the child learn by exploring and being creative, an approach that probably achieves more long-term results than the rote teaching of number facts or phonics.

Still, if you have a child who needs practice in math or reading skills, using the computer is a good way to combine drills with the reward of playing a game. Figures 9-1 and 9-2 show a typical "skill-drill" program from Math Blaster Mystery by Davidson. Skill drills come in different levels, from pre-reading and reading readiness on up. This one happens to be for older kids. The first example is a pretty straightforward one—you must select the proper steps to solve the problem. The second example is a familiar one, the puzzle—Towers of Hanoi—turned into an addition drill. The trick is to pile up the correct weights on the scale in as few moves as possible, without putting a larger one on a smaller one.

```
════════════ Follow the Steps Level 1 ════════════

Problem 11:
              "This 15 page report will be easier to do if I break
              it into smaller pieces," Jose realized. "I'll do just
              a little each day. If I do 1/6 today, 1/4 the next
              and 1/3 the next, what fraction of the report
              will I have completed?"

          What does the problem ask you to find?
  A    fraction of the report Jose will do the next day
  B    number of pages he will have to do each day
  C    fraction of the report done in 3 days
  D    fraction of the report still left to do after 3 days

  [ OK ]                    Step  ⦿1  ○2  ○3  ○4
```

9-1 *These problems are fairly difficult, but very good practice.*

There are two other activities within the program. One asks the player to guess a number based on "clues." The other involves a code that the player solves by putting numbers into an equation until the correct ones are determined. This program is rated for ages 10 to adult. It keeps track of the player's scores on different sections and will print out a certificate, declaring the player a Computation Cadet, or whatever level has been achieved. Older

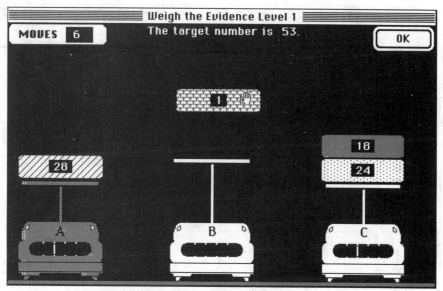

9-2 *This is a bit easier than the Tower of Hanoi puzzle.*

kids might find this rather patronizing, although the younger ones might actually enjoy it.

Number Munchers, shown in Fig. 9-3, is one in a series of Munchers programs from MECC. There are also Word Munchers, and even a Super Munchers Trivia game. The premise is the same in all—steer the Muncher around the screen to the correct answers, while avoiding being munched by a Troggle. They're cute, fun, and require some fast thinking. All in all, a good challenge for ages 8 and up.

Sierra On-Line's Ready, Set, Read features two friendly animated creatures, a monkey named Bananas and a talking jack-in-the-box. It introduces two-letter consonant and vowel sounds, rhyming words, recognizing some words on sight, composing words from parts of words, alphabetizing, and reading a simple story. It does so in a fashion that will probably hold the interest of younger children for quite a while.

Jack-in-the-box and Bananas both talk, with animated mouth movements so accurate a deaf lip-reading child was able to

9-3 *Oh, no! There's a Troggle about to munch you!*

understand them. They ask the child to point out certain words or
letter sounds. Every time the child gets one right, some sort of
animated "surprise" appears on the screen. Sometimes it's a
marching band crossing the screen, sometimes an airplane or
floating balloon. If the child clicks on the surprise, it does
something else unpredictable. This game is entirely mouse
driven. There are six activities in all, from finding two-letter
sounds, to reading the story. Figure 9-4 shows an example.

Parents can customize the speed at which it runs, whether or not
there's music, and even whether the letter "z" is pronounced
"zee," as it is in the United States, or "zed," as in most of the rest
of the English-speaking world. Ready, Set, Read comes with a
booklet that also suggests other non-computer activities to help
reinforce the new skills.

Other good "teaching" programs for the younger set include the
Stickybear series that, interestingly enough, is bilingual
Spanish/English. Your child could easily acquire the

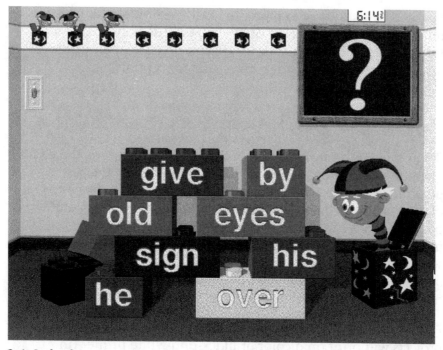

9-4 *Jack asks you to point out a word. If you click the right one, something fun will happen.*

fundamentals of a second language while having fun. ISM also has a bilingual bundle consisting of two storybooks about dinosaurs in English/Spanish or English/French. These are aimed at kids aged 3 to 8, and teach reading skills as well as correct pronunciation. The programs are animated with digitized human voices, and can print coloring-book pages with the child's own original stories about the same characters.

If bilingual means "two tongues," what's the word for four languages? On the Mac, it's Language Explorer, a new program from Nordic Software. The program includes word sets for English, French, German, and Spanish. These are presented in 42 topic areas with more than 500 animated picture tiles. You select a topic, and a language, and match the pictures to the words by placing them in the correct frames. Correct answers earn a "whooping" sound, while incorrect ones get the "try again" buzzer. Use Language Explorer to teach vocabulary, to brush up on what you already know or, if you're a true polyglot, as a multilingual race against time. This program is appropriate for anyone from age 5 to adult, according to its publishers.

The one to pick

If you could only buy one piece of child-oriented software, there's no question which one it should be. Kid Pix is absolutely the best program ever written for children aged 2 to 12. (Adults like it too.) It's a paint program, but it's a lot more fun than "grown-up" paint programs. Kids can paint in color using tools like the drippy brush, fractal brush, rubber stamps, and dozens more. Each tool has its own sound effects, and you can turn the sounds off when they get annoying. There's a small-kid mode that hides the Menu bar, making it less dangerous to leave your child alone with the program.

Figure 9-5 shows a picture drawn with the scratchy brush. Art projects will print on a color or black-and-white printer (in appropriate gray scale!). There are outlines to color and shapes to reveal by erasing for those times when they don't know what to paint next, but most kids immediately start creating their own masterpieces. By the way, this program is also bilingual. The menus and dialog boxes can be configured to be read in either English or Spanish.

Kid Pix Companion has more rubber stamps, more pictures to reveal, more outlines to color, silly sentences to illustrate, and a really neat feature that lets the kids turn their artwork into a slide show much like the fancy presentation packages grownups use. If your Mac has a built-in microphone, they can add a narration track along with the pictures and create a talking slide show, complete with Hollywood-style transitions between scenes. Sound effects and music are already part of the program, too. Figure 9-6 shows how the sounds are assigned.

Imager has packaged several sets of backgrounds and stamps to use with the Kid Pix program, under the name Kid Art. Among

9-5 *These drawing tools will inspire artists of all ages.*

9-6 *It might not replace Aldus Persuasion, but kids can create their own slide shows.*

the subjects represented are maps, highlights in U.S. history, sports, animals, monsters, and holidays. Since all Kid Pix files are saved in the PICT format, you could probably use these with another graphics program or as clip art for a newsletter or report cover.

Around the world

A study done a few years ago claimed that 10 percent of all the college freshmen surveyed couldn't locate the United States on a world map. Fifty percent couldn't find Brazil, Iran, or Korea. Over 90 percent couldn't locate Estonia, Libya, Honduras, or Tibet. If the same study is done about six years from now, the results should be very different, thanks in part to a fictitious lady criminal by the name of Carmen Sandiego. Brøderbund's Carmen series first appeared in 1985 and has mushroomed from a simple home-computer game into a TV series on PBS and a merchandising blitz worthy of Mickey Mouse. In the process, a total of over 2.5 million copies of the five Carmen programs have been sold.

Carmen is an ex-spy and leader of a gang of thieves who call themselves V.I.L.E. (Villain's International League of Evil). Players sign on as members of the Acme Detective Agency and chase Carmen and her henchpersons through time, around the world, or through American history. Along the way they uncover factoids about the countries they pass through. An upcoming Carmen game will place the junior sleuths in outer space, as Carmen goes intergalactic.

Despite the educational content, the games are fun and exciting. Each one comes with a resource book, like the *World Almanac*, or *What Happened When: A Chronology of Life and Events in America*. Players need to use the books to decipher many of the clues provided in the game scenarios.

The Carmen series features great graphics, including digitized photos like the one in Fig. 9-7 from the deluxe edition of Where

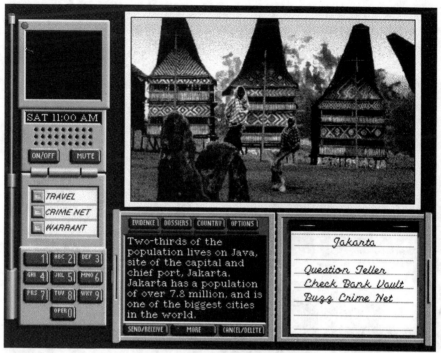

9-7 *Perhaps in the next version of Carmen she'll be using a Newton to keep notes and call headquarters.*

in the World is Carmen Sandiego. This game covers 45 countries on the disk version, and 60 on the CD-ROM version, which also includes authentic local musical backgrounds from Smithsonian/Folkways recordings.

As an Acme detective your goal is to identify the criminal, get a warrant, and catch up with him or her to make the arrest. You'll need to visit several countries each time. These criminals don't sit still for a minute. You'll be able to figure out where to go if you pay close attention to the clues. "She exchanged her money for pesos" tells you that the crook *du jour* is female, and is heading for some Spanish-speaking country. When you look at the travel options, the possibilities are Mexico, Myanmar, Norway, and the United States So you know your next stop is Mexico City.

Figure 9-8 shows the end of a round of Where in the World. Your crook has been caught. This time you've managed to identify him and get a warrant first, so you're a hero.

9-8 You caught another one! The Chief will be pleased.

Where in Time, shown in Fig. 9-9, sends you back through history in the Acme Detective Agency's Chronoskimmer 325i time-travel machine. Where in America's Past uses a similar time-travel machine. The basic game play is the same in all of the Carmen games. In the Where in Time version, you must know either the country you want to go to or the time period, preferably both. As Fig. 9-10 shows, you are offered a choice of four destinations.

In addition to the TV series, Brøderbund has licensed all kinds of Carmen merchandise. Carmen's young fans can be identified by their Carmen wristwatches, backpacks, T-shirts, and school folders.

9-9 *Time travel is easy, if you have the right tools.*

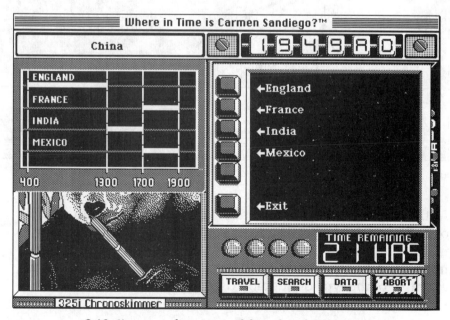

9-10 *You must choose one of these four destinations.*

The Carmen Sandiego series might be the best-selling geography games for kids, but they aren't the only ones. Swamp Gas Visits the USA and Swamp Gas Visits Europe are a couple of wacky adventures from Inline Design that feature a friendly little alien in a spaceship who travels from point to point on a map. He follows a different itinerary each time. You point and click to guide him around. The European version of the game is shown in Fig. 9-11. As you can see, it's reasonably up-to-date. All of the former Socialist Republics are properly identified.

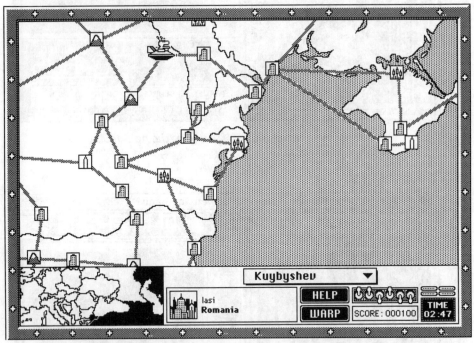

9-11 *Some of these places are way off the beaten track.*

At the beginner's level of the game you need only identify states or countries in Europe. At advanced levels, you'll be given city names and names of landmarks as well as countries. And you might be asked to answer trivia questions from time to time. An example of the type of question asked is shown in Fig. 9-12.

9-12 *If you give the wrong answer you lose a turn.*

At the end of each round of Swamp Gas you can enter the alien arcade and play one of three different arcade games, as shown in Fig. 9-13. The length of time you get to play is determined by how well you did on the previous round.

Kids learn about a different kind of travel in a simulation from MECC called Oregon Trail. If your child's school has an Apple II or Mac, there's a good chance that they've already played and enjoyed this game. But since it's never the same twice, it's still worthwhile for home use. In Oregon Trail, you are a pioneer, setting out with your family to make the trek from Missouri to Oregon. You have a certain amount of money for supplies for your trip, depending on what profession you've chosen to represent. You must choose a starting date for the journey. If you start too late in the season, you'll get caught in snow storms and end up like the tragic Donner party. You can purchase food at forts along the way, trade for supplies with other wagons you meet, or hunt for meat.

Now that you have completed your mission, what would you like to do?

Enter the
Alien Arcade™

Return to
Swamp Gas™

9-13 *There are three games in the alien arcade. You can only play one per round, though.*

The game shows a map and a diary of your trip, as in Fig. 9-14, and has icons you can click on to change the amount of rations you allow your family to use and the speed at which you travel. It's fascinating, and historically accurate. Even the weather is accurate for the dates shown. The Guide book will give you information about places you pass through and people you might meet along the way.

! Being a wealthy banker or doctor won't help you when your wagon axle breaks. Carpenters have a better chance of fixing broken wagons. Doctors, however, have a better chance of having the members of their party recover from broken bones and illnesses such as cholera.

Let's go exploring

Kids are curious. Like scientists, they'll try things just to see what might happen. For this reason, programs like Playroom and Treehouse are ideal. They contain lots of "educational" toys, but

9-14 *You could probably afford to increase the rations.*

the child discovers these on his own, and plays with them because they look interesting, rather than because a parent is sitting beside him saying, "Two and two are four; click on the bunny four times."

Brøderbund's Playroom is an example of an interactive environment. The child needn't be able to read to use the program, all that he needs to do is point and click a mouse, or find and press a letter on the keyboard. Doing so might turn on a sound, send an animated balloon floating across the screen, or select a word from a list. Figure 9-15 shows the main screen of the Playroom. Most of the items in the room will do something when the child clicks on them. The picture changes. The radio plays a song, and so on.

One of the more interesting Playroom activities simulates those vinyl stick-on picture boards. The child adds items to a predrawn picture. In the booklet that comes with the program, it's suggested that the parent ask the child to think in terms of

9-15 *Most of the things in the Playroom will do something when you click on them.*

making up a story about the scene he's creating. Another is the three-way "mixed-up" toy, shown in Fig. 9-16. It can make silly creatures, or have the sections aligned to make "correct" ones. The Treehouse has a different, but similar set of activities. Both are aimed at the pre-reader.

Older kids with a fondness for exploration will love Spelunx and the Caves of Mr. Seudo. Like Playroom and Treehouse, it's an interactive environment. There are lots of activities, mostly in the general area of science. Some are just for fun. Others will actually teach some aspect of science. One shows closeup pictures of planets from the Voyager mission. Another activity, shown in Fig. 9-17, uses the principles of gas spectrometry to show that different gasses will burn with differently colored flames.

There is a tree-growing experiment, and one that uses the physics of sound to determine how deep a cave is. It's shown in Fig. 9-18. There are musical games, animation machines, and a few "just plain" games, like Yodel Toasters, shown in Fig. 9-19. The little

9-16 This is the mixed-up toy.

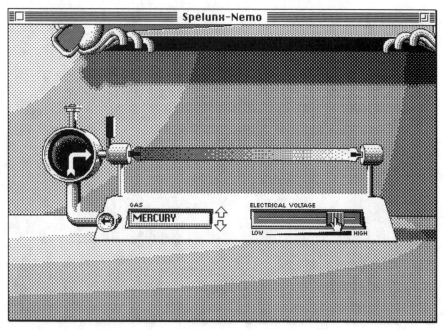

9-17 There are lots of gasses to test.

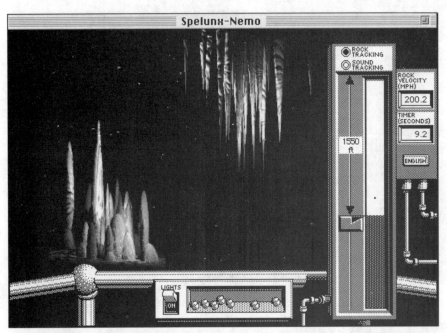

9-18 *You'll hear the splash when the pebble lands, after the appropriate delay.*

9-19 *If you return five in a row, he'll wave and give you an extra life.*

yodeler drops a slice of bread that you must catch with the toaster and bounce back to him. It's not as easy as it sounds. The toast slices bounce high. If you drop one, the game is over. If he catches five, you get a second life and can afford to drop a piece.

You can add new tunnels to the caves, if you know the secret of the Cave Builder machine, shown in Fig. 9-20. You need the program manual, both to know where to look for it, and to enter the correct combination on the lock.

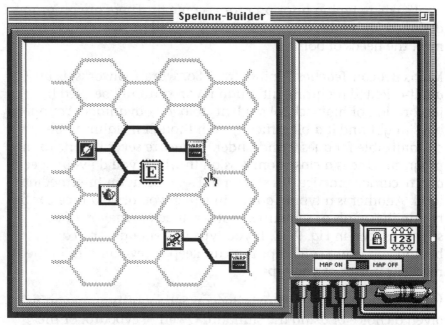

9-20 You can warp back and forth from one set of tunnels to another.

Many games require a password from the manual or from some sort of code device. If your family collects game manuals and other artifacts as readily as ours does, you need a place to keep them. A shoe box (or a more elegant plastic equivalent) is a good place to stash your decoders and manuals between game sessions.

Typing teachers

One of the easiest ways to improve your computing speed *isn't* to invest in a Quadra, it's learning how to touch-type. If you are still doing the two-finger tango on your keyboard or using the typing system developed by Messers. Hunt and Peck, you could find your speed increasing by 100 percent or more. Kids are beginning to need to know how to touch-type, too. As computers become more and more a part of the classroom environment, it becomes more and more important to be able to use them easily and efficiently. That's where typing tutor programs come in. There are programs designed for adults, and some clearly aimed at kids. Others try to meet the needs of both.

Mavis Beacon Teaches Typing, from Software Toolworks, is an adult-oriented program, although it can certainly be used by junior-high or high-school students to good advantage. Younger ones might find it a bit difficult, even though it claims to be customizable for ages 9 and under. There are several parts to the program. One is a classroom session in which you do your speed and accuracy practice. It's shown in Fig. 9-21 at an intermediate level. Another is a typing game, in which you drive a race car by typing the words or sentences that scroll across the top of the screen as seen in Fig. 9-22. If you type fast enough, the car behind you won't catch up. You can keep an eye on him in the rearview mirror as you type.

When you enroll in the Mavis Beacon School of Typing, you're given a choice of using the standard Qwerty keyboard, or the Dvorak keyboard, a different key layout that can improve your typing speed by as much as 20 percent or more, and your accuracy by a good 50 percent. Why? Back when the typewriter was invented, in 1872, its keyboard was alphabetical. The young ladies and gentlemen who were trained to use it (also called typewriters) kept having the keys jam together as they tried to use the machine. They were typing too fast.

The typewriter's inventor, Charles Latham Sholes, went back to his drawing board and came up with the most awkward

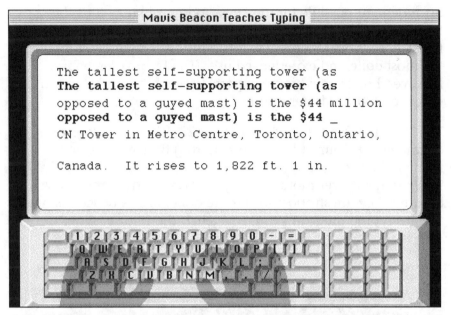

9-21 *The fingers on the keyboard move to show you which letter you're supposed to be typing.*

9-22 *If the other car passes you, type faster to catch up.*

arrangement possible for the keys. Today we know it as the familiar Qwerty keyboard. Since it was designed to slow down the typist, speeds over 75 or 80 words a minute are difficult for even the most agile and experienced user. The Dvorak keyboard, however, has enabled some experts to reach typing speeds in excess of 200 words per minute.

The Dvorak layout is shown in Fig. 9-23. It's a more logical arrangement. Your little fingers and ring fingers have one frequent key each, and the others are only used occasionally. The index fingers cover more territory and are used for more keys because they are stronger and more agile. Mavis Beacon is one of the few typing programs that will teach the Dvorak system.

9-23 *The Dvorak keyboard can be learned much more quickly than the Qwerty keyboard.*

Mavis also teaches the 10-key (adding machine) keypad, with a cleverly conceived activity that has you entering prices of items on a grocery-store cash register. If you make a mistake, or type too slowly, the item will go crashing to the floor instead of into the grocery bag.

The newest typing program, as of this writing, is Mario Teaches Typing, from MacPlay (formerly Interplay). Actually, you can choose Mario, Luigi, or the Princess . . . and run them through the three world levels as your typing speed increases. This program is really intended for use by younger kids, but in all honesty, I enjoyed it too and spent longer practicing typing with Mario than with Mavis. Figure 9-24 shows the middle of the three worlds. If you type fast enough, Mario can swim away and avoid being eaten by the fish. The music and sound effects are fun,

9-24 If you type too slowly, Mario is fish food!

although Mario's phony accent annoys me. The animation is terrific. It has the look and feel of a Nintendo game. The only problem is you're too busy concentrating on your typing to watch what's happening on the screen.

Actually, that's *not* the only problem. Mavis Beacon and most computer typing tutors let you decide whether to use one space after a period or two. Mario doesn't. Why do you care? Standard American typewriter letters look best if you use two spaces after a period because the type is monospaced. In other words, every letter is equally wide; for instance, the letter "l" takes up as much space in the line of type as the letter "m." Computer type, however, is generally proportionally spaced, and looks better with only one space after the period. So people who use computers need to learn to leave only one space. But with Mario Teaches Typing, and some other typing programs, if you don't leave two spaces every time you type a period, every letter you type after that is marked wrong, and your score goes down to the basement.

Save the World 101

So you want to save the world. Why not? You can have an ecological adventure without ever leaving your keyboard and mouse. There are two programs so far in the Eco-Adventures series from Chariot Software. One Eco-Adventure takes you to the rainforest (Fig. 9-25), the other to the world's oceans. Both come with stunning posters and comprehensive manuals. The rainforest adventure also includes a copy of *The Rainforest Book* from the Natural Resources Defense Council. These games will play in black and white or in color, and have nicely detailed graphics.

Your goal is more or less the same in both games: to stay alive. You must also try to photograph a particular item of the local wildlife. You gain extra points for photographing other interesting subjects. If you survive the rainforest or the ocean long enough to find your target animal, fish, or plant and photograph it, you'll be returned to the ranger station (or to port)

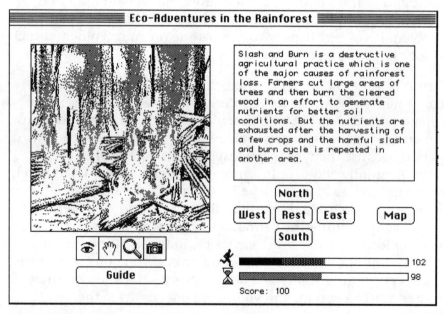

9-25 *Click on the icons for a closer look, help from the guide, or to use your hands to pick something up or climb a tree.*

for a press conference. You'll be able to get help along the way. In the rainforest game, there's a native guide who can help you with mapping and will scout for the animal you must photograph. You'll gain extra points by rounding up the poachers and leading them to the Rangers who will arrest them. You can also earn points and stop the logging, thus saving the rainforest by photographing a rare Sumatran Rhinoceros.

In the ocean game, you can get advice from One-Eyed Jack, an experienced sailor. (If he's so smart, why does he always fall overboard near the end of the game?) Your points will increase if you free the trapped dolphin (photograph him first!) and then photograph the fishing boat, or if you find the radioactive waste as shown in Fig. 9-26, or assist with the leaking oil tanker, the whaling boat, or the submarine.

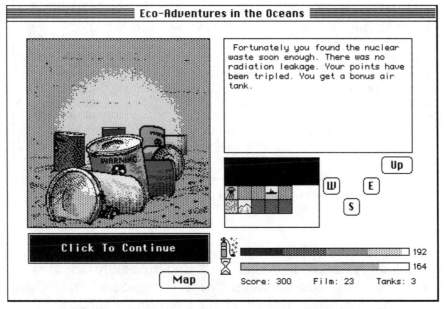

9-26 If you don't stay there too long you won't get poisoned.

If the Eco-Adventures get you interested in saving the world, as they are supposed to, your next step might well be to ask "How?" A charming freeware program called Kids Can Save the Earth

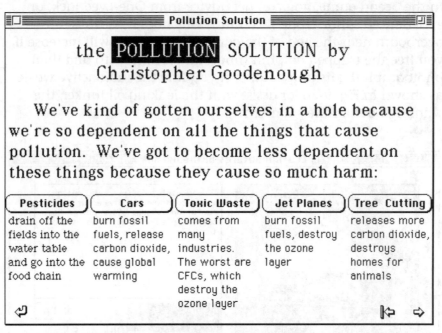

explains what the problems are and how we can help be part of the solution by recycling, using solar power, being careful how we dispose of toxic materials, and so on. Some good points are made. See Fig. 9-27 for an example. Most of the work on these stacks was obviously done by kids. Other HyperCard stacks with similar messages have names like Save the Planet and Save the Environment.

Pollution Solution

the **POLLUTION** SOLUTION by Christopher Goodenough

We've kind of gotten ourselves in a hole because we're so dependent on all the things that cause pollution. We've got to become less dependent on these things because they cause so much harm:

Pesticides	Cars	Toxic Waste	Jet Planes	Tree Cutting
drain off the fields into the water table and go into the food chain	burn fossil fuels, release carbon dioxide, cause global warming	comes from many industries. The worst are CFCs, which destroy the ozone layer	burn fossil fuels, destroy the ozone layer	releases more carbon dioxide, destroys homes for animals

9-27 Maybe we ought to listen to the kids a little more carefully.

These are just the tip of the iceberg of educational shareware. If you belong to America Online, you'll find incredibly rich and varied libraries of educational software. CompuServe and GEnie, although not as teacher-oriented, have reasonably good collections, too. Also, look into user-group libraries. There are often special interest groups (SIG) within a user group for professionals of one kind or another. The Boston Computer Society and the Berkeley Mac group (BMUG) both have huge collections of educational shareware and freeware.

Among the more interesting freeware educational tools are the Shakespeare stacks by Mark Zimmermann. These contain the full text of Shakespeare's plays and sonnets. An example is shown in Fig. 9-28. There are individual stacks for most of the plays and one for the sonnets, plus a huge stack that contains them all. (It's well over 5M of data, and should be used from a CD-ROM.)

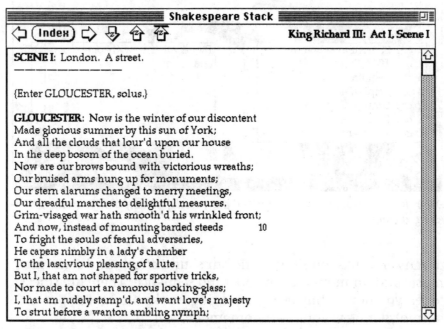

9-28 *Every word the Bard (or Bacon, perhaps?) wrote, in HyperCard.*

If you look long enough, you can find a HyperCard stack for just about anything you might want to learn, from Greek or Japanese to interpreting an EKG or understanding Mesopotamian art and architecture. There are stacks to teach safe boating, Morse code, and the Periodic Table. You can learn first aid on your Mac, or more than you ever wanted to know about the inner workings of the two-stroke engine.

You can even study bartending. Figure 9-29 shows a card from a stack called Tropical Drink Recipes. It comes with the recipes for

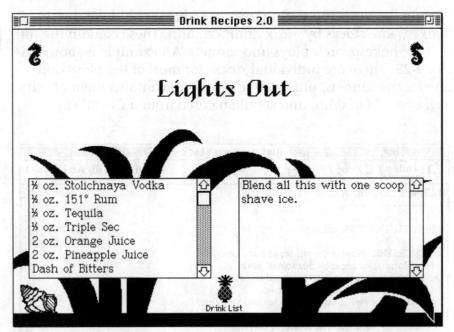

9-29 *Rum, vodka, tequila . . . this will put your lights out, and guarantee interesting dreams.*

dozens of drinks, plus authentic bar sound effects and some nice music and animation in the opening sequence. There are stacks to tell you how to buy a diamond ring, make origami paper animals, or brew your own homemade beer.

The oddest one I saw in the online files explains, step by step, how to tie a bow tie. Save it for formal occasions or send it to a preppie friend.

10
Multi-player games

The Mac is a tough but usually fair opponent, and always available when you want to play. Still it's sometimes more fun to play against a live opponent. Networks and modems have made multi-player games possible. You can sit at your Mac while your friend in the next office sits at his, and play any of dozens of different games over the AppleTalk network. If you have two Macs at home, you can hook them together with a very simple network, and play cooperative or competitive games with your family. Or, if you happen to have a modem connected to your Mac, you can play against a friend across town, across the country, or on the other side of the world (if you can afford the phone bills).

You gotta have connections . . .

If you're lucky enough to be playing Mac games in an office, you're probably already connected to a network and can skip this

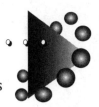

section. For you, playing a networked game is simply a matter of getting some colleagues to agree on when to play it, and logging in. If your luck holds out, the boss won't catch you.

But if you have two or more Macs in a home or small office that aren't networked, you should definitely wire them up. Not only will you enjoy the thrills of real-time multi-player gaming, you'll also be able to share printers and transfer files. Wiring a network is about as complicated as plugging in a couple of telephones.

Every Mac, from the earliest 128K machines to the newest Quadras, has AppleTalk networking capability. PowerBook Duos need a dock before you can network them, but every other machine has a jack on the back that looks like one of the two in Fig. 10-1. Networking is simply a matter of connecting one jack from each of your Macs together. If you've got a modem or serial printer like a StyleWriter, it's probably plugged in to one of these jacks already. Use the other one for your network. If you have a serial printer *and* a modem, you can get a Serial Switch at your computer dealer to add more jacks. If you have an AppleTalk printer (like most LaserWriters), you don't need this switch. The printer will join your new network, just like your game-playing family or office mates.

 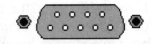 **10-1** *Network connections . . . the rectangular jack is found on only the oldest Macs.*

 Always make sure everything is turned off before you plug in or unplug any connectors. You could accidentally fry your Mac if you plugged into the wrong port or caused a spark with a live connector.

The AppleTalk signal has to be treated before it joins the network by running it through a *connector box*. The most popular ones are compatible with Farallon's PhoneNet system. Farallon boxes are available at most computer dealers for under $35, and come with complete instructions and an informative manual. Other PhoneNet-style boxes can be as cheap as $20. You can mix the Farallon and other brands; you'll need one for each computer or printer on your network. (Apple's own LocalTalk connector boxes cost about $50 each, aren't as good, and aren't compatible with other brands or standard cables. Save your money for shareware fees.)

Each connector box is a mouse-sized plastic gizmo with a short cord that plugs into your Mac, and two snap-in jacks like the one on the back of your telephone. Use the extension wires provided and run cables from each device on the network to the next—as we've done in Fig. 10-2. Depending on the brand of connector box, you might also have to snap a little plastic *terminator* onto the unused jack at each end of the line. If you need them, they're included with the boxes.

10-2 *These three Macs can talk to each other, and share one printer.*

You can purchase additional telephone wires from any electronics store (and most large hardware stores or drugstores), or build your own. Just make sure the ones you add have connections on the "outer" pins of the snap-in plug, usually color-coded yellow and black. You can also tap into unused telephone wires that already go through your home or office. In most cases, this is perfectly safe and legal. See the PhoneNet instructions, or a good book on networking.

Once all the Macs are wired up, all you have to do is give each one a *user name* (the name refers to the machine, not to the human user). This way AppleTalk will know which signals go to your computer and which go to the one in the next room. Obviously, each Mac on the network has to have a different user name. You can't just call them all "Macintosh" or "accounting department." Look upon it as a chance to be creative.

Figure 10-3 shows how the user names are entered. Open the Sharing Setup control panel in System 7 and type a convenient Macintosh name. In System 6, you do it from the Chooser desk accessory. When you close the window you'll be on the network, ready to play.

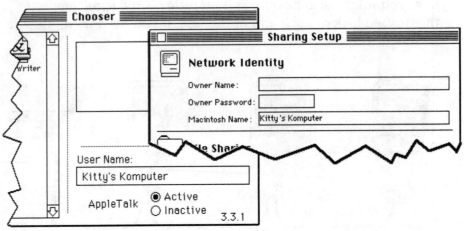

10-3 *Entering user names in System 6 (left) and System 7.*

Plug in and play

Sometimes a network is more than you need. If you have just one Mac, and you want to go head-to-head against your friend's (also non-networked) Mac, all you need to do is to get the two machines within a few feet of each other and plug one end of a standard 8-pin connector into the modem port of each Mac. (It's the same 8-pin connector, a mini DIN-8, that's shown in Fig. 10-1. By the way, the technical term for this kind of connection is *null modem*. You can borrow the cable from an ImageWriter II, if either of you has one.) Otherwise, your friendly local electronics or computer store will be happy to sell you a 6-foot cable with the proper connectors. Always make sure the computers are turned off before you do any plugging in or unplugging.

There's a certain advantage to both of you being in the same room. It's best if you can arrange things so you can't see each other's screens. Facing each other across a table is ideal. That way you can exchange comments, insults, and snarls while you play. Expert gamers refer to this activity as the "intimidation factor."

Games on the network

Once you get hooked up, one way or the other, you need something to play. Before you invest in new network games, check out a few of your old favorites. Spectrum Holobyte's 'Vette can be played in head-to-head mode, as can Battle Chess and Checkmate. WordTris, Faces, and Super Tetris can also be played on a network or by direct connection. Figure 10-4 shows how Super Tetris would be configured for a two-player, head-to-head game.

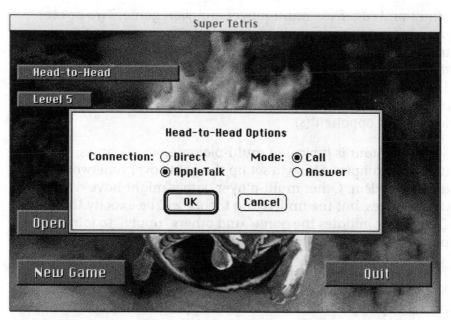

10-4 *One player will call or initiate the game and the other will respond.*

The Super Tetris set up is fairly typical of the kind of dialog box you'll have for any networkable game. When you're playing on a network, one machine has to be designated the *primary* or *originator* or *caller*. The reason for this has to do with how the communications are passed back and forth between the two Macs. One has to be "in charge." It doesn't matter which, unless one Mac is a lot "smarter" than the other. If you have an SE, and your friend has a Quadra, let the Quadra do the work. If the machines are relatively equal in terms of speed, it makes no difference at all.

> In most cases, you need two separate master copies of any game you're playing on a network, since most use a form of copy protection that polls the network for other active games with the same serial number. Making a back-up doesn't help here. Unless you've purchased a game that comes with disks for two players, like Minotaur from Bungie Software, you'll need a second master.

Lost in the labyrinths

Minotaur is a terrific multi-player dungeon game. Two or more players (up to seven in all) on different computers are thrown into a huge, randomly generated labyrinth that is loaded with the weapons, armor, and spells they'll need to defeat each other. There are monsters in the maze, too, but they're indestructible . . . and you're not. You can only attempt to avoid them while trying to kill your opponent(s).

Since Minotaur is typical of multi-player modem games, we'll use it as an example of how to set up the game over a network and/or modem. Other multi-player games might have different dialog boxes, but the underlying theory will be exactly the same. One player initiates the game, and others "apply" to join. The player who starts the game selects them or invites them in.

To set up an AppleTalk game, select Gather AppleTalk from the Minotaur pull-down menu, as shown in Fig. 10-5. The names of the other players on the network will appear in the dialog box.

```
┌─────────────────────────────────────┐
│ Minotaur                             │
├─────────────────────────────────────┤
│ One Player Exploration     ⌘E        │
│                                      │
│ ✓Ignore Serial Port                  │
│ Begin Serial Game          ⌘B        │
│ Serial Port                      ▶   │
│ Serial Baud                      ▶   │
│                                      │
│ Gather AppleTalk Game      ⌘G        │
│ Join AppleTalk Game        ⌘J        │
└─────────────────────────────────────┘
```

10-5 One player will "gather" the game. The others select "join" to add their names to the roster of available players.

Click on each to add them to the game, as shown in Fig. 10-6. Click OK when done to start the game. Multi-zone networks can also support the current version of Minotaur. If you are on a zoned network, you'll see a pop-up zone menu over the list of available players, as in Fig. 10-7. When you select a different zone, the names of characters waiting to play on that zone will appear. As

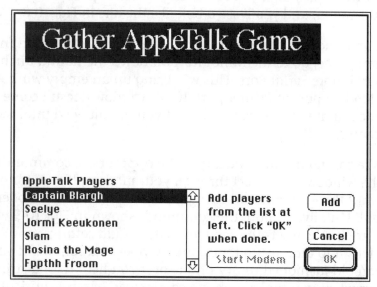

Gather AppleTalk Game

AppleTalk Players

Captain Blargh
Seelye
Jormi Keeukonen
Slam
Rosina the Mage
Fppthh Froom

Add players from the list at left. Click "OK" when done.

[Start Modem]

[Add]
[Cancel]
[OK]

10-6 If you're gathering the game, you'll see this dialog box. Select a player and click Add to put him in the game.

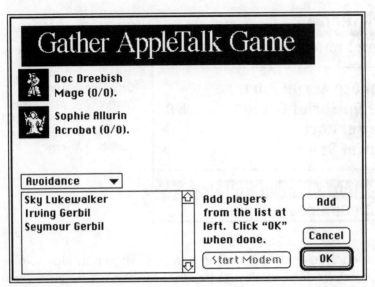

10-7 *Zoned networks appear on a pop-up menu. Players you've already added to the game are shown with their icons and record.*

you add new players, their icons, names, character types, and records are displayed. If you're waiting to join a game, select Join from the menu, and you'll see a box like the one in Fig. 10-8.

To set up a modem game, or a two-player direct-connection (null modem) game, go to the Minotaur pull-down menu and uncheck the item Ignore Serial Port. This will bring up an empty window titled Modem port or Printer port. If this window doesn't come up, the Mac might not realize which port you are plugged into. Use the menu to switch ports.

If you're calling another Mac, type the appropriate commands into the window to connect through your modem. If you're not sure what the AT command strings should be, check the modem manual. Usually, though, the commands shown in Fig. 10-9 will do the trick. ATZ resets the modem to its default settings, and ATDT tells it to dial, using tones, the number that follows. If you have an old-fashioned rotary phone or if you hear a long string of clicks when you make a phone call instead of semi-musical beeps, use ATDP for pulse dialing.

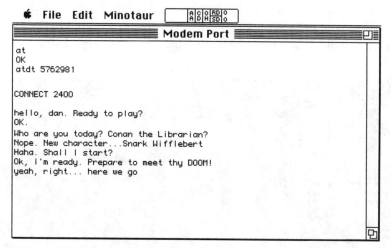

10-8 *After you've been added to the game, this box will disappear. Instead, you'll see one that tells you you're in.*

10-9 *Use the intimidation factor over the modem, too.*

The other Mac should already have Minotaur up and running and should be waiting for your call. Since you have already called (by voice) to arrange this, you and the other player should have agreed on a *baud rate*. This is the speed at which the two modems send data back and forth, and it should be set from the pull-down menu before you place the call. Generally, the fastest speed both can use is the best, although if you have a noisy telephone line, switching to a slower speed might help you maintain a connection.

If you are the recipient, and the modem doesn't automatically answer the incoming call (most will do so), force it to answer by typing ATA when you hear the phone ring or see the word "Ring." You can also place a call to your opponent with a regular telephone and then, when you're through talking, force the modem connection by typing ATD without the number. Have him type ATA. As soon as you hear the modem pick up the line, hang up the handset. The two modems should be fooled into believing they're connected. In any case, when you have a connection you can type messages back and forth to each other or just start the game.

Figure 10-10 shows what the playing field actually looks like. The game screen shows the maze map on the right, and your collection of armor, weapons, spells, and other objects at the left, as well as your targeted opponent, and the last four messages in the game. Important information might be displayed there.

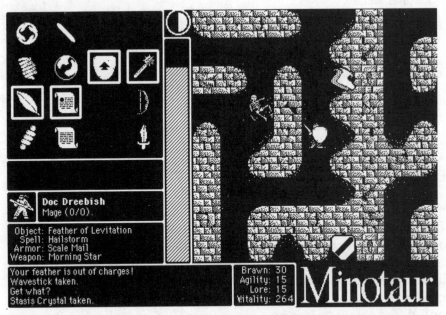

10-10 *Grab all the goodies you can. Otherwise your opponents will take them. If you have more than you can carry, drop the least useful ones first.*

While you're playing the game, you'll see your opponent's icon on your screen in the target box, and he'll see yours. In a two-player game, your opponent is always the target (and you are always his), but in a multi-player game you must designate a target for your offensive actions. If the target player appears on your screen, he will have a blinking crosshair drawn over his icon. To switch targets, use the tab key. You will cycle through the available players according to the following priority:

1. visible on your screen;
2. not dead, paralyzed, concealed by an illusion or rendered invisible;
3. not designated friendly.

Since temporary alliances tend to form during play, you can designate certain players as friendly to keep them from being targeted every time they appear on your screen. Mark friendly players by typing a plus when their icon appears.

To cycle through all players, whether friendly, dead, or otherwise, hold down the Shift key as you press Tab.

Remote robotics

RoboSport is one of those games you either love or refuse to bother with. It's complicated. In fact, it has nearly as much of a "learning curve" as SimLife or A-Train. The folks at Maxis must think we're all genius-level game players. But players who get into it, including my teenaged sons, consider it one of the best games ever written. It's a battle-strategy simulation, played out as a series of war games between two to four teams of robots. The game can be played human vs. computer, but more importantly, it can be played human against human by modem, direct connect, or over an AppleTalk network. Up to four human players can compete in a networked game.

In RoboSport, teams of robots battle each other in any of five different "sports": Survival, Baseball, Capture the Flag, Hostage, and Treasure Hunt. Figure 10-11 shows a game of Treasure Hunt. Any of the four teams can be controlled by a human or by the computer. There are three steps to the game. In Setup mode, you can choose from over 2,100 preset battles or customize the battle by choosing the arena, teams, and sport yourself. In Edit mode,

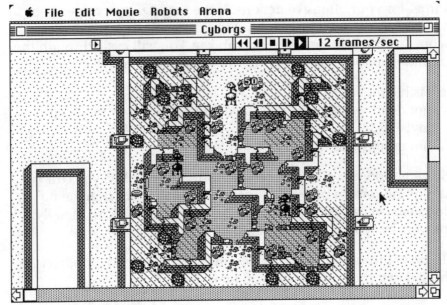

10-11 *Score points by finding the "gold coins" before the other side does.*

you program your team's moves for a certain time period, usually on the order of 10 to 15 seconds. All the moves of all the teams are combined into a movie.

In Movie mode, you play back the action from various points of view, add up your damages and assess your strategic position, and plan another set of moves. Then you return to Edit mode and program them, watch the results, and so on until there's a winner. Programming isn't complicated. You simply point and click. To make the robot shoot, click on the Aim and Fire button, and then on the target.

Armor Alley is an older game that runs in black and white or in 16 colors. It's still around, though, and still being played and enjoyed by military simulation fans. It runs over a network, by direct connect, or by modem for up to four players. It requires a combination of action and strategy. As shown in Fig. 10-12, you're fighting a war in the desert. Your opponent has equal strength and your goal is to try to eliminate him. His goal, alas,

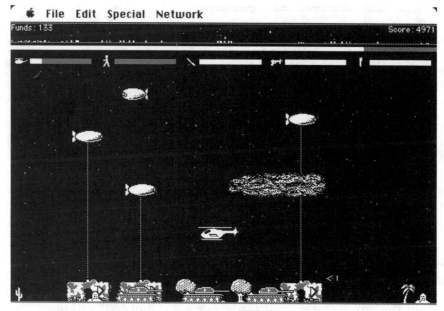

10-12 *Use your choppers to take out his tanks.*

is to do the same to you. You each have a certain amount of
money to spend for additional troops or equipment. How you
spend it, in many cases, determines the outcome of the game.

Bowled over by Bolo

Bolo is one of the most popular network games ever, for large
networks. It's a tank battle set on an island, and it supports up to
16 players at once, each using separate computers and monitors.
It's not a mindless shoot-em-up, but requires planning and
strategy. On the Mac it plays in black and white or in color. It
runs in UNIX as well, and is very popular at universities and in
businesses that run UNIX on workstations. Figure 10-13 shows
the network set up, including UNIX nodes.

Since Bolo is a multi-player game, team work is vital to your
success. You can't hope to defeat 15 other armies, but if you form
alliances with other players you'll have a better chance of

Welcome to Bolo, the multi-player
tank battle game. Please choose
your network connection method:

○ Single Player (no network)
○ Serial Port
◉ AppleTalk
○ UDP/IP
○ UDP/IP Multicast   [OK]

☐ Skip this dialog next time [Quit]

10-13 *The last two choices on the menu let you play against UNIX machines on a network.*

success. Also, if you get into trouble, you can shout for help and have your allies come and rescue you.

When the game starts, your tank is on a boat at sea. You must land it, either coming ashore on the beach (dangerous) or sneaking up one of the many rivers or canals on the island. In Fig. 10-14, Diving Dude is trying to get ashore, while Dan's trying to stop him. There are enemy pillboxes all over waiting to shoot at you. Since they can only shoot in one direction at a time, it generally takes two or more tanks to capture one. If you do capture one, you can then move it to territory you control and it will shoot at your enemies. You can also lay mines, and build your own bases. And of course you can send messages back and forth, as in Fig. 10-15. The game will also broadcast a commentary on what's happening. You have an unlimited supply of tanks (or lives), but only one at a time.

There are refueling stations that you can easily capture that will replenish your weapons and armor as well as fuel. The object of the game is to capture all of the refueling stations.

Once you've played Bolo for 10 minutes or so, it's easy to understand why it's so popular. At the lowest level it's easy to understand, but as you get into it you begin to realize how much more there is to it. In effect, it grows with you. The game is well documented, with an illustrated manual as well as several other

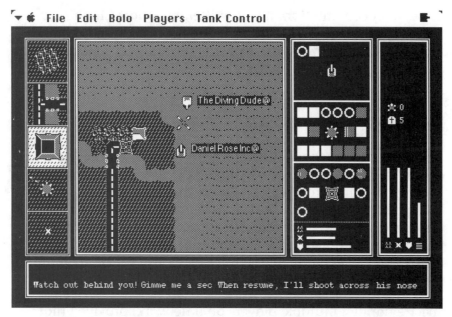

10-14 *Players can send messages to their allies to agree on strategy.*

10-15 *Send messages to some, all, or just one player.*

pieces of documentation. It was written by Stuart Cheshire, a
Ph.D. candidate at Stanford (probably post-doc by now . . .).
There's a $25 shareware fee, which is certainly reasonable for a
game this good. Pay the man.

Spectre Supreme

Before Bolo got such wide distribution, Spectre was the "game of
choice" for large groups of networked players. Spectre bills itself
as a "cyberpunk battle world." You're in a customizable tank-like
battle craft, a sort of wedge-shaped thingie that looks like the box
the game comes in. (The box doesn't fit on the shelf, and gets
thrown away immediately. The manual, also an odd shape,
doesn't fit conveniently on the bookshelf or in the game manual
file. Why they do this, I don't know.)

Spectre handles multiple players on a network, provided that
each player has his own copy of the game. There is serial number
protection, so you can't cheat and give copies to your friends. The
economical way to handle multi-player participation is to share
the cost of a LAN pack, which will give you two sets of game disks
for only slightly more than the cost of one. Setting up a network
game is shown in Fig. 10-16. Each player must choose a team,
either red or white.

Game play consists of choosing a vehicle from the dialog box
shown in Fig. 10-17, and then going into the arena shown in Fig.
10-18. The graphics are not spectacular, as they are in Stellar 7,
an almost 3D single-player game that is otherwise quite similar.
Spectre can be played as a single-player capture-the-flag game,
as well as a variety of multi-player games. Spectre Supreme, the
newest version, adds new weapons, new hazards, new multi-
player games, and better inter-player communication. It's not
compatible with the original Spectre, though.

Pararena—Soccer on skateboards

Well, it's not exactly Soccer, since you can pick up the ball, and
they're not exactly skateboards. They run on a frictionless air

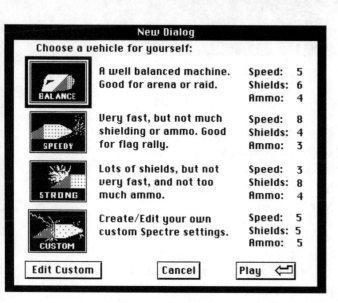

Network Options

Scenario:

Arena
Base Raid
Flag Rally
BitBall
Maze

Play for 10   ☒ Points
                 ☐ Minutes

Wait for other players, then
click Ready. Click Exit to
leave before other players
have joined.

Players:

Name   Team

Catris   Red

DanDude   White
Diver   Red
Krystal   White

Single Zone Mode

Ready   Exit

10-16 *Teams assemble on the network.*

New Dialog

Choose a vehicle for yourself:

BALANCE	A well balanced machine. Good for arena or raid.	Speed: 5 / Shields: 6 / Ammo: 4	
SPEEDY	Very fast, but not much shielding or ammo. Good for flag rally.	Speed: 8 / Shields: 4 / Ammo: 3	
STRONG	Lots of shields, but not very fast, and not too much ammo.	Speed: 3 / Shields: 8 / Ammo: 4	
CUSTOM	Create/Edit your own custom Spectre settings.	Speed: 5 / Shields: 5 / Ammo: 5	

Edit Custom   Cancel   Play ⏎

10-17 *Choose your vehicle from the ones shown or customize it.*

cushion, and the "stadium" is shaped like a bowl. Pararena is a
terrific game for two players. John Calhoun's game started out as
shareware several years ago, and is still around in that form. But
it was picked up by Casady & Greene, who provided money and
incentive for many improvements, and the commercial version is
well worth the price. For one thing, you can make network-only
copies for your friends or coworkers from your original disk. They

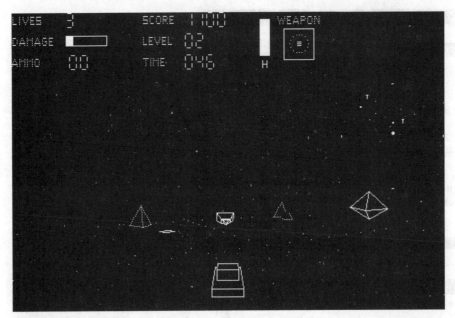

10-18 *The graphics are minimal, but help keep it a fast game, since screen redraws are so easy.*

won't be able to practice unless they buy their own copies, but you'll be able to compete with them over your network. Use the dialog box shown in Fig. 10-19 to set up a game. If you're playing on the network, click the network icon and the Mac will poll the network to see who's ready to play against you.

Play is controlled by the mouse. You have to try to block your opponent's goal shots and gain control of the ball so you can either kick it or throw it into the goal. Whenever a goal is scored, there's an (optional) instant replay. Because of the way the game is drawn, it's impossible to take a screen shot of the action, but Fig. 10-20 shows the shareware version, which looks similar but isn't networkable. Pararena is ridiculously addictive, and a lot of fun. In addition to the network opponents, you can play against the characters shown in the set up. Try to defeat them all in a tournament.

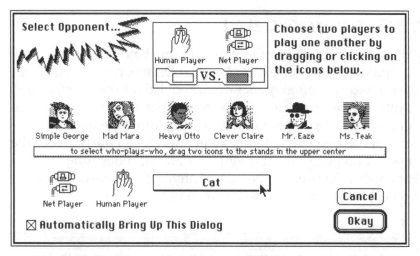

10-19 *The set-up box is the same for Pararena whether you are playing a single-player game or against a networked opponent.*

10-20 *The two players were jockeying for control of the ball when we stopped the game to take a screen shot.*

Games by modem

All of the online services offer games of one kind of another. Trivia is a popular activity on GEnie, America Online, and Delphi. Multi-player interactive trivia games are scheduled for the evening hours and attract players of all ages. Delphi's Trivia Quest (TQ) has had 50 or more people playing at once in regularly scheduled tournaments, and exchanging comments during the game as they compete for a prize, which might be a T-shirt, coffee mug, or some other goodie. TQ can also be played anytime, by one or more players. A TQ anytime game is shown in Fig. 10-21.

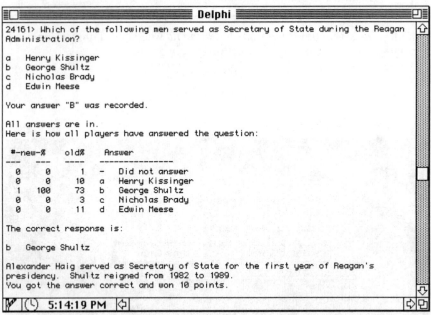

10-21 *All of the online services have games of one kind or another.*

America Online's conference rooms are limited to about 20 players each, but there are frequently several games of different kinds of trivia (movies, music, etc.) going on at once. Experienced players take turns hosting the games, and awarding prizes of free online time.

Word games are popular, too. Many Delphi users are addicted to Scramble, a game much like the board game Boggle. You have

16 letters from which to make as many words as possible in the time allowed. Words score points according to their length. In addition to trying for the highest scores, players compete to see who can find the longest word, or simply make up silly sentences out of the words they find. Since the game is played in a conference format, it's possible to chat during or after a round.

America Online players have their own word games, including some in which you must guess a word from clues, or try to find a common theme based on several one-word clues.

CompuServe has a full menu of games online, including some that are in their basic services area and don't incur an extra charge for playing. Since Prodigy doesn't offer real-time interactions with other players, its games are all played against the computer.

All of the services have some form of fantasy role-playing game (RPG) in process. America Online's Red Dragon Inn is a live conference area for role players who attend conferences at the Inn in character, and even engage in real-time mock battles. The Duel of Swords is run in a separate "room" of the inn, and pits two players against each other in a sword fight. The moves are determined by the contestants and sent to the referee who announces the outcome of each move according to an elaborate matrix of possible attacks and responses. Figure 10-22 shows an exchange in the Duel.

Poker is popular on Delphi. The interactive poker games are among the best online games anywhere, and the Thursday-night poker tournament attracts as many as 50 players at a time. There are 5 different card games that can be played at the poker tables, including Five and Seven Card Stud, Draw Poker, Straight Poker, and Texas Hold 'Em. Figure 10-23 shows a hand of Seven Card Stud, played against three of Delphi's robot players, all relatives of Max the Vax, the Delphi mainframe.

The bottom line to all of this is that no Mac is an island. Just because you're playing a game on a computer doesn't mean that you can only play against the computer. You can hook up with one other player directly, use a LAN to reach several, or find dozens of fellow gamers in an online conference. Competing with your family and friends is fun, and adds a new dimension to computer games.

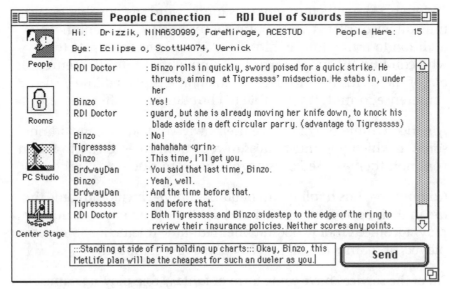

10-22 *The Duel of Swords is played most evenings on America Online.*

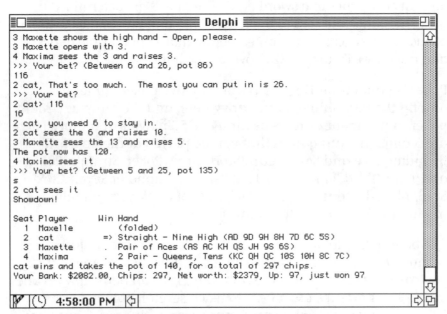

10-23 *I should have raised that last bet.*

11

Games on CD-ROM

If you've played any of the current crop of disc-based games, you've had the experience of doing a multi-disc install. A really "big" game, like King's Quest VI can take 15 minutes or more to install. You might as well be putting in PageMaker 5 or WordPerfect. Now, suppose you could play a huge game—color, sound effects, full-stereo score, QuickTime movies, the works—just by clicking on an icon. No dreary installers, no shut down . . . turn off the INITs . . . restart . . . install . . . restart again sequence . . .. Wouldn't it be great?

It's here, it's called CD-ROM, and it really is great. The alphabet soup stands for compact disc—read only memory. To use one, you need a CD-ROM player. Your Discman won't do. Audio disc players are not quite the same as data disc players, although there are many CD-ROM players that can handle musical discs, too.

The big advantage to CD-ROM is its storage capacity. A single disc can hold more than 600M of information. CD-ROMs are used for storage of fonts, clip art, photographs, and software, notably games. There are dozens, even hundreds, of CD-ROMs available for the Mac, with new ones coming out frequently. As of this writing, CD-ROM games are a bit more expensive than disc-based games, but that's likely to change as more game publishers get used to producing them, and as the game playing public (that's you) gets used to expecting stereo sound, color QuickTime, and so on.

Choosing a CD-ROM player

There are two differences between ordinary CD players and CD-ROM players. The first is that musical disc players lack the error-correction circuitry and SCSI interface necessary to talk to the Mac. The second difference is access time. The Mac can accept data much faster than your ears can listen to music. So a CD-ROM reader needs to be able to access data fast, and transfer it at a much higher speed than it would play an audio disc. Access times around 200ms (*microseconds*, or thousandths of a second) and data transfer rates of up to 330K per second are currently about the top of the line but, as with everything else in the computer industry, tomorrow's CD-ROM players will be smaller, faster, smarter, and probably less expensive than today's.

To run a CD-ROM game successfully you need a player with a minimum of 150K/second sustained transfer rate. Of course, faster is better. You'll see smoother animation with a faster drive.

Before you buy a CD-ROM player, check to make sure it has these attributes:

- a door that closes over the drive to keep dust out of the mechanism. A self-cleaning lens is a convenient, but expensive, feature.
- An easily set SCSI address. Some drives use internal dip switches, which are harder to set. Others use an external rotary switch.
- External SCSI termination. You have many more options in

fitting the player into the SCSI chain if there's no internal terminator to contend with.

- Audio CD compatibility, with appropriate software included. It's not necessary, but if you like, you can listen to music while you work on your Mac. Also, make sure there's a volume control.
- RCA preamp jacks if you want to hook the player up to external speakers for better sound. Otherwise, you're stuck with just the headphone jack.

Multi-session compatibility is on the way to becoming an important feature for CD-ROM players. It's of interest to you if you ever intend to use the drive to display the contents of photo-CD discs (Kodak's new image-storage medium). Ordinary "clip-art" photo-CDs are mass-produced, a disc full of images all at once. The new Kodak photo-storage system creates discs for you out of your own pictures, taken with your Nikon or whatever. It's "paperless" photography. You can view your photos on the screen of your Mac, use them in graphics or desktop publishing applications or in desktop video projects, or transfer them to videotape. You can even make prints on your color inkjet printer.

But since the CD-ROM can hold more pictures than you took on your trip to Disney World, when Kodak prepares the disc they leave the directory in a form that can be added to. When you shoot more pictures, you send the disc back to Kodak and they add the new ones to the existing disc. That's where "multi-session" comes in. The disc has been written to be used for more than one session. Some CD-ROM players can't deal with this. Some can. It seems to be the direction that photo-CD is going in, and it might be worthwhile to look for a player with this capability, even if you have no immediate plans to get into "paperless photography." (It's the ideal medium for taking pictures of the Christmas party in the paperless office.)

There's one more thing you need in order to use a CD-ROM player efficiently—extra caddies. When you put a disc into a CD-ROM player you must place it into a caddie first. The caddies look a little bit like the plastic cases the discs are usually sold in, but they're mechanically quite different. They have a sliding metal shutter somewhat like the ones on floppy disks. It moves aside when you insert the caddie into the player so the laser beam can read the disc. Your CD-ROM player probably came with one caddie, perhaps even two. Additional ones can be bought, at inflated prices, from your local computer store, or much less expensively by mail order. Look for ads in the back of your favorite Mac magazine. Be careful, though, there's at least one brand (Optical Access) of CD-ROM reader that uses a nonstandard caddie. Don't get stuck with something you can't use.

! Keep your frequently used CD-ROMs in their caddies instead of in the plastic "jewel boxes" they come in. You can buy plastic CD racks that hold 25 CDs vertically in their cases. The racks hold CD-ROMs in caddies just as easily; and keep them clean, out of your desktop clutter, and accessible, especially if you mark the name of the CD-ROM on the edge of the caddie.

Let's play!

Okay, you have your new CD-ROM player installed. You have the disc caddies, and you've gone down to the software store and put several hundred dollars worth of new goodies on your credit card. Time to settle down for some serious play, right? Wrong. Time to reconfigure your system and install QuickTime, if you don't already have it.

First things first . . . depending on how much RAM you have installed, you might need to remove all of your INITs (System Extensions in System 7) except the ones you need for the CD-ROM player and QuickTime. If you use an INIT manager, like the NOW Utilities Startup Manager or Baseline's INIT Manager, it's easy to assemble a CD-ROM game set with the minimum number of INITs enabled. If you have a machine with 5M or less of RAM, set the Disc Cache as low as possible (32K) in the Memory control panel, turn off the AdobeTypeManager, and remove any unnecessary fonts from the system. Now, you can play.

Sci-fi movies

There are two kinds of CD-ROM games: science-fiction stories and everything else. The "everything else" category includes the Sherlock Holmes detective games, educational CD-ROMs and shareware collections, as well as "seedy ROM" adult-porn discs, and a few that defy definition. Elaborate science-fiction scenarios are by far the most popular CD-ROM games on the market today. I don't know why. Perhaps it's just that the game designers who were the first to jump on the CD-ROM bandwagon were the ones most wrapped up in the future. Perhaps it's that the medium lends itself to futuristic animations, rather than medieval mazes. For whatever reason, many of the games currently released on CD-ROM require that you save the planet—your own or someone else's.

Iron Helix

In Iron Helix, from Drew Pictures/Spectrum Holobyte, the planet is an earth-like one called Calliope. Unfortunately, earth is preparing for war against an alien race and has equipped its spaceships with highly classified and extremely lethal weapons. One of these ships, the SS Jeremiah Obrien, is participating in war games. The weapon the Obrien carries contains a deadly virus that, unknown to the ship's crew, has attacked and altered their DNA. The ship's computers, no longer able to recognize the captain's and crew's DNA access codes, program themselves to attack Calliope. The virus kills off the crew, and the ship heads off to start a war that could end all life in the universe. Onboard the Science Ship Indiana you receive the Obrien's last call for help. As a science ship, you have no weapons, only three Darwin 5 zoological probes. Your only hope is to send one into the Obrien to try to interfere with the ship's computers and abort the mission before the ship reaches Calliope.

Inside the ship your probe can be steered by pushing buttons. The interface is shown in Fig. 11-1. You have a map of the level you're on, plus a video-camera view of whatever the probe is pointed at.

11-1 *There are three different map views available. Click over the map to see your options.*

To avoid the long wait when you're starting a game, the first time you play the game save it as soon as you get onboard the Obrien. Otherwise, you'll have to sit through the introduction every time you restart.

Once onboard, you must first locate some bits of crew DNA. Without it, you can't open certain doors or read the messages the crew has left on the computer view screens. There is quite a lot of nonhuman DNA scattered around. Don't bother to save it to your library. It does you no good. But, if you're persistent, you'll find the stuff you need. Figure 11-2 shows what a typical DNA scan looks like. If you find the assistant engineer's DNA, you can get into Aux. Eng. on level 2. Be sure to scan under the desk there. Sometimes, an initial scan of a room doesn't reveal anything, but if you move in closer, your scanner will pick it up.

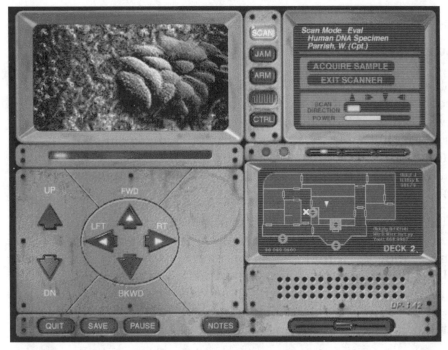

11-2 *This will help. You've found the Captain's DNA, and he has access to nearly everything.*

After you find the DNA you need, get as far away from the Defender as you can and start activating view screens. You can make him chase you down to level 6, and then take the elevator up to level 1 and have a bit of time before he gets back up again. Write down all the codes you get. You won't know, at least not at first, which one(s) you might have to use.

Iron Helix is a fairly difficult game only because you get zapped by the Defender so often, and have only three probes. You'll find yourself starting over quite a few times, but each time you'll know a little more about the geography of the ship, and where the most useful DNA samples are hidden. Eventually, you will find a screen that tells you how to get rid of the Defender. Once you've accomplished that, the rest is easy.

Spaceship Warlock

Suppose your planet was taken over during a pan-galactic war. Not merely plundered, or enslaved, it was kidnapped to some other part of space . . .. Wouldn't you want to get it back? Sure you would, even if it meant joining a band of the ugliest thugs ever to grace a Macintosh. Spaceship Warlock puts you onboard a space pirate ship under the leadership of the legendary Captain Hammer, battling the evil overlord Kroll, who has captured the planet Terra and hidden it deep in guarded Krollian-controlled space.

First, though, you need to find your way out of Stamboul. If you hang around dark alleys long enough, you'll get mugged. But that's what you want to happen. The mugger is none other than Hok Tuey, whose ugly green mug is plastered on "wanted" posters all over town. Defeat him with a few well-aimed blows to a sensitive spot. Search him before the cops arrive and get the credit chip. Without it, you can't collect your reward.

Now that you've got some credit, use it to get out of town. But remember what they say in the ads: "Let your fingers do the walking." Right. Find a phone. Call the spaceport and have them fax you a schedule and a ticket. Take a cab to the spaceport, and eventually you'll meet Captain Starbird and Stella on the Belshazzar. If you ask Stella about pirates, things will get interesting. Figure 11-3 shows what happens next.

You know what they say about pirates—if you can't beat them, join them. Good advice. You need to beat at least one, though. Go for Raskull's eyes and mouth, just as you did with Hok Tuey. Winner is the first to land 10 punches. Before you can fight him, you have to find him in the reactor room. Once you get to the engineering deck, there will be a map at the lower right of the screen, as in Fig. 11-4. Double clicking on it enlarges it.

If you get all the way to Terra, you'll be asked to make a speech. Can you say six good things about Terra? If the Terrans cheer six times, you can continue. Just don't insult them. They're sensitive.

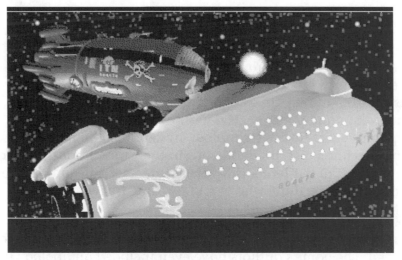

11-3 *The pirate ship attacks!*

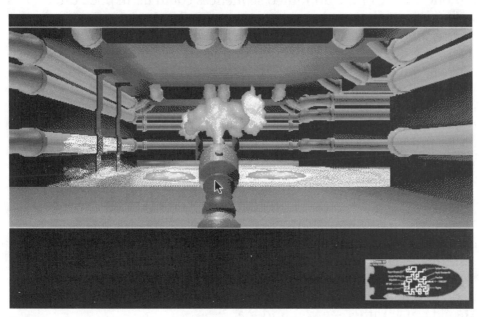

11-4 *Use the fire extinguisher, from the cabinet near the last gate, to cool off the deck so you can cross it.*

The Journeyman Project

According to Presto Studios, it's the world's first "photorealistic adventure game." The graphics are, admittedly, gorgeous; and the sound track is really more of a sound sculpture, with great music and sound effects. But the game stretches both imagination and patience. The Journeyman Project has taken the premise that earth's technology has enabled time travel. Like all new technologies, it's dangerous in the wrong hands. Your job, as a member of the Temporal Protectorate, is to safeguard history from sabotage by those who would use time travel to go back and alter the course of events.

There are a few problems with this game, one of which is its lack of speed. The game's authors have even included an apology in the introduction to the game. It's not so much their fault, although some of the animated sequences could be skipped after we've seen them once, but the fact that CD-ROM drives aren't fast enough to transfer the amount of data the game needs. And it admittedly runs very slowly on some of the older Macs. But the other problem is more serious. There seem to be some definite bugs in the game. I found a few while trying to play. Other people have reported the same ones and some that didn't happen for me. But despite these difficulties, it's an amazing game with wonderful music and beautiful pictures. In Fig.11-5 you are about to get into the transport to go from your apartment to your job. In Fig. 11-6 you've encountered a strange creature, one of many.

The plot is engrossing. There are rips in time. Someone has changed history and you have to identify the correct version and restore it . . . not just once, but at several times and places in the history of the galaxy. And you have a very limited time in which to do it. The people who did this don't want it undone, either. They'd much rather see you undone.

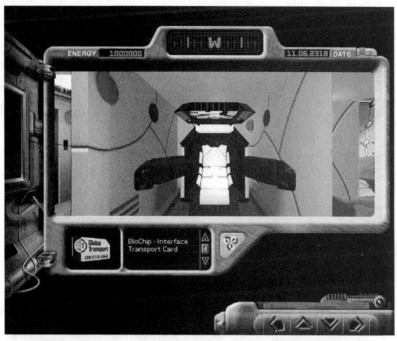

11-5 *There's the transport, waiting for you to climb in.*

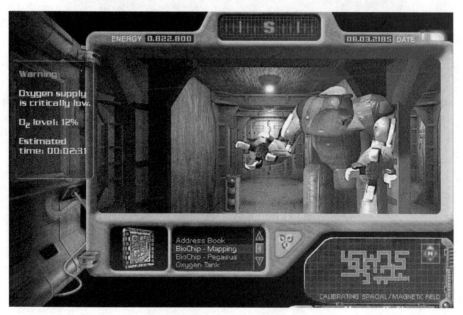

11-6 *Yikes! Here comes trouble!*

The cab ride from hell

If you're getting tired of roaming around the galaxy, here's a change of pace—a ride in New York City's strangest cab. You didn't notice the license plate—666—or the fiendish expression on the driver's face. (See Fig. 11-7.) Too bad, because now you're going on the cab ride to end all cab rides . . .. It'll cost you, either your money or your soul. Your goal is simply to survive, and it's not easy. Raul hits the high spots, like the Empire State Building; also some of the low spots . . .. How about a swamp full of dinosaurs for a low point? If Raul takes you to the Colosseum, expect to see the guy in Fig. 11-8, not the Knicks. You'll learn to appreciate the artwork in the lobby of the Empire State Building, if nothing else.

11-7 "I've got a special tour of New York for you."

11-8 *It's the Colosseum all right, but the Lions are playing instead of the Knicks.*

Elementary, my dear Watson . . .

"Tell me Holmes, in which of your many schools did you learn to be a detective?" ICOM's Sherlock Holmes series is now up to three volumes, with three complete stories in each. These are just plain fun. There are QuickTime movies with actors, sets, and costumes worthy of a feature film, plus a convenient point-and-click set of detective tools, shown in Fig. 11-9. You can send the Baker Street Irregulars to check out suspects for you, visit the promising ones yourself by calling for the carriage, browse the *Times* for clues, search your files, and gain access to the London Directory.

When you have gathered all the evidence you need, take your case to the judge. If you've gotten enough for a conviction, the case is solved. You'll need to answer the judge's questions correctly, though. If you can't, it's back to the streets to look for more clues.

Each of the stories on the three CDs in the series is complete, and actually taken from the stories by Sir Arthur Conan Doyle. They run better than most CD-ROM games, since they're less ambitious. They use QuickTime movies instead of full-screen animation, and

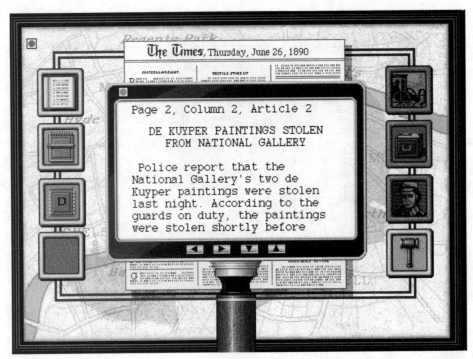

11-9 *Click on any of these icons to use Sherlock's detective "tools."*

sound other than with the movies is very limited. Still they're fun to play and don't demand too much mental effort.

Game, or gamy?

It's Virtual Valerie: the Director's Cut. Valerie's back (and her front, for that matter) on a CD-ROM with music, sound effects, and sophisticated 3D modeling. The plot is, well . . . .. Saying you bought this disc for the plot is like saying you read *Playboy* for the interviews. You meet Valerie at the door of her stylish (and unusually equipped) apartment. You interact with her in various ways, very few of which can be described in this book. Clicking on-screen objects causes amusing responses . . . .. It seems that word processors are not the only programs that use a mouse to set an insertion point.

PG
13

Graphic quality, dialog, and game play ranges from not-so-hot to somewhat interesting, if you're interested in that sort of thing. (There are, of course, some CD-ROMs sold in the back pages of magazines that would make Valerie look like a scene from a Disney movie.) If you've got a lot of money to spend and want a toy you can use to show your computer off to more-mature friends, get a copy. Otherwise—without even beginning to comment on the moral or 1st-Amendment aspects of Virtual Valerie—a magazine or video rental is a better investment. By the way, there's a panic screen, if your boss, mother, or 6 year-old comes wandering in while you're watching.

Games and more games

One of the great things about CD-ROMs is that they hold a lot of bytes, and they don't cost an unreasonable amount to produce. That makes them a good distribution medium for user groups with large collections of shareware. The BMUG (Mac user group in Berkeley, CA) and BCS•Mac (Boston Computer Society) shareware collections include hundreds of games, as well as lots of other useful stuff like fonts and clip art, utilities, and system software (everything except System 7.1, alas) and more. Arizona Mac User Group's BBS in a Box is legendary. They're up to Volume VIII now, with over 9,000 files that decompress to 1.4 gigabytes of good stuff.

The MACnificent 7.1 CD-ROM (See the terrific discount offer in the back of this book!) has 280M of games and educational shareware and freeware for all ages. The good thing about these is that most can be used right from the CD. You don't have to copy them onto your hard drive and expand them, they're all ready to play. This disc was complied by the National Home and School Mac User Group, the absolute authority on what's good in shareware and freeware games. Most of the shareware games in this book came from this disc.

Wayzata's CD Funhouse 8 is another great shareware game compendium. Since it runs on both PC and Mac platforms, it has a lot less in it than the MACnificent 7.1 disc. If you happen to have both a Mac and a PC, and one CD-ROM reader that they share, this would be an ideal purchase.

Even though you've probably heard this before, I'll say it again. Pay your shareware fees! Just because you bought the disc doesn't mean that you don't owe the author anything. The only people who make money from shareware compilations are the people who sell the discs. The program authors usually don't get a penny from the disc publisher. In many cases, they aren't even asked if they want their programs included. Shareware authors have chosen this method of distribution to avoid the hassles of dealing with big companies, not because they don't think their games are worth anything. In many cases, the shareware games are as good as, or better than, commercial ones. If nobody pays shareware fees, pretty soon there won't be anymore shareware, and that would be too bad.

Non-game fun stuff

Fun and games go together like pie and ice cream, but that doesn't mean you can't have one without the other. There are a lot of CD-ROMs that are fun to play with, but aren't games. For instance, there's Funny: the Movie in QuickTime. Its producers went out and asked 100 famous and not-so-famous people to tell their favorite joke, and videotaped the results. It's hilarious. You can watch the whole thing as a movie, or search for individual gags by topic, by rating (and yes, some are X-rated), or by who told them. Some of these stories are so old my grandfather told them. Others I heard here for the first time.

Get even more laughs from QuickToons. It's classic cartoons, like Betty Boop in Wonderland, Porky's Cafe, and more, in QuickTime format. All are public domain, so you can use clips to liven up your own multimedia presentations.

Kid stuff

Are there CD-ROMs just for kids? Yes, lots of them, and some are really terrific. Brøderbund was the first to take a favorite kid's book and animate it on a CD-ROM. Mercer Mayer's *Just Grandma and Me* is a delightful story about a day at the beach. Grandma and Little Critter swim, dig in the sand, and have a wonderful time. The pictures come to life as the child clicks on them. There are music and sound effects, too, and the story can be read in English, Spanish, or Japanese, as in Fig. 11-10. Brøderbund's come out with several more, including *Arthur's Teacher Trouble*, guaranteed to make every third grader grin, giggle, and groan at Arthur's troubles with Mr. Ratburn, World's Meanest Teacher.

11-10 *The starfish dances, a fish jumps out of the pail, and Grandma speaks Japanese!*

The Discis Kids Read series has about a dozen different titles, ranging from *Peter Rabbit* to *Scary Poems for Rotten Kids*. They're not as interactive as the Brøderbund books, but the stories are kid pleasers.

Cosmic Osmo and the Manhole are two remarkable interactive environments on CD-ROM. Like Spelunx and the Playroom, described in chapter 9, these are places for a kid and a mouse to explore.

Anybody can learn . . .

Educational CD-ROMs aren't just for kids. Atlases and encyclopedias of all kinds come in CD-ROM versions. One of the more unusual ones is called Small Blue Planet. It's an electronic satellite atlas, integrating a collection of maps with striking satellite images of Earth as seen from above. Cruise the world and zoom in at the click of a mouse. Figure 11-11 shows one of my favorite spots.

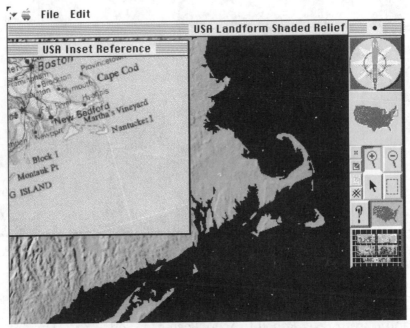

11-11 *There are views of Earth from all angles.*

There are CDs about every kind of animal from whales and dolphins to butterflies to dinosaurs. How about a tour of the San Diego Zoo, or Mammals of Africa? Creepy Crawlies covers 74 of the ugliest, most horrible creatures on Earth, from lizards to beetles. Beatles of a different sort appear on the Hard Day's Night CD-ROM, a QuickTime version of the film.

Art and music are well represented, too. There are discs of such works as Brahm's *German Requiem*, Beethoven's *String Quartet #14*, and many more, with pictures, background, and facts about the composers. A Survey of Western Art includes beautiful photographs of great paintings and sculpture and stories about the artists who created them. No matter what your interest, politics to poetry, there's a CD-ROM for you.

12

Toys for your Mac

It comes as little surprise that most Macintosh owners perceive their computer as having some sort of personality. Macs tend to get decorated with stickers and little stuffed mascots on top of the monitor, and many of them get nicknames. Customizing your Mac is a way of acknowledging that it's more than just a tool. And, of course, it makes it more fun to work on and play on.

There are lots of things you can add to the Mac to make it uniquely your own. Some, like screen savers, even help keep it healthy while they entertain you. Others, such as custom icons, might even make you more efficient. If nothing else, they'll give you something to smile about as you work.

Saving your screen, and your sanity

You could argue that a screen saver isn't a toy, it's a necessity. And, of course, you'd be right . . . up to a point. Computer screens are just like any other kind of television screen. A chemical phosphor is sprayed on the flat glass inside the front of the picture tube. When a beam of electrons hits the phosphor, it releases energy. The phosphor glows, creating the image you see. Overuse exhausts the phosphor, leaving dark spots that technicians usually call *burn-ins* or *ghosts*. You might have seen them at a bank's automated-teller machine, where the opening message screen is on most of the time. After a while it gets so badly burned-in that you can read it right through any other message on the screen.

Screen savers work either by dimming the screen, or by keeping something in motion on it so that different bits of phosphor are on at different times. If you could remember to turn down the screen contrast every time you stopped work for a few minutes, you wouldn't need one. But, that wouldn't be any fun.

The other thing that a screen saver does, in addition to saving the screen, is that it gives your Mac something to do when you aren't using it. The screen might be filling up with geometric designs, showing you a rainy city night, or a tank of tropical fish. It might be slowly melting your last page of text, or sending your spreadsheet swirling gently down the drain. It might be sending you messages in Klingon, or showing Mickey Mouse. There might be flying appliances, fractals, or a blizzard. Some screen savers are pretty; some are comic relief; and some are simply strange. But if you can save your screen and get an occasional laugh in the process, you've gained more than just a healthy monitor. You've helped your own mental health, too.

Berkeley Systems, although they've published many different kinds of programs, are best known for their screen savers. After Dark, first released in 1989, was the program that really started it all. It was the first modular screen saver, meaning that it could do more than one or two kinds of picture. (Pyro, from Fifth Generation Systems, gave its users a choice of digital fireworks or a floating clock.) After Dark's control panel, shown in Fig. 12-1, listed dozens of different kinds of pictures. After Dark gave us the tropical fish, string art, and flying toasters that made Mac owners

12-1 *To see a preview of any of the After Dark modules, click the Demo button.*

realize that their computers were just as much fun to watch as to use. The flying toaster, in all its chrome glory, is a sort of icon for the technological explosion that gave us the Mac itself.

Berkeley realized they had a good thing going when they started to receive copies of After Dark modules that users had written and/or drawn to go with the basic set. Soon there were dozens of "unofficial" After Dark modules, some as good as or better than the company's originals. Berkeley decided to have a contest for the best ones. The result of the contest was More After Dark, a second set of screen-saver modules that featured the contest winners.

Since then there have been two more additions to Berkeley's screen-saver software. Star Trek: the Screen Saver is a collection of 15 animated displays ranging from tribbles, to burrowing horta, to the sickbay monitors, and more. Join Captain Kirk on the bridge as you warp through the galaxy. Browse through Scotty's technical files containing the blueprints for the Enterprise,

Klingon battle cruisers, and other 23rd-Century hardware. Check out the Planetary Atlas showing dozens of strange new worlds, or test your knowledge of Star Trek trivia by taking the Starfleet Academy Final Exam. You can even send "subspace" communications to your coworkers with the Messages display in the official Klingon alphabet.

Berkeley's very newest screen savers use Disney characters. Mickey, Goofy, Donald, and the whole gang are there, plus scenes from some of your favorite Disney films. The Dalmatian puppies from *101 Dalmatians* are irresistible . . . even to a cat fan. Berkeley also has jumped onto the merchandise bandwagon with T-shirts featuring fish, toasters, or Boris the Cat from More After Dark. You can go to business meetings in style with an embroidered flying toaster necktie. How about an inflatable gold-winged toaster for your desktop or bookcase? They're silly, but they are cute, and they let the world know that you're taking care of those phosphors.

Are we having fun yet?

Now Fun, from the makers of Now Utilities, Now Up-to-Date, and Now Compress, is a package of three disks with all kinds of stuff to customize your Mac. There are FunScreenSaver modules that run alone or with After Dark, as well as FunColors, to let you change your Mac's color scheme, FunCursors and FunPictures to decorate your desktop, and FunSounds to attach to specific events on your Mac. The screen-saver application will also run any After Dark modules you happen to have. When you install it, it turns off After Dark (if After Dark is present) and adds After Dark's list of modules to its own. By the way, it's compatible in the other direction, too. FunScreenSaver's modules will add themselves to After Dark's menu.

If you also use Now Menus, all of your screen-saver modules will be available from a submenu when you select FunScreenSaver from the Control Panel submenu. You can also open the Control

Panel for FunScreenSaver to demo any of them, or to change parameters if necessary.

Both After Dark and FunScreenSaver give your Mac another kind of protection, too. They can both use password protection, so if you're out for lunch your boss or a curious co-worker can't come along and click your mouse to see what you were working on. This feature could be especially important if you were "working on" a game of some kind or revising your résumé.

Desktop toys

People who sit at desks all day are likely to have something that they play with while they're thinking. Some of us twirl pens, twist paperclips, or doodle. Some have actual desktop toys, like those little water-filled plastic things that send up interesting streams of bubbles when you flip them over. On my desk right now I have a little tiger, a squeaking penguin, and a wind-up mouse. The Mac has a desktop, so it ought to have some toys for its desktop.

One of the first things a new Mac owner does is to customize the desktop pattern. The trouble with the desktop patterns is that you're limited to 8-by-8 pixels. Patterns have to be very small. That is, unless you have something like Wallpaper. Wallpaper is an interior-decoration program for your Mac. It lets you create and display any number of large desktop patterns in 2 to 256 colors. You can also use any of the hundreds of desktop patterns that come with the program, or invest in More Wallpaper, Wallpaper Zebra for black and white monitors, Wallpaper Wraptures, or Wallpaper Light and Dark for a total of well over 1,000 different desktop designs. You can even subscribe to Wallpaper and get disks sent to you twice a year with more patterns! Each Wallpaper pattern fills a square 128 pixels on a side. Wallpaper installs easily as a CDEV. Its control panel is shown in Fig. 12-2.

Now Fun includes a utility called FunPictures that displays all kinds of images as desktop patterns. It will accept your Wallpaper

12-2 *These are a very small sample of the Wallpaper patterns supplied.*

patterns, as well as any PICT, EPS, MacPaint, StartupScreen, GIF (CompuServe's Graphic Image Format), or photo-CD image you care to open. The program comes with a few sample images, but the main point of this one is to bring in your own favorite pictures. Essentially, it's a graphics viewer that works in the background so you see the picture you have selected whenever the viewer is active. You can return to your standard desktop at any time by unclicking the Activate box in the FunPictures control palette, shown in Fig. 12-3. The map behind it is one of the sample desktop pictures. It's even better in color!

! If you're creating your own full-screen pictures to use as desktop patterns, you'll find it's much more efficient to save them as PICTs. They'll take up less storage space than in any other format. If space is a problem, use Now Compress to compact the files. Now Fun can automatically uncompact the one you're using while keeping the rest of the art files small.

There are other interesting things you can do to your desktop, too, but here's one you can do to someone else's. If you are on a

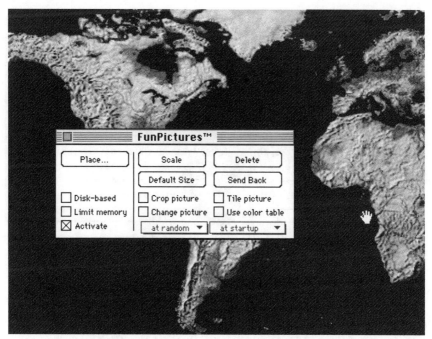

12-3 *This one is even more beautiful seen full-screen in color.*

network, look for an application called NetBunny. Your local user group or online service will probably have it. To use NetBunny properly, sneak the NetBunny INIT file into a friend's (or your whole office's) system folder and restart. Wait for an appropriate moment and open the StartRabbit application on your own machine. Select a rabbitized Mac or group of Macs, and press the "Energize" button.

In a few moments, your co-workers will see a two-inch high, pink, battery-operated rabbit march across their open applications, looking just like the one in Fig. 12-4. If their speakers are turned on, the whole office will reverberate to one of the tinniest bass drums ever sampled on a Mac. The whole thing takes about two seconds, and then the rabbit disappears back into his system-folder hole to await another energizing.

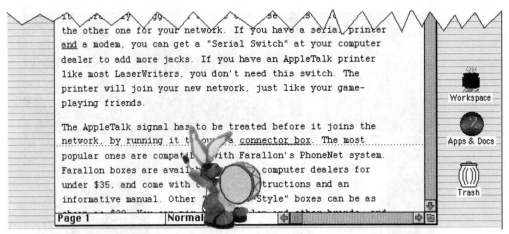

the other one for your network. If you have a serial printer
and a modem, you can get a "Serial Switch" at your computer
dealer to add more jacks. If you have an AppleTalk printer
like most LaserWriters, you don't need this switch. The
printer will join your new network, just like your game-
playing friends.

The AppleTalk signal has to be treated before it joins the
network, by running it through a connector box. The most
popular ones are compatible with Farallon's PhoneNet system.
Farallon boxes are available at computer dealers for
under $35, and come with instructions and an
informative manual. Other "Style" boxes can be as

Page 1   Normal

12-4 He keeps going and going . . ..

Custom icons
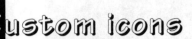

Do you have trouble finding the things you're looking for in a
nest of open folders? Do you ever wish that the files you create
could have neat, custom icons like some of your favorite
applications do? They can, and there are several ways you can
accomplish it. The simplest, if you're using System 7, is to create
a custom icon in your favorite graphics program. Copy it to the
clipboard. Select the file, folder, or disk you want to customize,
and type command+I to Get Info about it. You'll see the plain
vanilla icon in the Get Info box along with the information
about the selected item. Simply paste the custom icon over it.
Figure 12-5 shows the "before and after." If you aren't yet ready
to switch to System 7, you can still use ResEdit to customize
application icons. It's fairly easy to do, but remember always to
work on a copy of the application.

You can go even further toward customized icons with a program
from Baseline called I Like Icon. It lets you add QuickTime mini-
movies to your icons, as well as create and edit icons of all kinds.
Figure 12-6 shows the Icon Editor in use. I Like Icon comes with a
collection of icons, plus an icon installer that lets you switch back
and forth, and an easy tutorial to help you figure out what you're

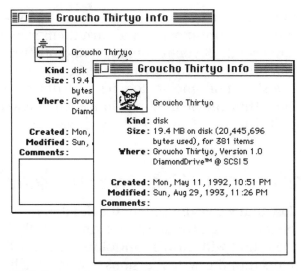

12-5 *I named my hard-disk partitions after the Marx Brothers, and gave them appropriate icons.*

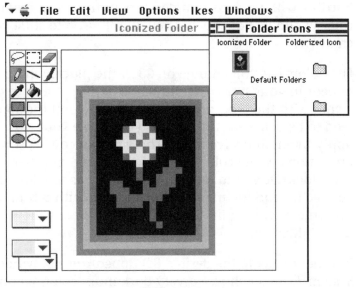

12-6 *Don't worry about details. The finished icon is only a half-inch high.*

doing. The program also teaches you to make your own animated mini-movies, and turn them into active icons to dazzle your friends. If you're already doing other things with QuickTime, you can turn any existing QuickTime movie into an icon-sized mini-movie, too. It's a great way to index your QuickTime movie files. Just link each one to a mini-movie icon of itself.

What's on the menu bar?

Now that we've dressed up the desktop and customized the icons, the menus and windows look kind of drab. We can do something about that with Now's FunColors, which will let us change the colors that the system assigns to colors we like. Or don't like. (Maybe you want to use this to make somebody else's Mac really ugly. We won't tell.) If you've poked into all of your standard Apple-issue control panels, you have found the one that lets you change the highlight color, and the color tint around the edges of windows. Some fun, huh? Well, don't blame Apple...they just didn't realize that your standard window color was going to clash horribly with your custom desktop, or that your ideal highlight color would be pale puce. They didn't *mean* to stifle your creativity.

FunColors lets you change all 23 of the places where colors appear in your system displays. (A pop-up menu of color sets comes with the program.) Some of these combinations must be seen to be believed! You can also assemble your own color sets, apply them, and save them. There are, of course, some limitations. Some colors don't work as well as others in some situations. Don't make menu backgrounds too dark or you won't be able to read the menus. Highlighting with a bright color gets tiresome after a while. Choose a paler tint of yellow, instead of the brightest one.

 In order to create the desired 3D appearance of windows in System 7, if you choose a very dark main color, you need to be able to choose a still darker color for the "shadow" effect. So you'll find some of the colors in the FunColors palette are crossed out. You can still use them, but they won't look right.

Are you getting tired of the Apple, or the help balloon? You're not alone. Lots of people have looked for ways to change them. A shareware INIT called Fruits of Passion can change your Apple to a banana, cherry or other fruit, and Zipple lets you customize the Apple, Help, or Application icon in the Menu bar into an animated icon. Use the ones provided or create your own. Figure 12-7 shows a frame from the Zipple icon I use instead of the balloon. It's a dancing cat. Zipple icons are also a convenient way to tell when your Mac has frozen, as all Macs do from time to time. Whenever the cat isn't dancing, I know I need to restart.

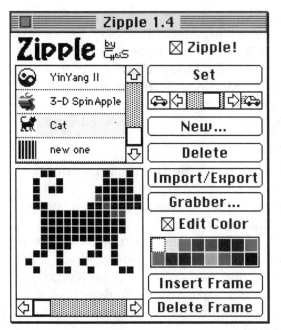

12-7 *Since I never use Balloon help, the dancing cat is more helpful.*

Do you hear a moose?

One of the very first toys I ever installed on my first 128K Mac was a thing called the Talking Moose. The Moose originated up in Canada, where winter nights are long and lonely. It put a little animated moose head up in the corner of the screen, and every few minutes it spoke to you. The Moose used MacinTalk, a phonetic speech program that was part of the Mac's system. It said "hello" when you started up, and "good-bye" when you shut down. In between, it kept you entertained with a string of wisecracks, insults, and non-sequiturs. It was fun.

By the time I'd graduated to an SE and System 5, the new system software had left the moose speechless. Careful breeding by Moose author Steve Halls and Baseline Publishing brought the beast back from extinction. The Moose lives on, in color too, along with a bunch of strange characters including Major Tom Beaver, Stinko the Evil Clown, a camel, a mouse, and Herb the corporate jester.

The Moose and his friends come with a collection of quips for most occasions, and a speech editor that lets you write your own Moose phrases. Control him from the Moose Control Panel shown in Fig. 12-8. To open the Moose application (in System 7) and change his voice, or switch to one of the other characters, click the Go Moose icon. Figure 12-9 shows two of the alternate characters.

The Moose might be one of the noisier Mac toys, but he's not the only noisemaker you can install. Ordinarily, your Mac makes noises only when you do something you shouldn't. If you try to do something else without closing a dialog box, you get an indignant chirp. Well, okay, maybe you get a harp glissando, but it somehow manages to be an "annoyed" harp glissando . . . as if it's saying, "You blew it again, dummy." Wouldn't you like to have your Mac say thank you when you open a folder, cluck like a chicken when you launch an application, or reward you with a happy sound when you hit save?

There are several ways to accomplish these things, but the least expensive is a shareware program called SoundMaster. It's a widely available shareware INIT ($15) by Bruce Tomlin that constantly watches for various Mac actions like mouse clicks, resizing a window, ejecting a disk, or any one of a couple of

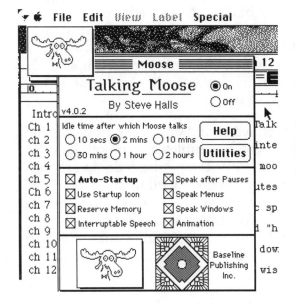

12-8 *The Moose comes with a control panel that lets you decide how often to hear from him.*

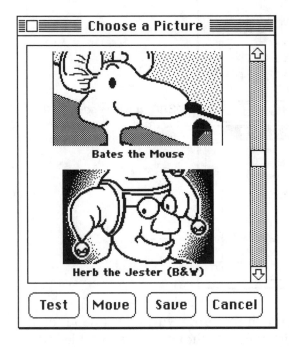

12-9 *Would you rather see a Moose or a Mouse?*

dozen other things. When one of the actions happens, SoundMaster plays a sound you specify. While this description might seem somewhat bland, very few things compare to the thrill of hearing a toilet flush when you empty the Trash, or having the system say "Gee, thanks Boss!" when you shut down for the night.

Tomlin has supported and refined SoundMaster through many revisions, and the current version is completely compatible with System 7 and the newer Macs. While the program doesn't come with any sounds of its own, you can download them from bulletin boards or create them with a sound-editing program. Figure 12-10 shows its intuitive control panel. Select an action and a sound, and then use the volume and sample-rate sliders to adjust it to your liking. When you restart your Mac, the sound will be installed.

12-10 *If you're going to flush the trash, perhaps you should make an icon that has a flush handle?*

Now's FunSounds work in much the same way. The FunSounds control panel has a long list of events that could be heralded with a sound. You might choose any or as many of these events as you wish, and install a different sound for each. Some of these sounds are even useful. For instance, do you wander off to do other things while you're copying disks, but have to keep coming back to see if the copy's done? Why not have the Mac call you when it's ready? How about giving your PowerBook a gentle snore to play to let you know when it's going to sleep? FunSounds comes with a collection of well over 100 different sounds you can install. Some are great, others suggest that one of the programmers has a 3 year-old who wants to break into show biz.

Pay careful attention to which sounds you've installed. If you come back to your office after a coffee break and hear breaking glass, you don't want to have to wonder whether it's your calendar program reminding you of a meeting, or a fed-up co-worker putting a hammer through your monitor. Some people just don't like noise. But on the other hand, some do better *with* noise.

It's quiet out there . . . too quiet

Parents of teenagers are constantly amazed at how their progeny can study with such noisemakers as the television, tape player, and other kids providing constant distraction. If your mind works the same way (and studies show that a soft background noise can help certain people concentrate), you need Digital Eclipse's Zounds—a disk jockey for your Mac.

Zounds loads as an INIT, works in the background like a screen saver, and its controls resemble After Dark. Once activated, it plays random sounds through your Mac's speaker. But unlike a screen saver, Zounds works all the time. If you've turned on its waterfall, you'll hear a Niagara of sound even while you're working on the driest spreadsheet. Fortunately, the controls let you set volume (independent of any system or game volumes), whether Zounds waits for a few seconds or as much as an hour of inactivity before working, and how often it'll mellow out and not make any noise at all.

Zounds' control panel also lets you choose from a library of background sound modules, everything from the expected crackling hearth and rainstorm to Italian lessons. In Fig. 12-11, we've selected Kitty on the Keys—some very realistic typing and system sounds designed to convince an eavesdropping boss that your fingers are flying, even while you're taking a coffee break. You can also add your own sounds, if you're handy with ResEdit and follow the sometimes obscure documentation (more about that in a moment). The price of all these sounds is memory. A full install adds about 5M to your system folder, and depending on the module, requires a ⅓-to ½M of RAM to run. Fortunately, you can shrink the installation to save disk space.

12-11 *Don't use Kitty to fool the boss if she types faster than you do.*

Just don't expect the documentation to tell you how. While the 20-page booklet tells you custom installation is possible, it doesn't even hint at how you get there. It also doesn't describe any of the sound modules—you have to run the installer for that—and doesn't warn how the installer crashes unless you disable normally-benign INITs. More disturbing is the ReadMe file on the first installation disk. The disk is shipped locked, with the file scrolled off the window. Unless you go looking for them, you won't even know these instructions exist.

Still, some of the sounds are pleasant and relaxing. If you must work in a noisy environment, you might find it helpful to find some neutral sound like the waterfall or crackling fire, plug in a decent pair of headphones, and listen to a Zound instead of the random office or household roar.

Insanity

You know how there are heroes and anti-heroes? Well, you've seen lots of Mac toys, so here's one that could probably be called an anti-Mac toy. Ever had one of those days when the system crashes and takes your whole (irrecoverable) day's work with it? Ever wanted to let the Mac know what you really think of it? I have. And it's fairly obvious that Patrick Bertinelli and John Fitzpatrick have. Insanity is a control panel that lets you configure a key combination to shoot bullets (fake, of course) through your screen, to fling cow pies at it, or to dive bomb it with a particularly incontinent seagull. It's a riot, and good therapy on days when everything goes wrong.

Frame it

We've pretty well covered software toys, which leaves hardware toys. There aren't many. You can get a plastic gadget that snaps over your mouse and makes it look like a Ferrari, or a fuzzy mouse cover with ears and whiskers. You can even get slipcovers for your Mac to keep dust out of the CPU, keyboard, and monitor. These come in a variety of prints. I've seen tropical fish designs, plain colors, neon colors, and even camouflage, both jungle and desert varieties. (If they ever come out with a print that combines coffee cups, used Kleenex, and stacks of disks, it'll be the perfect camouflage for my desktop.) And there are mouse pads of all descriptions, including some with the guys from Chippendales, and some young ladies dressed for skinny dipping. There's one with liquid crystals in the cover that change colors with the heat of your hand. My current favorite is the Moose Pad, with a portrait of guess who . . . .

One of the best toys I've ever seen for the Mac II is a piece of cardboard, about 14-by-15 inches square. It's a frame for your monitor, and comes in at least 50 different designs. They're called Screenies. Mine has a collection of cats in various poses. It's shown in Fig. 12-12. One's eating sardines; one's napping; and a couple of others are artistically draped over the top of the screen. Other Screenies include a baroque gilded frame, a frame that makes your screen look like a giant Etch-a-Sketch, graffiti, and a whole lot more. They're wonderful. They attach with velcro so you could buy several and change them according to your mood or the job you're doing.

12-12 *Cats rallying around the screen, and a collection of Mac mascots on the monitor.*

A last word

Everybody plays differently. My husband enjoys programming and likes to go for long walks. My older son is happiest when he's 50 feet or more underwater with a scuba tank on his back and a bunch of lobsters in his loot bag. When he can't dive, he draws pictures of tropical fish in SuperPaint. The younger one likes to fight online duels at the Red Dragon Inn, and play piano and clarinet in a jazz band. My idea of play is to walk the dog, or join my online friends and family in a group exercise of virtual reality we call "the Yellow Submarine." Yours might be to shoot down marauding Klingons, collect antique silver, play trivia games, or compete in the Iron Man/Iron Woman Triathlon.

Not all of your play should be or can be done on a Mac. Computer games and simulations aren't reality. Playing 18 holes of MacGolf might relax you—and it should—but it doesn't count for fresh air and exercise. Zapping aliens doesn't solve day-to-day problems. Interacting with a Talking Moose is no substitute for one-on-one conversation with another human being. Play computer games. Make friends with your Mac. Decorate it, relate to it, enjoy it. And know when to quit.

Index